W0035960

SAGE was founded in 1965 by Sara Miller McCune to support the dissemination of usable knowledge by publishing innovative and high-quality research and teaching content. Today, we publish over 900 journals, including those of more than 400 learned societies, more than 800 new books per year, and a growing range of library products including archives, data, case studies, reports, and video. SAGE remains majority-owned by our founder, and after Sara's lifetime will become owned by a charitable trust that secures our continued independence.

Los Angeles | London | New Delhi | Singapore | Washington DC | Melbourne

POLITICS, IDEOLOGY & NATIONALISM

POLITICS, IDEOLOGY & NATIONALISM

JINNAH, SAVARKAR & AMBEDKAR VERSUS GANDHI

BIDYUT CHAKRABARTY

SAGE

Los Angeles | London | New Delhi
Singapore | Washington DC | Melbourne

Copyright © Bidyut Chakrabarty, 2020

All rights reserved. No part of this book may be reproduced or utilized in any form or by any means, electronic or mechanical, including photocopying, recording or by any information storage or retrieval system, without permission in writing from the publisher.

First published in 2020 by

SAGE Publications India Pvt Ltd
B1/I-1 Mohan Cooperative Industrial Area
Mathura Road, New Delhi 110 044, India
www.sagepub.in

SAGE Publications Inc
2455 Teller Road
Thousand Oaks, California 91320, USA

SAGE Publications Ltd
1 Oliver's Yard, 55 City Road
London EC1Y 1SP, United Kingdom

SAGE Publications Asia-Pacific Pte Ltd
18 Cross Street #10-10/11/12
China Square Central
Singapore 048423

Published by Vivek Mehra for SAGE Publications India Pvt Ltd. Typeset in 10.5/13 pt Berkeley by Zaza Eunice, Hosur, Tamil Nadu, India.

Library of Congress Cataloging-in-Publication Data

Name: Chakrabarty, Bidyut, author.
Title: Politics, ideology and nationalism: Jinnah, Savarkar and Ambedkar versus Gandhi/Bidyut Chakrabarty.
Description: Thousand Oaks, California: SAGE Publishing, 2020. | Includes bibliographical references and index.
Identifiers: LCCN 2020016180 | ISBN 9789353883843 (hardback) | ISBN 9789353883850 (epub) | ISBN 9789353883867 (ebook)
Subjects: LCSH: Gandhi, Mahatma, 1869–1948. | Savarkar, Vinayak Damodar, 1883-1966. | Ambedkar, B. R. (Bhimrao Ramji), 1891–1956. | Jinnah, Mahomed Ali, 1876–1948. | Identity politics—India—Biography. | Nationalism—India—History—20th century—Biography. | India—History—20th century—Biography.
Classification: LCC DS430 .C445 2020 | DDC 320.540954092/2—dc23
LC record available at https://lccn.loc.gov/2020016180

ISBN: 978-93-5388-384-3 (HB)

SAGE Team: Rajesh Dey, Sandhya Gola and Rajinder Kaur

Dedicated to Professor W. H. Morris-Jones,
Professor Thomas Nossiter and Professor Meghnad Desai,
my teachers-cum-mentors in a foreign land,
who steered me towards an academically fulfilling life.

Thank you for choosing a SAGE product!
If you have any comment, observation or feedback,
I would like to personally hear from you.

Please write to me at **contactceo@sagepub.in**

Vivek Mehra, Managing Director and CEO, SAGE India.

Bulk Sales

SAGE India offers special discounts
for purchase of books in bulk.
We also make available special imprints
and excerpts from our books on demand.

For orders and enquiries, write to us at

Marketing Department
SAGE Publications India Pvt Ltd
B1/I-1, Mohan Cooperative Industrial Area
Mathura Road, Post Bag 7
New Delhi 110044, India

E-mail us at **marketing@sagepub.in**

Subscribe to our mailing list

Write to **marketing@sagepub.in**

This book is also available as an e-book.

Contents

Preface

There is a saying that good food leaves one with food for thought, which is more likely if you have delicious food in the company of someone who is admired for his scholarship and human qualities. This book would not have been in the public domain without the lunch meeting that I had with Professor (Lord) Meghnad Desai in a South London pub in June 2018. While eating the sumptuous English lunch chosen by Professor Desai in a secluded corner of the pub, the idea of this book was mooted. He wanted me to take up this project and probe into the Gandhi critique that his nationalist critics, Mohammad Ali Jinnah (M. A. Jinnah), V. D. Savarkar and B. R. Ambedkar, offered to pursue their respective life-long missions. According to Professor Desai, the nationalist discourse would have been less complex had it not been exposed to multiple politico-ideological priorities. During the discussion over lunch, it came out very sharply that though they pursued completely different modes of nationalist campaigns, they drew on more or less similar ideological predilections presumably because they were raised in a context in which Enlightenment values were privileged. The fact that Jinnah and Ambedkar had accepted liberal constitutionalism as an empowering device for significant sociopolitical changes is evident if one scans the devices that they designed for political mobilization. For Savarkar, the argument needs to be nuanced since there are two starkly different phases in his political career. First, being baptized in revolutionary nationalism, he endorsed violent resistance to colonialism. Once released from his long incarceration in the Cellular Jail in Andaman, he appeared to have abdicated the path of violence and was happy in following the constitutional means of struggle. What was striking, as Professor Desai pointed out, was the relevance of Gandhi during this phase of India's nationalist struggle to understand even the views of his fierce critics which means that the Mahatma remained critical even in conceptualizing the critiques that his colleagues offered to put forward a counter to his politico-ideological preferences. It was not a single- but two-way traffic which helped build the views that Gandhi had articulated and also his detractors who created their own conceptual universe in contradiction with and appreciation for the mode of nationalism that gradually emerged as the mainstream political response.

Without Professor Desai's mentoring since my days at the London School of Economics (LSE), where I successfully finished my doctoral studies, it would not have been possible for me to complete many challenging academic works. I am grateful to him for liberally sharing his ideas with me, which helped me undertake many book projects. By dedicating this book to my teacher-cum-mentors, I express my heartfelt gratitude to them for having kindled my curiosity and encouraging me to tread an untrodden path along with many at LSE and elsewhere. I have no hesitation in putting on record that much of my stay in London during the period when I was engaged in academic pursuits would have been dull had Meghnad (he prefers to be addressed by his first name by his students) not been around to stand by me; many evenings that I had spent with him at LSE's Beavers' Retreat remain memorable simply because I had had the privilege to be with him for longer hours in the evening.

My students, Dr Bhuwan Jha of University of Delhi and Dr Rajendra Pandey of Meerut University, deserve to be complimented for their help in procuring materials and helping me persuasively set out the argument for the book. Dr Nemai Saha of Visva-Bharati Library was always a phone call away whenever I needed books or articles available online. I am privileged to have a colleague like him at Visva-Bharati, which is now my place of work. For sustaining my energy, I remember the contribution of Gopal in the office of the Vice-Chancellor and Tublu, Gaurav, Tapash, Anuj and Sanatan, who, with their support, made my stay away from family most enjoyable. It was possible for me to concentrate on my writings for hours together since they extended whatever help I required as instantaneously as possible. I express my gratitude to my colleagues in office who never allowed me to be over-hassled with administrative pangs. My colleagues in the academic segment at Visva-Bharati are always a source of inspiration. I owe a great deal to them. I owe a debt of gratitude to Professor Amrit Sen, my colleague at Visva-Bharati for his contribution in the refinement of the text.

By raising pertinent issues, especially regarding my written texts, my daughter Urna/Barbie was there as a committed teacher who helped me to significantly improve the language in which the arguments were presented. Pablo, my son, had also a role in sustaining my energy by being deviant of what I wanted him to do. Sanchita, my wife, may have not appreciated my being glued to the computer, though she is happy that I spend my time in creative writings. My Kolkata-based sisters, Mini and Tinku, and their daughters, Debiparna and Sreeja, have not allowed me to feel lonely even when I am here at Santiniketan all by myself by making my stay with them in Kolkata as enjoyable as ever.

My students in India and abroad always provide useful inputs to view Indian nationalism in a new perspective. This is true of my students whom I taught in India and also those who took my courses in Indian nationalism, Indian politics and Gandhi's sociopolitical ideas in foreign universities where I spent considerable time as a teacher. I am privileged to have had this opportunity which would not have been possible, I strongly believe, without providential endorsement. Finally, I heartily thank Mr Vivek Mehra at SAGE and his competent team for having had faith in me as an author. Without their support, I would not have appeared as an author and most of my ideas would have gone with me to the grave. Because of their constant prodding and adequate care, it was possible for me to put my views forward in black and white on such a complex theme that the book has dealt with and also to add one more book to the list of books that I have published with SAGE so far.

If this book is useful in unearthing new dimensions in Indian nationalist trajectory, I shall have achieved the purpose for which I undertook the exercise.

November 2019 **Bidyut Chakrabarty**
West Bengal, India **Visva-Bharati, Santiniketan**

INTRODUCTION*

Mohandas Karamchand Gandhi (1869–1948), popularly known as Mahatma, is considered as both a global icon for the resolution of conflict through peaceful means and an unparalleled mass leader of the 20th-century India. He is the one person who has been credited in the popular imagination as having, single-handedly, secured independence for India. This is reflected, for example, in the popular song of the 1954 Hindi film *Jagriti* (or awakening) written by the famous poet Pradeep. Referring to Gandhi as fakir (one without any worldly belongings), it says 'you gave us independence without using sword or shield. In doing so, O' Saint of Sabarmati, you created a miracle'. He inspired passionate devotion and loyalty from those who were his followers; it is also striking that he drew on to him those who dissented with his views. Jawaharlal Nehru, for instance, remained with Gandhi despite having criticized him for using the expression '*Ram Raj*' and also for withdrawing the 1920–1922 Non-cooperation movement.[1] For decades after his death in 1948, leaders around the world were inspired by his life, writings and political activities. Martin Luther King Jr, Nelson Mandela and Dalai Lama are just few iconic leaders who had drawn on Gandhi's teachings while pursuing their respective

* I am thankful to Dr Bhuwan Jha of Satyawati College, University of Delhi, and Dr Rajendra Pandey of Meerut University (Uttar Pradesh) for their inputs which helped me a lot in putting the argument upfront while introducing the theme of the book.

[1] Jawaharlal Nehru, *Autobiography* (New York: John Day Company, 1941), 72 (on the use of phrases like *Ram Raj* by Gandhi) or 80–83 (on the sudden suspension of the Non-cooperation movement in February 1922).

politico-ideological missions. Honoured as 'Father of the Nation' by Indians almost universally, the Mahatma is known to have charted a unique style of political mobilization based on his own assessment of the situation in which he rose to prominence. His political education and activity began in South Africa in the late 19th century. It got him into local struggles as well as advocacy and lobbying with the Imperial government in London. This combination of mass struggle involving the peaceful breaking of unjust laws along with patient negotiations and lobbying with those in power remained his modus operandi. It was also entirely his innovation that loomed large before the British as the battle for freedom in India progressed under his care.

Even so, during his long political life spanning 60 years, starting in South Africa in the 1890s and ending in the late 1940s, Gandhi encountered three people or leaders in their own right who never fell for his charm and cunning, and strongly disagreed with him—his ideas or strategies. Of course, many more people at various times strongly disagreed with him or defied him. Subhash Chandra Bose, for instance, was a victim when he was forced out of the Congress Party presidency because of his differences of opinion with Gandhi. But their disagreements were of minor or no consequence. The three singled out here had major and consequential disagreement with Gandhi. They were Vinayak Damodar (Veer) Savarkar, Bhimrao (Babasaheb) Ambedkar and M. A. Jinnah, also known as Quaid-i-Azam.

All the three as well as Gandhi were barristers-at-law having fulfilled the required terms in one or the other of London's Inns of Court. Savarkar had kept terms at Grey's Inn, but he was removed from the list when he was convicted; he made an appeal to be restored after he was released from his life sentence in Andaman but did not get success. Both Jinnah (1876–1948) and Gandhi (1869–1948) were Gujaratis hailing from the Kathiawad (now Saurashtra) region. Both Savarkar (1883–1966) and Ambedkar (1891–1956) were Maharashtrians. The continued disagreements between Gandhi and these three leaders affected not only the course of the national movement but also the shape of things to follow post 1947. The three represented separate streams of thought in direct opposition to Gandhi. While Savarkar, a revolutionary turned Hindu nationalist icon, was debatably the most militant face of a resurgent political Hinduism, Ambedkar became the voice of the millions of the so-called untouchables seeking an equal social and political space, and Jinnah rallied the Muslim separatist forces, arguing vociferously and determinedly in favour of the two-nation theory. That the Gandhi-led Congress and the national movement failed to contain the growing appeal of these three leaders also denoted important weaknesses of their anti-British struggle.

Another division among them, Gandhi and the three leaders, relates to the notion of modernity or for them which was similar to Europeanization. Gandhi was the exception in his total opposition to the idea of modernity as reflected in the Western world of that time. This feeling was expressed in his first major book *Hind Swaraj*, published in 1909. He was opposed to mechanization and modern industry, even railroads and modern medicine. The other three were modernists and rationalists. Jinnah spent much of his life as a westernized liberal politician who was at ease with modernity. Ambedkar was all for modernization and industrialization—very much like Jawaharlal Nehru. Savarkar was also very impressed by European civilization and espoused a rational, scientific attitude.

Born in Bhagur village near Nashik, Savarkar spent much of his later life in the Ratnagiri district of the then Bombay province (now Maharashtra state). Interestingly, after his birth in Mhow (Central Provinces, now Madhya Pradesh), Ambedkar too came to the Ratnagiri district along with his parents. All three were younger than Gandhi who was the first to die in 1948, just months ahead of Jinnah. Savarkar was one of the accused in the trial of Gandhi's assassins—Godse and his associates—but was acquitted subsequently. Even so, for some Indians, he carried the opprobrium of being somehow responsible for Godse's attack on Gandhi.

Savarkar was active since his early days in India in the revolutionary militant movement which was in favour of armed struggle, using bombs and guns, smuggled or stolen, in a country which had been officially disarmed by the foreign rulers, to show defiance by injuring or killing the British officials in India. This agitation, which spanned Bengal, Punjab and Maharashtra, was in full swing after the Partition of Bengal in 1905. Savarkar was known to be an activist, watched by the British. He was known to be an admirer of the Chapekar brothers who were convicted for the murder of a British official. Other young rebels like Aurobindo Ghosh and older leaders such as Lala Lajpat Rai, Bal Gangadhar Tilak and Bipin Chandra Pal (popularly known as Lal–Bal–Pal), though not openly advocating the use of arms, did not show aversion to the path of violence. Gandhi, on the other hand, had arrived at his weapon of Satyagraha in South Africa by 1907. He totally disagreed with the violent path as a tactic or a strategy or a philosophy for winning independence from the British. Jinnah and Ambedkar preferred the constitutional path for winning independence. Ambedkar organized the Dalits in their continuous fight against orthodox Hindu groups, but in dealing with the British, he was a liberal constitutionalist. Jinnah, late in his political life, during 1946–1947, incited mob violence as a political weapon to win his demand for Pakistan. Otherwise, he was also a liberal constitutionalist.

Savarkar and Gandhi: Hindutva versus Congress Politics

Drawn on the writings of the Italian nationalist Mazzini, for whom masculinity, race, culture and nationalism were aligned and had to be asserted against perceived otherness or foreignness,[2] V. D. Savarkar (1883–1966) outlived the other three. He was also the first of the three to meet Gandhi in London in 1909 during one of Gandhi's periodic visits to London from South Africa while lobbying for the cause of Indians in South Africa. It was the time that many revolutionary nationalist expatriates in London were celebrating the killing of Curzon Wyllie (a British official) by Madan Lal Dhingra and a scholarship had been instituted after the latter. Shyamji Krishna Verma was a major leader and inspiration. Savarkar and Gandhi met in a dinner party organized by the former to celebrate Dussehra on 24 October 1909. In this conversation, Gandhi said that he considered Savarkar's teaching as injurious to the country, and that the real oppressor—the 10-headed monster—was within every individual and not outside.

[2] Vinayak Chaturvedi delved into the history of V. D. Savarkar's masculinist nationalism in Vinayak Chaturvedi, 'Vinayak & Me: Hindutva and the Politics of Naming,' *Social History* 28, no. 2 (2003): 155–73.

Savarkar, while criticizing Gandhi's opinion, said by pointing to Gandhi's interpretation of Ramayana, that Ram did not invade Ceylon (aka Sri Lanka), the island of tyrant, for the sake of peace, and did not carry the war abroad to kill the 10-headed monster within himself, but instead fought for Sita the chaste, for Sita the freedom of India.[3] It is not incidental that this was also the year which saw the publication of *The Indian War of Independence of 1857* by Savarkar and *Hind Swaraj* by Gandhi. While the former was written to arouse the Indian revolutionaries in their war against the British rule, the latter contained, among others, a firm critique of the violent methods deployed by them.

Both Gandhi and Savarkar were (upper caste/*savarna*) Hindus but very different in their attitudes towards religion. Savarkar is known for having championed Hindu nationalism; he was an atheist, a rationalist and a modernizer. On the other hand, Gandhi was a deeply religious person; he fashioned his own version of Hinduism, a stripped down, almost Christianized version. He did not visit temples or take part in any ceremonies. His prayer meetings which were ecumenical with the singing of *bhajans* resembled Methodist Church services with singing of hymns. The difference between Gandhi's attitude towards Hindu religion and that of Savarkar has shaped India's history over the century and more since they met, more than is realized or, if realized, admitted. The anathema that Savarkar is for the liberal–tolerant–secular–elite has led people to demonize and/or ignore his thoughts. Hindutva, the ideology of Hindu nationalism associated with Savarkar, was ignored for 50 years after he first propounded it, dismissed as un-Indian and later as anti-Indian, but has come to centre stage during the 21st century, *malgré tout*. Yet Hindutva as a word denoting Hinduness (i.e., *tatva* or essence of Hinduism), the quality of being a Hindu was used by Gandhi as well. Mahadev Desai records in his diary that before meeting Ambedkar for their crucial talks in Yerawada, Gandhi expressed the view that Ambedkar seemed to be lacking in Hindutva. This was a shrewd observation, but Gandhi did not realize that Ambedkar did not approve of the merits of being a Hindu.

[3] National Archives of India, New Delhi, Weekly report of the Director of Criminal Intelligence, Simla, 20-11-1909, Home (Political) Files, January 1910, nos. 46–52, B, 18–19.

Yet there are similarities between Gandhi and Savarkar. They both wanted to reform Hindu society. Both were opposed to untouchability and, in their own ways, fought for temple entry and access to water sources for the 'untouchables'. Savarkar initiated a practice of all caste brethren dining together and helped open a temple for entry by all castes. He organized pan-Hindu festivals focusing on granting entry to the 'untouchables'. In one of his public speeches, he took the menace of caste hierarchy head-on:

> From today I shall not believe in highness or lowness of caste. I shall not oppose the intermarriage between the highest and lowest castes. I shall eat with any Hindu irrespective of castes. I shall not believe in caste by birth or by profession and henceforth I shall call myself a Hindu only—not Brahmin, Vaishya, etc.[4]

He himself was an atheist and had no time for what he believed were old superstitions and mythologies associated with Hinduism. But Savarkar disliked the process of conversion of Hindus to other faiths such as Islam or Christianity. He was keen on their conversion back to Hinduism (*shuddhi*, i.e. purification). Savarkar is reported to have had Muslim friends while in London during 1906–1910, and where he also made friends with the British. Indeed, in his seminal 'History of 1857', Savarkar praises many Muslim soldiers and officers for their bravery fighting for an independent India against the British.[5] Under the 'Author's Introduction' in this book, while dwelling upon the significance of the consciousness of their past, Savarkar asked the countrymen to be a master and not a slave of this past:

> The nation that has no consciousness of its past has no future. Equally true it is that a nation must develop its capacity not only of claiming a past but also of knowing how to use it for the furtherance of its future. The nation ought to be the master and not the slave of its own history. For, it is absolutely unwise to try to do certain things, simply because they had

[4] Walter K. Andersen and Shridhar D. Damle, *The RSS: A View to the Inside* (New Delhi: Penguin Viking, 2018), 80.

[5] T. C. A. Raghavan, 'Origins and Development of Hindu Mahasabha Ideology: The Call of V. D. Savarkar and Bhai Parmanand,' *Economic and Political Weekly* 18, no. 15 (9 April 1983): 595–600.

> once been acted in the past. The feeling of hatred against the Mahomedans was just and necessary in the times of Shivaji—but, such a feeling would be unjust and foolish if nursed now, simply because it was the dominant feeling of the Hindus then.[6]

But after his hard life imprisonment in Andaman, bullied by Pathan prison guards, according to his biographer Dhananjay Keer, his attitude changed.[7] Further, in between, many new issues, most significantly related to the field of electoral representation, had worked to adversely affect the inter-community relationship. By the time he returned to mainland India in 1922, the leader most regarded in India was his old sparring partner Gandhi. The principal and massive agitation going on then was the Khilafat movement which Gandhi chose as a platform for Hindu–Muslim unity, as an important part of the non-cooperation, to fight the British. Although this movement had been suspended in February 1922, fierce communal riots had taken over in the Malabar area where a large number of Hindus had been converted to Muslims. An important Marathi public figure B. S. Moonje, who later on became a frontline leader of the Hindu Mahasabha, made on-the-spot assessment of the conversions in this region and pointed out that the Hindus of Malabar were 'mild and docile' in sharp contrast to the Moplahs who were 'domineering in spirit and ferocious'.[8] Another significant Marathi leader M. R. Jayakar called the Moplah riots one of the 'darkest chapters' in Indian nationalism which, nonetheless, taught the Hindus to 'organize themselves'.[9] Inclusion of the issue of Khilafat in the national movement alarmed Savarkar. For him, as a Maharashtrian, the Mughal Empire had been the enemy of Shivaji, and later the Peshwas. The Maratha ideal was *Hindu-pada-padashahi*—a Hindu Empire. Liberation of India from the Muslim rule had been the dream. To harness Muslims in a struggle for independence of India, a

[6] V. D. Savarkar, *The Indian War of Independence of 1857* (London, 1909), vii–viii.

[7] Dhananjay Keer, *Savarkar and His Times* (Bombay: India Printing Works, 1950), 38–41.

[8] Moonje's report on 'Forcible Conversions in Malabar', 4-8-1923; Moonje Papers, Nehru Memorial Museum and Library, Subject Files No. 12.

[9] 'Oral Evidence of M. R. Jayakar (President, Bombay Presidency Hindu Sabha) before the Bombay Riots Enquiry Committee', 24-7-1929; Jayakar Papers, National Archives of India, File No. 437.

Hindu land, by invoking religious symbolism of Khilafat, was against his principles. Freedom for India meant freedom from all present and previous non-Hindu rule. (Savarkar wrote a book on the military exploits of the Marathas in the 17th and 18th centuries. *Hindu-Pad-Padashahi* reads like a hastily written book with little else than a serial account of Maratha victories in battles starting with Shivaji. Little is said about other governance aspects or contemporary situation in rest of India. Muslims are the main and indeed only enemy as far as Savarkar's history is concerned.

The interaction between Savarkar and Gandhi was fruitful in an odd way. Gandhi's *Hind Swaraj* is in some ways a dialogue with Savarkar. Savarkar's influential essay on Hindutva is a reaction to Gandhi's Khilafat movement and the idea of an ecumenical fight against the British uniting Hindus and Muslims. Given his global perspective on the Empire, it should not have caused surprise (though it did at the time) that Gandhi had chosen an issue whose location was far away in Turkey to fight British imperialism. But he realized that for the Muslims of India, as elsewhere across the Sunni Umma, the Khilafat was a valuable, if not sacred office. If the British were to change it, there would be distress. Ironically, it was Mustafa Kemal Pasha, the new ruler of Turkey, who abolished the Khilafat as a move towards the European-style modernization of Turkey, thereby indirectly agreeing with Savarkar rather than with Gandhi. But by then Gandhi had suspended his movement due to violence in Chauri Chaura.

Ambedkar and Gandhi: Dalits' Right to Equality versus Independence from Foreign Rule

B. R. Ambedkar (1891–1956) usually attracts the same kind of reverence in contemporary India as Mahatma Gandhi. It is a paradox of history that the leader who was a fierce critique of Gandhi, his ideas and leadership of the national movement, especially his ideas on *varnashram* and caste system, including the method of eradication of untouchability, has an equally large number of statues at public and private places. Ambedkar's influence has increased beyond Gandhi's and indeed his own during his lifetime since his death. Especially in the politics of the 1990s and after, Ambedkar has acquired new significance. To a large number of people, he remains the most ardent advocate for providing equal status to Dalits, while for others, he remains the leading architect of the Indian Constitution which provides a sound basis for equality of all citizens. (Most of his statues show him holding a copy of the Constitution.) He was bestowed with Bharat Ratna in 1990, and over the last few years, several institutions have been named after him, and very recently, a fitting memorial has been set up in his name in the heart of the Indian capital.

B. R. Ambedkar has carved a space for himself as he put forward a distinct school of thought that sought to privilege the social and economic emancipation of the oppressed classes of Indian society in a sharp contrast to the mainstream discourse of political independence of the country from the yoke of British colonialism. This, however, does not mean that he did not put forward his political ideas and presented his perspective on the shape of future of Indian polity. Politically, Ambedkar emerges as a 'rebel-liberal' in the Gandhian universe who sought to reinvent his ideas on social justice in tune with his firm commitment to liberalism.[10] In fact, the evolutionary nature of the social and political thought of Ambedkar has, to a large extent, been conditioned by the unfolding situations in the course of Indian national movement. His ideas, indeed, appear to be contextualized in the unique framework of his Western education, on the one hand, and his felt experiences of the social and political as a person belonging to one of the oppressed classes, on the other. In other words, being a scholar-activist keeping a vigilant eye on the happenings of his times and responding to them at both theoretical and practical plains, it was obvious for Ambedkar to have written and commented on a wide range of issues pertaining to the political scenario of the country. The political thought of Ambedkar, therefore, does not come as a body of organized and systematic theorization. On the contrary, the political thought of Ambedkar consists of the views expressed by him in the form of numerous statements, speeches, books and monographs coming in the wake of a particular issue being raised at the specific

[10] Bidyut Chakrabarty, 'B. R. Ambedkar: A "Rebel-Liberal" in the Gandhian Universe,' *Indian Historical Review* 43, no. 2 (2016): 289–315.

point of time. For instance, during the 1950s when the problem of linguistic reorganization of states became a burning issue in the wake of agitations and fasts primarily in the southern part of country, he was prompted to pen down the book *Thoughts on Linguistic States* to articulate his intellectual understanding of the problem and the probable solution to it. Nevertheless, Ambedkar as a political thinker appears liberal, but not a dogmatic, one to the core as his context-driven critical beliefs in the liberal values underpin almost the entire body of political thought as reflected in the main strands of the political thinking Ambedkar articulated in various contexts and forms from time to time.

A cardinal principle of Ambedkar's political ideas related to the rights of the people in general and special rights and protection for the oppressed sections in particular. Clearly, while articulating his views on the annihilation of caste, Ambedkar repeatedly expressed himself in favour of a social order based on the ideals of liberty, equality and fraternity[11] presumably to highlight the absence of and the need for the same in the Indian society, especially in the case of untouchables. Rooted in this contextual framework, he went on to explain the imperative, nature and limits of the rights. The imperative of individual rights, for Ambedkar, appears to have become evident due to its democratizing impact on the society. As a firm believer in an egalitarian and democratic sociopolitical system, Ambedkar was convinced that such an order can be ordained only by having the ideals of liberty, equality and fraternity indissolubly ingrained in the law of the land of the country. To him, right of an individual appears to be the ameliorating agent set to bring about fundamental changes in the social and political standing of the person in the society.

Presumably, in order to emphasize the indissolubility of the rights, Ambedkar stood by the natural theory of rights instead of the legal theory of rights which ought to have been the case given his comprehensive training in the legal profession. Hence, taking the rights as natural and inherent in the human personality, he stressed on the

[11] For details see, B. R. Ambedkar, *The Annihilation of Caste* (New Delhi: Arnold Publishers, 1990).

social sanction instead of the legal support as the true perspective of securing the rights of the people. As he explains,

> Rights are protected not by law but by moral conscience of society. If social conscience is such that it is prepared to recognize the rights which law chooses to enact, rights will be safe and secure. But if the fundamental rights are opposed by the community, no law, no parliament, no judiciary can guarantee them in the real sense of the word.[12]

However, the absoluteness and rigidity of the prevailing social inequalities, indignities and discriminations against the untouchables seemed to have weighed heavily in the minds of Ambedkar as he vehemently argued for the constitutional protection of the fundamental rights of the people. Thus, the theoretical understanding of the nature and practical manifestation of the concept of rights seemed to differ ostensibly for Ambedkar in view of the contextual imperatives of different times.

The context-driven fluctuations in the perspective of Ambedkar on rights again became evident at the time of the debate on the issue in the Constituent Assembly. Thus, surprisingly, a champion of the natural and inherent rights, believing in the inalienability of certain rights such as right to life and liberty, was seen arguing for antithetical provisions such as preventive detention and suspension of such basic rights like the right to constitutional remedies during abnormal circumstances. As he explained,

> There can be no doubt that while there are certain fundamental rights which the state must guarantee to the individual in order that the individual may have some security and freedom to develop his own personality, it is equally clear that in certain cases, where for instance, the state's very life is in jeopardy, those rights must be subjected to a certain amount of limitation.[13]

In sum, despite appearing contradictory at times, Ambedkar's ideas on rights seem to reflect the perspective of a prudent realist who remained conforming to the dynamics of varying times.

[12] B. R. Ambedkar, *Ranade, Gandhi and Jinnah* (Jalandhar: Bheem Patrika Publications, 1964), 34–35.

[13] *Constituent Assembly Debates*, Vol. VII, p. 950 (New Delhi: Lok Sabha Secretariat).

The basic framework for the articulation of the political ideas of Ambedkar had been provided by the idea of constitutional democracy whose vibrancy he had seen in the Western countries. In other words, as a liberal thinker, Ambedkar was a hard-core believer in the value of the constitutional democracy having irrevocable elements of social and economic democracies, in addition to the political democracy. Indeed, the notion of social democracy, situated in the framework of the constitutional democracy, appeared dearer to him than the political democracy, presumably because of the fact that for this he fought for throughout his life. Quite evidently, to him,

> [Social democracy] means a way of life which recognizes liberty, equality and fraternity which are not to be treated as separate items in a trinity. They form a union of trinity in the sense that to divorce one from the other is to defeat the very purpose of democracy. Liberty cannot be divorced from equality; equality cannot be divorced from liberty. Nor can liberty and equality be divorced from fraternity.[14]

The complex web of democracy, thus, for Ambedkar was expected to consist of not only the sterile inputs, mainly political in nature, but also the dynamic elements of social and economic democracies with the balance weighing heavily in favour of the social democracy.

Though as a framework of life, Ambedkar emphasized the social component of democracy, as a system of government, he explicitly expressed himself in favour of the British parliamentary model of democracy. Taking it as a system of providing ample scope for the reconciliation of the individual good and the social good, he was keen on imbibing the basic liberal values which underpin the functioning of parliamentary democracy. For instance, he seemed overwhelmed by the virtue of rule of law as the foundational characteristic of a democracy as it lays down the basic functional domain of various actors in the polity. Under the rule of law, as he explains,

> all citizens are equal before law and possess equal civic rights. No state shall make or enforce any law or custom which shall abridge the privileges or

[14] Cited in, Bidyut Chakrabarty and Rajendra Kumar Pandey, *Indian Government and Politics* (New Delhi: SAGE Publications, 2008), 10.

> immunities of citizens; nor shall any state deprive any person of life, liberty and property without the process of law; nor deny to any person within its jurisdiction equal protection of law.[15]

Showing the wisdom of a realist thinker, Ambedkar was quick to conceptualize the notion of democracy within the peculiar contextual framework evident in India. For instance, he was in no case ready to afford the rule of majoritarianism, as has been the case with the classical notion of parliamentary democracy for the sake of stability, good governance and efficiency of the government, as he was convinced, 'efficiency combined with selfish class interests instead of producing good government is far more likely to become a mere engine of suppression of the servile classes.'[16] Similarly, in a clear departure from the British context, Ambedkar was a clear in his mind to locate parliamentary democracy in India in the framework of a federal set-up, keeping in mind the Indian circumstances. Moreover, never hesitant to borrow from other constitutions to make the suitability of the Indian Constitution best for India, Ambedkar seemingly retrofitted the parliamentary constitutional democratic arrangements of India with a number of plausible and patently suitable provisions drawn from the Presidential system of America, such as the supremacy of the Constitution and the provision of an independent judiciary. In sum, Ambedkar's views on democracy appear quite pragmatic and free from theoretical dogmas usually attached with such conceptualizations.

Ambedkar's confrontation with Gandhi and indeed with the entire Congress and their approach to independence was based on the argument that even if the foreign rulers went away, there was an internal un-freedom as far as the Dalits were concerned since they were oppressed by the caste Hindus. Their oppression preceded Muslim or British rule. For the Dalits to enjoy the fruits of independence,

[15] B. R. Ambedkar, *States and Minorities: What are Their Rights and How to Secure them in the Constitution of India* (Bombay: Thacker & Co., 1947), 9.

[16] B. R. Ambedkar, *What the Congress and Gandhi have Done to the Untouchables* (Bombay: Thacker & Co., 1945), 240.

they needed to secure reserved seats in the Parliament, along with other rights. Gandhi was against separating the Dalits from the Hindus. He believed that he could convince caste Hindus to give up the practice of untouchability by non-violent persuasion. As far as electoral politics was concerned, he preferred the Dalits to be part of the Hindu fold for the time when in future Independence came with some form of franchise. Gandhi could not and would not admit that the Hindu caste system was internally oppressive *in principle as well as in practice*. These were later-day deviations, and he could persuade the Hindus to voluntarily give up such practices. But he was against compulsory or bloody enforcement. Ambedkar was convinced that without some form of political struggle the Dalits would not get justice after Independence. His view of the Indian 'nation' saw it as a mixture of upper castes and the oppressed Dalits and lower castes. The central problem for him was not the British rule, which had treated Dalits better than ever before by recruiting them in the army and other jobs and providing access to education which previously had been denied. For Ambedkar, the problem was the inequity of the Hindu society. Independence and Hindu rule would not be enough to guarantee justice for the Dalits.

Ambedkar developed a powerful (and also persuasive) critique of Gandhi's notion of Hinduism and his conservative defensive attitude towards Hindu caste society. Ambedkar read the old religious manuscripts *Manusmriti* and others to expose the dubious defence of unequal practices. He was prolific in his analysis of the philosophical supports for Hindu practices and saw the deconstruction of the traditional foundations of Hindu social practices as one of his principal tasks. The Gandhi–Ambedkar interaction thus opens out a different dimension of the idea of the nation in which Savarkar, Jinnah and Gandhi all had different views. Their attempts to define a nation as a community differed but shared the notion that a nation had to be a community. Ambedkar from his unique vantage point saw the Hindu society as inherently divided and hierarchical where equality can come only via a modernist movement along the lines of European struggles for the emancipation of the lower classes and neglected groups.

Jinnah: Enigma in India and Hero across the Border

M. A. Jinnah (1876–1948) was the most ardent advocate of the two-nation theory that eventually turned out to be the intellectual justification for the partition of the country into two independent republics of India and Pakistan in 1947. Jinnah, a successful career lawyer, took up the cause of Muslim minority in India and keeping this in mind he adopted and readopted his strategies vis-à-vis imperial power as well as freedom struggle led primarily by the Congress under the leadership of Gandhi. The readily available solution was provided by the communal award of 1932 that was prepared and preceded by the 1909 Government of India Act. Again, the rights of the Muslims had extraordinary significance in the eyes of Jinnah, whereas the civilizational significance of the Indian subcontinent was of paramount significance for Gandhi. In addition to this, the idea of nation was also held differently by both of them. To Gandhi, Hindu and Muslims constituted the same nation, of course, with two different religions heavily influenced by each other over the course of centuries of living together. Precisely this is the reason the way Islam practised in the Indian subcontinent is qualitatively different from that it is practised in Arabia. But Jinnah's insistence on the two-nation theory eluded any kind of convergence with Gandhi's broader view of Indian nationalism. The convergence became almost impossible with the aid and abetment to Jinnah's position by the colonial government. The historical congruence with long cultural intermingling that Gandhi insisted to hold was forced to meet its Waterloo by the unholy nexus between colonial power and the Western-educated enthusiast Jinnah and his Muslim League. Gandhi, even at the strong displeasure of his own Congress colleagues, agreed to make Jinnah the first Prime Minister of independent India to avoid the partition of the country. That establishes the undiluted moral conviction of the man, and his ever-undiminishing human quality for the generations to come. It is evident in inexhaustive creative historical interpretations of the man ever since he took the pledge of the moral upliftment of human beings. On the contrary, the historical evolution of Jinnah and others is apparently a long-settled account.

The story of M. A. Jinnah's growing up in British India shows that he followed the same path as Gandhi. A trained lawyer who joined the Lincoln Inn, he is also known as Quaid-i-Azam, was nurtured in the Enlightenment tradition. Inspired by British liberalism, he admired the moderate nationalists, such as Dadabhai Naoroji and Pherozeshah Mehta. Like some of his nationalist colleagues, he was keen to forge a common politico-ideological platform against the British which, he thought, was needed to combat colonialism. As a regular participant in the Congress meetings, he neither had support for separate electorates nor had ever shown enthusiasm for this when it was granted by the constitutional arrangement that the 1909 Morley–Minto Reforms had devised. Being closely affiliated with the Congress, he did not seem to have favoured the creation of a separate political outfit for the Muslims. Only in 1913, six years later than the foundation of the All India Muslim League, he became its full-fledged member. During the 1916 Lucknow Congress Session when the famous Lucknow Pact was executed to bring together Hindus and Muslims, he even declared himself as 'staunch Congressman first and later a Leaguer'.[17] Being opposed to sectarian politics, the Quaid-i-Azam had hardly shown the inclinations that gradually unfolded in the course of the nationalist campaign for a separate Muslim land. The evolution of the Gandhi-led nationalist movement saw reversal which was the product of those processes that gained momentum in the context of the divide-and-rule strategy which the British ruler had deployed to strengthen the colonial authority. This is one part of the story; the other part can be understood with reference to the prevalent circumstances in which the Hindu–Muslim chasm flourished largely to the unbridgeable socio-economic gulf between these two communities. There were hardly any serious attempts to bridge the gulf, and, consequently, did Muslims not only remain marginalized but they were also alienated. As studies show, the Congress leadership, especially C. R. Das in Bengal where Muslims constituted a demographic majority, made attempts to generate brotherliness among the members of these communities; but with his untimely death, none of his political successors pursued

[17] Ayesha Jalal, *The Sole Spokesman: Jinnah, the Muslim League and the Demand for Pakistan* (Cambridge: Cambridge University Press, 1994), 7.

this line of thinking, which further estranged the Muslims from their Hindu counterparts. With the constitutional guarantee of the separate electorate for the Muslims following the acceptance of the Communal Award in 1932, the British government helped consolidate the separatist sentiments that so far remained dormant. Once the Muslim League emerged as a strong contender for power, the situation became far more complicated. M. A. Jinnah became powerful and bargained strongly with the Congress for power-sharing in Bengal and Punjab where Muslims, being demographically preponderant, fared well in the 1937 election. In view of their class prejudices, complemented by their religious differences with the Muslims, a majority of the Congress leaders, particularly in Bengal, seem to have underplayed the inevitable consequences of this separation. The Congress always remained a second fiddler in institutional politics in Bengal. M. A. Jinnah was a major player during this period, and as an astute strategist, he projected those leaders who had organic linkages with the grassroots in Bengal and Punjab; picking up A. K. Fazlul Haq from among the Muslim leaders in Bengal and Sikander Hayat Khan in Punjab was not his random choice. By 1940, the Muslims became a formidable force in Indian politics which helped the Quaid-i-Azam argue for his two-nation theory in support of his claim for a separate Muslim state. The 1940 Lahore Resolution was a benchmark event in the history of Pakistan and India's freedom struggle because this was the resolution which formally presented the idea of Pakistan. Moved by A. K. Fazlul Haq, perhaps the most popular Muslim leader in Bengal, the resolution was also illustrative of how M. A. Jinnah created a conducive political space for his separatist argument which was inconceivable in the early part of the 20th century.

Since the 1940 Lahore Resolution was an effective challenge to Gandhi's nationalist design, it was a milestone in India's freedom struggle. As is now a matter of common knowledge, Gandhi, being opposed to the 1947 Partition, was never persuaded by Jinnah's model of two-nation theory since, for the Mahatma, Hindus and Muslims were inseparable communities. Nonetheless, the Lahore Resolution was a momentous event for Jinnah because it was a definite direction towards geographically demarcating areas for Pakistan. Insisting on Muslims being culturally separate, the Resolution thus resolved that

> it is the considered views of [the 1940] session of the All India Muslim League that no constitutional plan would be workable in this country or acceptable to Muslims unless it is designed on the following basic principle, namely that geographically contiguous units are demarcated into regions which should be so constituted, with such territorial readjustments as may be necessary, that the areas in which the Muslims are numerically in a majority as in the North-Western and Eastern Zones of India, should be grouped to constitute 'independent states' in which the constituent units shall be autonomous and sovereign.[18]

The tone and the texture of the Resolution were unmistakably a clear statement for Pakistan which, for the first time, identified the areas that were earmarked as those for Muslims. Jinnah was its principal priest, though he remained in the periphery, while A. K. Fazlul Haq read the Resolution as its prime mover. Nonetheless, as available literature demonstrates, it was the Quaid-i-Azam who was the main political force behind the scene. Two important developments took place in the wake of the adoption of the 1940 Resolution. On the one hand, it was a masterstroke that Jinnah pulled off which, by rejuvenating the Muslims, created a momentum for the campaign for Pakistan during the time when the internal squabbles within the Muslim League appeared to have weakened its organizational base, especially in Bengal which was the citadel of the League. The Resolution electrified the League supporters to a significant extent. The Resolution had, on the other hand, another significant outcome: with its endorsement by the Muslims at large, Jinnah firmly established his claim as a widely accepted leader of the Indian Muslims, supporting his campaign in opposition to the claim that the Congress, and Gandhi in particular, made to represent them in the nationalist movement. This had significant implications. The divide-and-rule strategy that the British deployed put the Hindu and Muslims in two watertight compartments; with the adoption of this Resolution, the processes towards permanently separating them had begun, and Jinnah by applying his astute sense succeeded a parallel power centre which, so far, remained elusive given the hegemonic presence of the Mahatma in the nationalist universe. Not only did the Quaid-i-Azam

[18] https://historypak.com/lahore-resolution-1940/, the 1940 Lahore Resolution.

evolve a space in which the claim for Pakistan gained legitimacy, but he also firmly established himself as an effective leader who was capable of challenging the Mahatma and the Congress. In view of its tremendous impact on the campaign for Pakistan, the 1940 Lahore Resolution stands out in the plethora of resolutions that are critical in comprehending the processes leading to the dismemberment of India and the creation of a separate Muslim land on the basis of Jinnah's widely hyped two-nation theory. Furthermore, it was also a powerful critique of the Mahatma who vehemently opposed partition by stating that if it had happened, it would have been on his dead body. As history shows, neither Gandhi nor his secular colleagues in the Congress were able to halt the processes that finally culminated in the emergence of Pakistan in the aftermath of the 1947 British withdrawal.

The evolution of Jinnah from a Congress loyalist to an architect of India's partition appears to be baffling, at least on the surface for two complementary reasons. First, as evidence indicates, he was an ardent supporter of the Congress and its ideological priorities. His endorsement of the 1916 Lucknow Pact ensuring a separate electorate for the Muslims in electing representatives to the Imperial and Provincial Legislative Councils was a testimony to his effort to carve out an independent electoral space for them. By persuading the Congress to grant one-third seats in the Councils and the commitment that no act affecting the Muslims was possible without the support of the unless three-quarters of the Muslim members in the Council, Jinnah succeeded in formally recognizing the Muslims as an electoral entity which was a significant step in India's constitutional history. The Pact was also seen as a beacon of hope for Hindu–Muslim unity since it was endorsed politically by both the Congress and Muslim League. In view of the fact that the League and Congress came together to address the Muslims' concerns, it was also one of the first instances showing that it was possible for the two major religious communities to devise a mechanism to jointly fight for their legitimate claims. Second, the post-Lucknow Pact scenario, however, had undergone a sea change. The endeavour that Jinnah had undertaken to bring together two communities seems to have lost its steam as history progressed. Besides the failure of the mainstream nationalist leaders to create an ambience in which Muslims felt drawn, the schism between the Hindus and Muslims appeared unbridgeable given the well-entrenched socio-economic differences at the grassroots that caused a permanent fissure between the communities. The point is being made here to challenge the claim that had Jinnah not been there, Pakistan would not have been possible. It is true that Jinnah had a critical role in putting forward the well-justified scheme for creating a separate Muslim homeland. But this is the one half of the argument; the other half comes to light when one refers to the stark class differences between the Hindus and Muslims, clearly alienating the latter from the former. So, Jinnah became a beacon of hope for the Muslims who strongly believed that his two-nation theory was justified since they were denied their legitimate claims despite being integral to the polity. Hence, the argument that Jinnah was a context-driven phenomenon seems to be persuasive.

Jinnah's transformation from a loyalist to an opponent is also a testimony to how the Congress nationalists, including Gandhi, failed to sustain the goodwill between the two communities that the 1916 Lucknow Pact had generated. Historically speaking, Gandhi appears to have lost the battle to Jinnah in the Second Round Table Conference in 1931 in which Gandhi was present. With the acceptance of the 1932 Communal Award for the Muslims, the idea that Muslims were a separate electoral group was now constitutionally recognized, the reversal of which was no longer possible. Given Jinnah's critical role in persuading the British authority to grant a separate electorate to the Muslims, he now had emerged as an unassailable leader of the Indian Muslims in opposition to the claim of Gandhi being projected as a nationally acceptable leader of all the communities. As a result, not only did Jinnah's rise as an undisputed Muslim leader across the country create a parallel power centre, but it also unleashed socio-economic and political forces supportive of the Muslims' demand for a sovereign Muslim state. Gandhi endeavoured hard to halt the processes leading to India's partition in 1947 which did not work presumably because Jinnah's emotional appeal for division of the country was far more effective in a socio-economic milieu in which it had adequate backing at the grassroots. The purpose here is not to deal with how Pakistan was formed, since it has been extensively analysed by many scholars, but to comment on their interaction to understand how they shaped the historical processes which finally led to the creation of 'a moth-eaten Pakistan',[19] as Jinnah described once the new nation came into being, and a partitioned India which neither Gandhi nor his nationalist colleagues accepted, as it was contrary to what they so far assiduously pursued.

Gandhian Hegemony

The common thread that runs among Gandhi, Ambedkar, Savarkar and Jinnah is their early exposure to the Western culture and civilization which makes and binds them together as political thinkers. Yet, they have their own specific trajectory of philosophical development that constitutes their own world views. Much of the history of India's freedom struggle, which places them in the galaxy of great political thinkers, provides them the contextual perspective in which they have been able to evolve their thought process. Ambedkar, the first effective voice of the oppressed classes in modern India, well articulated their position and made the Indians realize not only the futility of the persisting caste system but also its inhuman aspects. He himself experienced the indignities hurled upon him at different stages of his life that constituted his initial psychology and approach to Indian society. His primary mission was to obliterate the social stigma of his caste fellows at any cost, sometimes even in collaboration with the British government. He did not stop there but found merit in demanding, like Muslim League, a separate electorate for the oppressed classes. This prepared the ground for the Poona Pact between Gandhi and Ambedkar. The first one-to-one exchange between them highlighted their different social views and methods of resolving the problems faced by India without any interference triggered by the colonial power. It was both arduous and painful exchange of ideas that ultimately forced Gandhi to undertake fast unto death at Yerwada Jail in Poona. Finally, Ambedkar agreed, though reluctantly, to Gandhi's

[19] https://www.nationalarchives.gov.uk/wp-content/uploads/2014/03/fo371-635331.jpg, M. A. Jinnah's statement on the partition of Bengal and Punjab, 4 May 1947.

position that led to the ending of his fast. To Gandhi, it was not that he was averse to the idea of liberation of the oppressed classes; in fact, his commitment to their liberation was as intense as Ambedkar's. Gandhi believed that a conscious split in the structure of religion for the realization of political goals was an immoral act and also at the same time was creating deliberate schism between the political and the moral. In opposition to this, Ambedkar strongly held his political position and, contrary to Gandhi, his own painful personal experiences led him to believe that the realization of political rights was more important than keeping the religious structure intact—religion that historically places them at the bottom of social hierarchy. Eventually, he agreed reluctantly, but somehow he also realized the significance of integrity of religion that shapes to a large extent the moral world view of the community. Gandhi was well aware of the position of Ambedkar and had all his sympathy for his traumatic experiences as a human being that equally made him convinced to join together the struggle against the inhuman practice of untouchability. But at the same time he was equally adamant to hold the intrinsic moral values of Hinduism. In other words, to him, the way to solution does not lie in creating binary but in transcending the bitterness created by the binary.

Savarkar, a progenitor of the philosophy of Hindutva, presented a somewhat circumscribed vision of Hinduism. Although he was a revolutionary and his commitment to India's freedom is unblemished, his political construction of great religion is not of its immense benefit. The inherent pluralism of Indian society was somewhat undermined with too much emphasis given to the faith of the majority community. However, the sacredness of Hindu religion was also appreciated and strengthened by his positive contribution in articulating this religion that has made him not only a great patriot but also attracted unflinching loyalty of millions of Indians. Here again, Gandhi's view of Hinduism is methodologically different from all such narratives of religion. Unlike such constructions, Gandhi believed in symbiotic relation among all religions of the world.[20] To him, they do not necessarily conflict with each other; rather they complement each other in innumerable ways.

[20] Vikram Sampth, 'Gandhi, Savarkar: Two Irreconcilable Poles in Indian History,' *The Week*, 22 June 2019.

His prayers are reflective of this fact; the hymns of all religions were collectively sung to highlight the fact of the organic unity of the human beings of all faiths—different paths but the same destination.

As in the case of Savarkar, Jinnah's world view regarding Indian nationalism as well as the theoretically grounded views on the identity and interests of Muslims in comparison to Hindus did not gel with the composite cultural conceptualization of the Indian nationalism by Gandhi. As had been well established in the historical accounts, Gandhi stood in firm opposition to the idea that Hindu and Muslim constituted two separate nations within the country and undertook many fasts in order to bring about harmony and cordiality between Hindus and Muslims—both during and after the partition of the country.[21] In fact, Gandhi could never have approved the partition of the country if he were allowed to have his way during the penultimate days of the Indian national movement. Nevertheless, when the mainstream leadership of the Congress accepted the partition of India as the fait accompli of the country, Gandhi just became helpless. But he could never reconcile with the view of Jinnah that Hindus and Muslims are two nations and there stood perfect intellectual justification for the creation of a Muslim homeland in the form of Pakistan.

The juxtaposition of Gandhi among the views of his contemporaries is, thus, a fruitful exercise in the sense of its undiminished relevance as well as a readily available corrective to the course of resolution of contemporary conflict and unease. The fecundity that Gandhi possessed was constantly used to morally uplift human beings irrespective of his social, economic, political as well as spatial locations. His epistemology engenders a corresponding ontology, or there is absolutely no mismatch between them. He abhorred any kind of act that did not give chance to rectify mistakes that inadvertently creep into. He put violence in this category by arguing that even when one realized that they erred in killing somebody, they did not even have a chance to regret, let alone reverse the consequences of killing. That made him absolutely convinced in the idea of non-violence and its unwavering practice even at the face of brutal tyranny.

[21] A. G. Noorani, 'Ambedkar, Gandhi & Jinnah,' *Frontline*, 12 June 2015.

The prevalent perception of the idea of political is pejoratively marked even by great minds. But Gandhi transcends this limitation and makes politics a potent means of realizing ones' rights along with its corresponding duties. Such characterization is further expanded by him by combining political and moral values together. He believes what is ethically wrong cannot be politically right. The idea of statecraft conceived purely in terms of power trivializes the meaning of politics which Gandhi does not subscribe. To him, politics is a means of realizing ones' potentialities as well as empowering others to realize the same. In other words, social equilibrium and harmony can be easily attained through politics which would ever move in the direction of realizing the political goal that is the moral upliftment of each and every individual. Gandhi also marks the trajectory of truth in this way—attaining it inherently lies in its unfatigued pursuance.

Unveiling different layers of modernity reveals the fact that it cannot sustain itself as a concept without creating its own opposite. Therefore, the conceptual visualization of good is not possible without the similar comprehension of evil. Gandhi long envisioned this inherent limitation of modern world view that seriously contradicted his moral position of transcendentalism. He believed in the intrinsic goodness of human beings as Swami Vivekananda emphatically put—every soul is potentially divine. Modernity gets stuck only to the level of politics and political where they always need a foe to undermine the friend and in the process appreciates the value of friendship. But Gandhi goes far ahead where the difference between the friend and foe gets obliterated once and for all, and finally things get integrated with the intrinsic goodness being possessed by both as human beings. That is what makes Gandhi's ideas hegemonic in a commonsensical way, but in a deeper way, its unending significance as always remains intact for posterity.

Comprising four chapters besides the Introduction and Conclusion, the book delves into interactive dialogues involving Gandhi and his critics, M. A. Jinnah, V. D. Savarkar and B. R. Ambedkar. At one level, they held compatible ideational views by being appreciative of the Enlightenment values; at the level of practice, they however differed radically: while Gandhi was never persuaded to champion sectional interests, his nationalist critics devised strategies for fulfilling the interests of specific communities. By insisting on the exclusive identity of the Hindus, V. D. Savarkar, for instance, did not seem to be fair, on occasions, to India's diverse social texture. The principal argument that the text provides is about the processes that informed the evolution and articulation of the mainstream nationalist ideas. There is no denying that the ideas that Gandhi evolved by being engaged with the campaign against artificially nurtured design of exploitation of one section of humanity against another remained prominent during the nationalist intervention. How did Gandhi become the Mahatma is the main concern of Chapter 1 which, by dwelling on how he conceptualized and also put into practice the non-violent Satyagraha, seeks to contextualize the dialogic interaction that the Mahatma had with his detractors. Chapter 2 is directed to capture the complex arguments that Savarkar offered to defend his claim for recognizing Hindus as a cultural construct and not merely a religious group. Based on his own written texts, the chapter is also an elaboration of a distinct approach to India's past recalling Savarkar's own assessment of the nationalist context and Gandhi's leadership. Being a protagonist of social justice, B. R. Ambedkar put forward his model of emancipation by being deviant from what the Mahatma suggested. A hard-core liberal, Ambedkar, as Chapter 3 argues, designed a mechanism to seek to create a template for equity and fair play. Being a staunch believer in liberal constitutionalism, he translated his ideas into reality by incorporating them in the 1950 Constitution of India, which was possible as Gandhi supported him first to become a member of the Constituent Assembly and later the chairman of the Drafting Committee. Of all Gandhi's critics, M. A. Jinnah stands out for the success that he attained by carving out a separate Muslim land to the chagrin of his nationalist colleagues. Despite Gandhi's vehement opposition to partition, the Quaid-i-Azam, as Chapter 4 illustrates, had won the battle since the British withdrawal was accompanied by the creation of two independent states, India and Pakistan, much to the annoyance of the Congress nationalists and to the satisfaction of League claimants. Focusing on how a loyalist Jinnah became a bête noire of the Congress and Gandhi, Chapter 4 draws on the complex interplay of socio-economic processes that aided the Quaid-i-Azam to accomplish his mission. It is true, as the chapter argues, that the peculiar unfolding of inter-communal relations between Hindus and Muslims created an ambience in which Jinnah's clarion call for dismemberment of India gained credibility. Out of these three critics, Jinnah became a nemesis for Gandhi who, despite being opposed to India's vivisection, became helpless when the Muslims of Bengal and Punjab rallied behind Jinnah's two-nation-theory. By shaping the transfer of power in the format that Quaid-i-Azam preferred, he charted a specific course in India's freedom struggle which was, at least in the mainstream nationalist perspective, inconceivable as late 1940 when Jinnah, along with his colleagues, formally adopted the infamous Lahore Resolution at the annual session of the Muslim League, held at Iqbal Park in Lahore.

Arguments

There are two major arguments and one peripheral argument that *Politics, Ideology and Nationalism: Jinnah, Savarkar and Ambedkar versus Gandhi* offers. First, the book claims that Gandhi would not have become Gandhi independent of the intellectual interventions, made by his equally illustrious nationalist colleagues such as M. A. Jinnah, V. D. Savarkar and B. R. Ambedkar. True that they drew different conclusions on how the struggle for freedom was to be designed, but what brought them together was their firm commitment to the widely accepted Enlightenment values and principles. Second, by delving into the complex interplay of socio-economic and political processes in the nationalist context, the book also makes the point that the individual existential experiences play a critical role in shaping individuals' distinct socio-economic and political priorities. For instance, the Dalit identity of B. R. Ambedkar remained a determining influence in conceptualizing his idea of social justice around caste atrocities. The peripheral argument defends the contention that the Gandhian ideas are transcendental in nature and texture since finality in thoughts was alien to Gandhi. As history has shown, not only did Gandhi's non-violent *Satyagraha* inspire the African Americans in the context of civil rights movement in the USA in the 1960s to successfully challenge the racial segregation, but it also helped the protestors mobilize the masses in the context of the Arab Spring (2010–2011) against the brutal political authorities despite being threatened and also severely punished. The claim substantiates the argument that Gandhi is an ideational battle for justice and equity for humanity; it may have had varied manifestations due to contextual peculiarities though, the kernel remains the same since it is based on ahimsa or non-violence. Hence, the claim that Gandhism can never be conclusive because it is drawn on the belief that the attainment of truth is contingent on its constant pursuance.

This book is a continuity with the past and reinforcement of India's well-entrenched argumentative tradition. Defending an aim-driven voice, the argumentative tradition enriches the discourses in which views and ideas are articulated. It is in this conceptual universe the dialogic design of thinking has flourished in India since time immemorial. The Indian nationalist leaders, including Gandhi 'emphasized the need to be vigilant in defence of this open-minded tradition and to help it flower more freely'.[22] Appreciative of cultural heterogeneity Rabindranath Tagore (1861–1941) felt proud to have belonged to a family representing 'a confluence of three cultures, Hindu, Mohammedan and British'.[23] While defining the idea of India, both Gandhi and Tagore strove to develop a collective template by seeking to creatively blend multiple cultural traditions because privileging one tradition over the rest was contrary to what was instinctive to the Indians by being Indians. Based on mutual borrowings from different cultural traditions, Indian identity is thus naturally multicultural. India's nationalist discourse that evolved in response to colonialism is a testimony to this claim. As evidence shows, the nationalists

> developed a new language of discourse in which old and long familiar words were revived, given new meanings, and adapted to modern concerns. [Hence], they talked of swaraj rather than liberty, freedom or independence; *naya* rather than justice; *adhikar* rather than right; vikas rather development;

[22] Amartya Sen, *The Argumentative Tradition: Writings on Indian History, Culture and Identity* (New York: Picador, 2005), 32.

[23] Rabindranath Tagore, *The Religion of Man* (London: Unwin, 1961) (reprint), 105.

> sanskriti rather than civilization. These were not vernacular translations of English words, … [r]ather they had indigenous cultural roots and history, and their cognitive and emotional connotations differed from those of their corresponding Western concepts.[24]

Ideationally unique and ideologically refreshing, these ideas gradually became part and parcel of the nationalist thinking. *Politics, Ideology and Nationalism* is an attempt to articulate the dialogic voice and also conceptualize the endeavour by reference to the public debate involving Gandhi and his detractors. It makes an analytical statement on the complex texture of India's nationalist ideas that evolved in the wake of the freedom struggle. The book argues that in the conceptualization of the mainstream nationalist counter-attack against colonialism, Gandhi remained one of the principal architects. His nationalist colleagues, M. A. Jinnah, B. R. Ambedkar and V. D. Savarkar, had also played a critical, if not determining, on occasions, role in shaping the nationalist voice and its vocabularies. As available evidence shows, they held contrasting ideological positions notwithstanding being inspired by compatible intellectual inclinations in the sense that they drew on the core Enlightenment values. The battle that they had lodged for equity and fairness was directed to create a society free from discrimination. Their ideological concern was partly derivative since by being politico-ideologically baptized in Western liberalism, they seem to have instinctively acquired concerns for empathy, care and compassion for all. There were two levels at which they pitched their ideational battle: at a rather visible level, their contrary views were drawn on sociopolitical imbalances leading to segregation of one section of society from another. In other words, it was a challenge to the artificially created socio-economic hierarchy which they were determined to do away with. For Jinnah, since the well-entrenched schism between Hindus and Muslims was organic to the Hindu society, no option was left but to fight for a separate Muslim homeland; given the widely nurtured caste segregation, Ambedkar had also embarked on similar course correction by strongly arguing for reservation for the Dalits who remained socially segregated due to the accident of birth;

[24] Bhikhu Parekh, *Debating India: Essays on Indian Political Discourse* (New Delhi: Oxford University Press, 2015), 26.

the perception that led Savarkar to mobilize the Hindus was not exactly the same though he was also persuaded to battle for the beleaguered Hindus since they were sociopolitically marginalized largely due to the Congress being overprotective of the Indian Muslims. Mahatma, however, stood out because he transcended the views supportive of sectional interests which is evident when he, regardless of politico-ideological priorities, had built an epistemological bridge by being engaged with the seemingly contradictory ideas. It was easier for Gandhi to interact with those colleagues in the nationalist struggle who held diametrically opposite views since the notion of finality was alien to the Gandhian politico-ideological priorities as the Mahatma believed in experimentalism that enabled him in his quest for truth. Being open to debates and discussions, Gandhi had an edge over his colleagues as he had always given adequate importance to views, contrary to his. His views and ideas were thus primarily interactive in the sense that they evolved out of the interface involving him and his critics. This further means, at the level of conceptual congruity, that since Gandhi and his nationalist colleagues were dialectically interconnected, the views that they evolved were drawn on each other. Keeping this in view, *Politics, Ideology and Nationalism* can thus be said to have made a long analytical statement reconfirming the claim on the basis of a thorough study of the ideas that the Mahatma and his critics had generated while effectively challenging the British rule and its ideational foundation.

Gandhi (1869–1948)

Unfolding of an Ideational Search*

1

Mohandas Karamchand Gandhi (1869–1948), popularly known as Mahatma Gandhi, continues to evoke interests even several decades after his death in 1948. It is true that Richard Attenborough's film *Gandhi* immensely popularized Gandhi all over the world, though Gandhi remains an important topic of research and discussion among those interested in exploring alternative ideological traditions. The task is made easier simply because Gandhi's own writings on various themes are plenty and less ambiguous. His articulation is not only clear and simple but also meaningful in similar contexts in which he led the most gigantic nationalist struggle of the 20th century. He wrote extensively in *Young India* and *Harijan*, the leading newspapers of the era, where Gandhi commented on the issues of contemporary relevance. These texts frequently address matters of everyday importance to Indians in the early and middle parts of the 20th century that may not appear to be relevant if seen superficially. Writing for the ordinary folks, he usually employed metaphors and engaged in homilies to teach Indians about their abilities and also their strong traditions. This is one of the ways in which he involved the Indians in non-violent struggles against the British imperialism, untouchability and communal discord. It is now fair to suggest that Gandhi created an ambience in which the nationalists became Gandhian by being appreciative of 'Gandhiana', the set of

* Drawn on my earlier works (*Social and Political Thought of Mahatma Gandhi*, Routledge, Oxford, 2006 and *Confluence of Thought: Mahatma Gandhi and Martin Luther King Jr*, Oxford University Press, New York, 2013), this chapter shows how Gandhi evolved his model of political mobilization by being involved in the nationalist campaign against the British which finally culminated in India's independence in 1947.

principles that he evolved by being dialectically interconnected with the context in which he rose to prominence. As soon as he arrived in South Africa, he confronted a brutal racist regime that privileged one section of the population over the rest purely due to the accident of birth. Being baptized in the Enlightenment values, Gandhi strongly opposed the regime since it was pursuing discriminatory policies which were contrary to the fundamental ethos on which the Westminster system of governance rested. It was a battle that he had waged for those who, despite being the citizens of the British empire, were deprived of being treated as her citizens. For him, it was a first experience of how a racist regime functioned when he was thrown out of the train compartment at the Maritzburg station in South Africa at the height of the winter. How did he react to the incident which did not seem to be very uncommon given the official recognition of racial segregation there? In his words,

> I began to think of my duty. Should I fight for my rights or go back to India, or should I go on to Pretoria without minding the insults, and return to India after finishing the case? It would be cowardice to run back to India without fulfilling my obligation. The hardship to which I was subjected was superficial—only a symptom of the deep disease of colour prejudice. I should try, if possible, to root out the disease and suffer hardships in the process. Redress for wrongs I should seek only to the extent that would be necessary for the removal of the colour prejudice.[1]

The aforementioned text is revealing: on the one hand, it is illustrative of how Gandhi viewed the emotional torture that he had undergone after having been thrown out the train despite being a legitimate passenger in the compartment. He had his dilemma which, however, was instantaneously resolved when, he, on the other hand, resolved to lodge a battle against colour prejudice; it was a battle that was required to be waged, he felt strongly, to combat the foundational values that nourished racism. A rebel was born who raised his voice against the regime which also derived its legitimacy from the Enlightenment values on which the British system of governance rested.

[1] M. K. Gandhi, *An Autobiography or the Story of My Experiments with Truth* (Ahmedabad: Navajivan Publishing House, 2008) (reprint), 104.

The Texture of Gandhiana

There is no dearth of text to decipher what Gandhi stood for. The problem lies in the language in which his ideas were articulated. The language is so simple that it is notoriously open to diverse interpretations. For instance, Gandhi's critique of modernity and modernization in his *Hind Swaraj* is constantly referred to as illustrative of his obscurantism. And the only correct way of reading him is, therefore, 'to see him arguing that India must return to a simple agrarian economy and simple society'. This interpretation appears to be overstretched and fails to capture the complex nuances in Gandhi's thought that flourished in a context when India, as part of the British colony, had adopted the path of capitalist development. It is true that Gandhi's insistence on rural economy and uncomplicated life was perhaps logical in his conceptualization of Indian society and economy. Hence, his arguments supporting a particular society and economy are not only criticisms of the dominant organizing principles of the era but also provide 'idealized alternatives to them which he wants men and women to enlist in their struggle to protect their own autonomy'.[2] In so doing, Gandhi was simply critical of the contemporary civilization that drew on a total rejection of what he defined the perennially valid 'traditional values'. His oppositional views upheld a new theoretical enquiry that is meaningful only in a colonial context in which the politically dominant ideas tend to swallow the countervailing ideas with indigenous roots. Gandhi's peculiar genius lay in his understanding of how the complex fabric of traditional Indian society could be 'related to the essentially modern phenomenon of the movement for political independence'.[3]

Furthermore, Gandhi's charisma had 'a cultural referent'. His success as a leader was less to his 'oratorical or theatrical skills' than to the reputation that preceded him and 'the ideal he embodied'. As Rudolphs argue 'the authenticity with which he sought virtue and the highest

[2] Ronald J. Tarchek, *Gandhi: Struggling for Autonomy* (New Delhi: Vistaar Publications, 2000), 3–4.

[3] Ainslie T. Embree, *Imagining India: Essays on Indian History* (Delhi: Oxford University Press, 1989), 165.

religious goals through self-control, truth and non-violence re-enacted a familiar but rarely realized cultural model, that of the saintly man'.[4] What he represented was 'saintly politics'[5] that acquired salience in the British-ruled India where the indigenous cultural traditions had a natural appeal to the peripheral masses. Many were struck by the contrast between his remarkable physical appearance and the aura surrounding him. In his first meeting with Gandhi, Lord Reading, the Viceroy, expressed surprise at his growing popularity among the Indians by saying

> There is nothing striking about his appearance. He came to visit me in a white dhoti and cap, woven on a spinning-wheel, with bare feet and legs, and my first impression on seeing him ushered into my room was that there was nothing to arrest attention in his appearance, and that I should have passed him by in the street without a second look at him. When he talks, the impression is different.[6]

By playing upon a very varied symbolic register, Gandhi was able 'to establish with the Indian public a rapport of profound complicity which often escaped the eyes of the British, who were not very sensitive to the nuances of Gandhian symbolism'.[7] To the Indian masses, he was a renouncer, a *sanyasi* who adopted a life style that was entirely different from those Anglicized politicians so far controlling the anti-British campaign in India.[8] While his typical life style endeared Gandhi

[4] Lloyd I. Rudolph and Susanne Hoeber Rudolph, *The Modernity of Tradition: Political Development in India* (Chicago and London: The University of Chicago Press, 1967), 159.

[5] According to Morris-Jones, Gandhi represented saintly politics in which his image as a renouncer mattered a lot. W. H. Morris Jones, 'India's Political Idioms,' in *Politics and Society in India*, ed. C. H. Philips (London: George Allen & Unwin, 1963), 140.

[6] Oriental and India Office Collections, London, Mss Eur. F238/3, Reading Papers, Reading, the viceroy to Montague, the Secretary of State, 19 May 1921.

[7] Claude Markovits, *The Un-Gandhian Gandhi: The Life and Afterlife of the Mahatma* (New Delhi: Permanent Black, 2003), 32.

[8] For a quick summary of Gandhi's role in Indian freedom struggle and the ideas he stood for, see Judith Brown, 'The Mahatma and Modern India,' *Modern Asian Studies* 3, no. 4 (1969): 321–42.

to the masses,[9] those who so far led the Congress failed to understand him. As Lajpat Rai commented, 'such of his countrymen as have drunk deep from the fountains of European history and European politics and who have developed a deep love for European manners and European culture, neither understand nor like him. In their eyes, he is a barbarian'.[10] Yet, Gandhi gradually became the centre of the nationalist activities in opposition to the typical constitutional means of protest against colonialism. In fact, his rise to the leadership of the Congress in 1920 radically altered its social composition by simply allowing the politically peripheral groups in contrast with the anglicized elite of the great metropolitan cities. A new middle class—some of whom came from the smaller cities and towns and were prone to express themselves in the vernacular rather than in English—joined the Congress that so far remained confined largely to the metropolitan cities of Calcutta and Bombay. This non-metropolitan middle class with close links with the countryside was 'better-placed to draw rural India into the struggle, thanks to its contacts with an upper strata of relatively rich peasants'.[11] Judith Brown thus argued that Gandhi's rise did not symbolize 'a radical restructuring of political life' or emergence of mass politics; rather it signified the rise of Western-educated and regional language literate elites of backward areas, in place of the Western-educated leaders of the presidency towns. It was the loyalty of these local leaders or the so-called 'sub-contractors' that enabled Gandhi to extend the constituency of the nationalist politics.[12] What is wrong in such an interpretation is the failure to comprehend the

[9] R. K. Narayan, the novelist who was in his early 20s provided a first account of Gandhi's arrival in a small town in Tamil Nadu. He was amazed by the electrifying presence of the Mahatma who was impressive neither in terms of his 'attire' nor 'the speech', he delivered. What perplexed the young Narayan was how the Mahatma struck an emotional chord almost instantaneously with those waiting for him for long hours. Narayan was drawn to him appreciating Mahatma's charisma and the ideology of non-violence. R. K. Narayan, *Waiting for the Mahatma* (Chennai: Indian Thought Publications, 2003) (reprint).

[10] Dhanki Joginder Singh, ed., *Perspectives on Indian National Movement (selected correspondence of Lala Lajpat Rai)* (New Delhi: National Book Organizations, 1998), 31.

[11] Markovits, *The Un-Gandhian Gandhi*, 34.

[12] Judith M. Brown, *Gandhi's Rise to Power, Indian Politics, 1915–22* (Cambridge: Cambridge University Press, 1972), 356.

mass appeal of Gandhi as a leader who could also appeal directly, beyond the ranks of this elite leadership, to the Indian peasantry and draw their support for his struggle against the British. Gandhi was not merely a leader, he also became a part of the masses. His simple attire, use of colloquial Hindi, reference to the popular allegory of *Ramrajya* 'had made him comprehensible to the common people'. In popular myths, he was, as Shahid Amin has shown, invested with supernatural power, which could heal pain and deliver common people from their day-to-day miseries. The masses interpreted Gandhi in their own ways drawing meanings from their own lived experiences and made him a symbol of power for the weak and underprivileged.[13] As evident on various occasions, the masses 'crossed the boundaries of Gandhian politics and deviated from his ideals of non-violence, while believing at the same time that they were following their messiah into a new utopian world of Gandhi raj'.[14] This also suggests that the introduction of Gandhi to Indian politics radically restructured its nature that was hardly confined to the presidency towns. Not only did he inculcate new styles of political articulation but he also enlarged the nationalist constituencies by incorporating new actors, so far peripheral in the anti-British struggle. So, Gandhi was a symbol of radical changes both in the nationalist political articulation and its constituencies that expanded beyond the Western-educated elites in metropolitan towns.

Thus he was a man of both thought and action, a rare combination. As a man of thought, he was highly critical of the madness of modernity and articulated 'an alternative vision [combining] the best insights of both the pre-modern and modern world-views while avoiding the naïve individualism and moral vacuum of the currently fashionable post-modernism'.[15] He also discovered a uniquely moral method of political change in the form of Satyagraha, and provided an effective alternative to violence, perpetrated by the ruling authority. As

[13] Shahid Amin, 'Gandhi as Mahatma: Gorakhpur District, Eastern UP, 1921–2,' in *Subaltern Studies: Writings on South Asian History and Society*, ed. Ranajit Guha, Vol. III (Delhi: Oxford University Press, 1984).

[14] Sekhar Bandyopadhyay, *From Plassey to Partition: A History of Modern India* (New Delhi: Orient Longman, 2004), 292–93. This point is elaborated in Chapter 2.

[15] Bhikhu Parekh, *Gandhi* (Oxford: Oxford University Press, 1997), 92.

Rudolphs put it, 'Indian nationalism had tried the paths of loyal constitutionalism and terrorist violence and found them wanting. Gandhi's answer was Satyagraha (truth force), expressed through non-violent but non-constitutional direct action'.[16] He also spoke about 'structural violence and the violence of the status-quo'.[17] Poverty was, for instance, violence to him. Human-caused, unnecessary suffering and doing nothing to alleviate suffering when one has the means remain the basic pillars of his analysis of violence. As a man of action, he led perhaps the most gigantic nationalist struggle of the 20th century on the basis of what he thought was morally acceptable. Without compromising one's integrity, he also demonstrated how to build a strong political platform drawing upon moral strength of the Satyagrahees.

Hind Swaraj

Written in 1909, *Hind Swaraj* or *Indian Home Rule* is Gandhi's own assessment of human civilization that evolved in the wake of industrial revolution. A careful analysis of the issues that he raised suggests that he was vehemently opposed to artificial mechanization of human life that inevitably was the consequence. One of the core points of his critique was linked with his stern opposition to colonialism that, he felt, came piggyback with industrialization. Since industrialization was contingent on the exploration of new markets, colonial expansion did not appear to have been an aberration which also justified the ruthlessness of the colonizers to fulfil their partisan aims. For the Mahatma, it was demeaning because it helped construct and also consolidate a hierarchy that was deliberately designed to protect the interests of one segment of humanity at the cost of the rest. Being born and raised in colonial India, it came naturally to him that colonialism was anything but a prejudicial system of socio-economic and political priorities. His sojourn of 21 years in racial South Africa (1893–1914), where he went to work, reinforced some of the ideas that he internalized while being in India. An outcome of his engagement of colonialism in practice in India and later in South Africa, *Hind Swaraj* or *Indian Home Rule* was

[16] Rudolph and Rudolph, *The Modernity of Tradition*, 183.

[17] Douglas Allen, 'Discovering Gandhi,' *The Times of India*, New Delhi, 4 July 2004.

a black-and-white representation of what the Mahatma articulated on the basis of his own appraisal of colonialism and its role in causing devastation to human civilization.

Given the dialectical interconnection between what Gandhi confronted and what he wrote, one can safely argue that what is unique in Gandhian thought is its drive to combine theory with practice. During his career as a political activist, Gandhi experimented with his ideas in the context of perhaps the most well-entrenched nationalist movement of the past century. While the activist Gandhi deployed Satyagraha to mobilize masses in adverse circumstances, the theoretical Gandhi grappled with the reality in a very rigorous manner. In other words, the activist Gandhi drew on the theoretical search for appropriate models in a particular context. Unlike those who launched the anti-British campaign before his arrival on the political scene, Gandhi appeared to have undertaken a thorough study of the Indian reality and also of the people who gradually became participants in the movements following Gandhian methods. So, Gandhian social and political ideas involve a thorough grasping of both reality and its articulation in the writings of the Mahatma. This is where the book is unique because not only does it deal with relatively unknown dimensions of Gandhian thought, but it also demonstrates the gradual but steady evolution of the man who dwelled on issues that remained relevant even after India became free.

A manifesto of what later became Gandhism, *Hind Swaraj* or *Indian Home Rule* is perhaps the most systematic exposition of Gandhi's ideas of state, society and nation. For the colonial authority, it was 'an incendiary manifesto' that was banned in 1910 because (a) it was a scathing critique of Western civilization and (b) it also provided a vernacular model of action against 'unlawful' oppression. For his nationalist colleagues, *Hind Swaraj* or *Indian Home Rule* was clearly 'an archaic text' seeking to reverse the cycle of history. Nonetheless, the point remains that it was perhaps the most authentic nationalist voice that charted out a new course of nationalist struggle in a context when the battle for political freedom was a distant goal. What needs attention is also the claim that it was Gandhi who created a nationalist template which was readily acceptable to the people at large. There were certainly efforts that his colleagues in the Congress had made to pursue their limited nationalist goal; with Gandhi on the scene, the nationalist struggle had undergone a sea change since it was no longer confined to the metropolitan cities of Calcutta and Bombay, but had spread out to the small towns and villages that remained peripheral insofar as the anti-British campaign was concerned.

Although *Hind Swaraj* is an original tract, Gandhi while writing this was heavily influenced by some of the leading Western thinkers. As he himself admitted, 'whilst the views expressed in *Hind Swaraj* are held by me, I have but endeavoured humbly to follow Tolstoy, Ruskin, Thoreau, Emerson and other writers, besides the masters of Indian philosophy'.[18] It contains a statement of some of the fundamental tenets in Gandhi's politics. In other words, Gandhi stated his position quite clearly in *Hind Swaraj* and held onto it all this life. *Hind Swaraj* laid, in fact, the most crucial theoretical foundation of his entire strategy of winning *Swaraj* for India. As the book deals with Gandhian ideas, a brief discussion of the issues raised in the *Hind Swaraj* will perfectly be in order. Aware that this tract revealed the foundational ideas of Gandhian thought, Gandhi, in a significant comment on the *Hind Swaraj* in 1921, explained the purpose behind the book by saying,

> It was written … in answer to the Indian school of violence, and its prototype in South Africa. I came in contact with every known Indian anarchist in London. Their bravery impressed me, but I feel that their zeal was misguided. I felt that violence was no remedy for India's ills, and that her civilization required the use of a different and higher weapon for self-protection. The Satyagraha of South Africa was still an infant hardly two years old. But it had developed sufficiently to permit me to write of it with some degree of confidence. … [*Hind Swaraj*] teaches the gospel of love in the place of that of hate. It replaces violence with self-sacrifice. It pits soul-force against brute force.[19]

[18] Gandhi's preface to the English edition of the *Hind Swaraj* in Anthony Parel, ed., *Hind Swaraj and Other Writings* (Cambridge: Cambridge University Press, 1997), 6.

[19] *The Collected Works of Mahatma Gandhi (CWMG)*, Vol. 19, (New Delhi: Ministry of Information and Broadcasting, Government of India), 277.

The aim of *Hind Swaraj* was 'to confront the anarchist and violence-prone Indian nationalists with an alternative to violence, derived from Gandhi's earliest experiments with satyagraha'.[20] As Gandhi wrote,

> Hind Swaraj [was] written in order to show that [his countrymen] are following a suicidal policy [of violence], and that, if they but revert to their own glorious civilization, either the English would adopt the latter and become Indianised or find their occupation in India gone.[21]

Even the title of the book was most significant; he dealt with his version of Swaraj that was relevant to India. This was the first and perhaps most elaborate discussion of *Swaraj* or freedom from Gandhi's point of view. This was also the most authentic text of Gandhian social and political ideas dealing with Swaraj and Satyagraha. Furthermore, in *Hind Swaraj*, Gandhi drew 'the dichotomies between the spiritual, moral fabric of Indian society, and the violent, politically corrupt nature of European state even more dramatically than any of his predecessors'.[22] While condemning 'the brute force'[23] of Western powers, Gandhi distanced himself from the militant nationalists for their support to violence which was suicidal as a strategy as it would provoke 'an organized violence' by the ruling authority.[24] Violence was, therefore, counterproductive. *Hind Swaraj*, as evident, served two purposes: on the one hand, this was a detailed commentary on Western civilization that thrived on naked force; this also laid down,

[20] Dennis Dalton, *No Violence in Action: Gandhi's Power* (Delhi: Oxford University Press, 1998) (reprint), 16–7.

[21] Parel, ed., *Hind Swaraj and Other Writings*, 7.

[22] Dennis Dalton, 'The Ideology of Sarvodaya: Concepts of Politics and Power in Indian Political Thought,' in *Political Thought in Modern India*, eds. Thomas Pantham and Kenneth L. Deutsch (New Delhi: SAGE Publications, 1986), 283.

[23] In his *Hind Swaraj*, Gandhi extensively commented on 'Brute Force'. Parel, ed., *Hind Swaraj and Other Writings*, Chap. 16, pp. 79–87.

[24] While comparing the Western brute force with his conceptualization of 'soul-force or truth-force', Gandhi charged the Extremist political leaders with nurturing 'narrow ends, infected by British methods'. Gandhi, 'the doctrine of the sword', reproduced in *CWMG*, Vol. 10, pp. 42–4. He further argued, 'violence is the law of the brute. The spirit lies dormant in the brute and he knows no law but that of physical might. The dignity of man requires obedience to a higher law—to the strength of spirit'.

on the other, the fundamental pillars what later became basic precepts of Gandhi's social and political ideas. Although his Satyagraha experiment in South Africa contributed immensely to *Hind Swaraj*, he was influenced by other sources. As he himself admitted, 'whilst the views expressed in Hind Swaraj are held by me, I have but endeavoured humbly to follow Tolstoy, Ruskin, Thoreau, Emerson and other writers, besides the masters of Indian philosophy'.[25]

Hind Swaraj is a foundational text for understanding Gandhi and his ideology. An outcome of a cross-fertilization of ideas, both Indian and Western, *Hind Swaraj* was perhaps the most powerful exposition of Gandhian social and political ideas. A rather 'incendiary manifesto'[26] to galvanize the masses into action, *Hind Swaraj* was banned in 1910 by the government for fear of sedition. Whether it was a seditious tract is debatable, but it is certainly a significant text with refreshing ideas (a) critiquing the Western civilization and also (b) seeking to build 'a vernacular model of action'[27] that the people of India understood.

Hind Swaraj provides a scathing critique of Western civilization. The three recurrent themes are (a) colonial imperialism (b) industrial capitalism and (c) rationalist materialism. According to Gandhi, colonialism triumphed in India not because of its strength but because of our weaknesses that allowed 'this intimate enemy' to strike roots in India. He was probably the first to have attributed the British rule in India to 'moral decline' that affected the entire nation. For Gandhi, the aim of his project was, therefore, to recover 'the self under colonialism'.[28] Attributing colonialism in India to 'our weaknesses', Gandhi thus argued,

> The English have not taken India; we have given to them. They are not in India because of their strength, but because we keep them. … Recall the

[25] Gandhi on *Hind Swaraj* in D. G. Tendulkar, *Mahatma*, Vol. 1 (Delhi: Government of India Publication Division, 1960), 100; *CWMG*, Vol. 9, p. 182 and Vol. 10, p. 189.

[26] Erik H. Erikson, *Gandhi's Truth: on the Origins of Militant Non-violence* (New York: Norton, 1966), 217.

[27] Bhikhu Parekh, *Gandhi's Political Philosophy: A Critical Appreciation* (Delhi: Ajanta Publications, 1995), 211.

[28] These expressions are borrowed from Ashis Nandy's, *The Intimate Enemy: Loss and Recovery of Self Under Colonialism* (Delhi: Oxford University Press, 1983) 31, 48.

> Company Bahadur. Who made it Bahadur? They had not the slightest intention at the time of establishing a kingdom. Who assisted the Company's officers? Who was tempted at the sight of their silver? Who bought their goods? History testifies that we did all this. ... When our Princes fought among themselves, they sought the assistance of Company Bahadur. That corporation was versed alike in commerce and war. It was unhampered by questions of morality. ... Is it not then useless to blame the English for what we did at the time? ... it is truer to say that we gave India to the English than that India was lost.[29]

According to Gandhi, the British conquest of India was solely due to our moral failure. Imperialism struck roots in India in course of time because of the cooperation of the Indians with the British government. There was no restraint presumably because of a moral decadence of the race, known as Indians. There is another side of the argument. Gandhi was contemptuous of Western civilization that under the garb of civilizing the colonial 'subjects' pursued its 'selfish interests' and nothing else. Based on 'brute force', the Western civilization was thus both 'narrow' and 'perverted'. So, in Gandhi's perception, by providing legitimacy to colonialism, the so-called modern civilization subverted 'the natural evolution' of societies clinging to the so-called traditional ways of life. Drawn on the civilizational resources of a traditional society like India, Gandhi produced perhaps 'the most effective trans-cultural protest against the hyper-masculine world view of colonialism'.[30]

Hind Swaraj was the most creative response to the perversion of industrial capitalism. For Gandhi, industrialization remained the driving force behind Western civilization. 'Machinery is' he characterized, 'the chief symbol of modern civilization; it represents sin. [Hence] if the machine craze grows in our country, it will become an unhappy land'.[31] Condemning the role of machine in 'de-humanizing' the workers toiling in the factories for 'profit' in which they had no share, the Mahatma thus argued that 'it is necessary to realize that machinery is bad. We shall then be able to do away with it. ... If, instead of

[29] Parel, ed., *Hind Swaraj and Other Writings*, Chap. VII, pp. 39–41.

[30] Nandy, *The Intimate Enemy*, 48.

[31] Parel, ed., *Hind Swaraj and Other Writings*, Chap. XIX, p. 107.

welcoming machinery as a boon', he further mentioned, 'we would look upon it as an evil, it would ultimately go'.[32] According to Gandhi, 'a snake-bite is a lesser poison' than 'the mill industry' because while the former merely harmed the body, the latter 'destroys body, mind and soul'.[33] Gandhi's critique of machine civilization was a creative response and thus most original than his erstwhile colleagues in the nationalist movement. While the earlier nationalists attributed the Western conquest of India to 'a superior military strength', Gandhi actually probed into the processes that led to such a dramatic rise of the Western powers. Unlike his colleagues, Gandhi had no doubt that 'the source of modern imperialism lies specifically in the system of social production which the countries of the Western world have adopted'. It is the limitless desire for 'ever-increased production and ever-greater consumption and the spirit of ruthless competitiveness' that not only sustained the system but also impelled these countries to establish colonies that could be exploited for economic gains.[34] Industrialism was an evil simply because the purpose of production was not to create an egalitarian but a capitalist society. For industrialism to survive and thrive, these Western industrial nations needed colonies to market their goods. Since colonialism and industrialism were complementary to each other, industrial capitalism was, as Gandhi saw, inherently harmful to human civilization.

According to Gandhi, there remained a tension between 'true civilization' and 'a civilization based on machine'. While the former is based on brute rationalist materialism, the latter draws its sustenance from dharma. In modern civilization, *artha* (money) and *kama* (desire) are totally divorced from dharma on the basis of the alleged superiority of 'rational materialism'. Critical of the unbridled march of 'reason', Gandhi was never agreeable to abdicate his 'faith' for reason. Instead, he would test his faith with his reason, but would not allow reason to destroy his faith. In other words, 'technological rationalism', defending 'crude materialism' lay at the root of destruction of true civilization

[32] Ibid, 111.

[33] Ibid, 108.

[34] Partha Chatterjee, *Nationalist Thought and the Colonial World: A Derivative Discourse* (Delhi: Oxford University Press, 1986), 87.

where dharma was a device to ascertain morality. 'To observe morality is', argued Gandhi, 'is to attain mastery over our mind and our passions'.[35] Religion was the template for morality. He never compromised with the importance of religion in our social life though he opposed religious superstitions which, according to him, were 'cruelties, practiced in the name of religion'.[36] But there was no end to this process and 'they will happen so long as there are to be found ignorant and credulous people'.[37] Although there was no space for religious superstition, for obvious reasons, Gandhi was not 'irreligious' either for he argued that 'we will certainly fight tooth and nail, but we can never do so by disregarding religion. We can only do so by appreciating and conserving the latter'.[38] While criticizing rationalist materialism of the West, Gandhi appeared to have drawn heavily on the Hindu tradition in which dharma in the sense of morality and religion remained crucial. He, therefore, condemned the modern civilization because it

> takes note neither of morality nor of religion. Its votaries calmly state that their business is not to teach religion. Some even consider it to be a superstitious growth. Others put on the cloak of religion and prate about morality. ... Immorality is often taught in the name of morality. This civilization seeks to increase bodily comfort by pursuing crude [rationalist materialism], and it fails miserably even in doing so.[39]

As shown, *Hind Swaraj* is Gandhi's creative response to the theoretical basis of Western civilization. Drawn on the civilizational resources of Hindu religion and its tradition, he put forward a new theoretical framework to conceptualize both colonialism and industrial capitalism. His articulation helps us understand that Gandhi, in this text, endeavoured to conceptualize his ideas in the format of four major

[35] Parel, ed., *Hind Swaraj and Other Writings*, 67.

[36] Ibid, 43.

[37] Ibid.

[38] Ibid, 43–4.

[39] Ibid, 37. He further noted, 'The tendency of Indian civilization is to elevate the moral being that of Western civilization is to propagate immorality. The latter is godless, the former is based on a belief in god. So understanding, so believing, it behoves (sic) every lover of India to cling to old Indian civilization even as a child clings to its mother's breast'. Parel, ed., *Hind Swaraj and Other Writings*, 71.

contradictions which are (a) contradiction between competition and cooperation, (b) nature versus machinery, (c) consumerism/consumption versus self-denial and (d) state-centric versus community-driven discourses.[40] A careful account of these contradictions reveals that Gandhi, being influenced by indigenous socio-economic and religious traditions, seems to have instinctively evolved his ideas which had connected him with his supporters in India since they immediately understood what he meant. An astute strategist, the Mahatma stood out in the history of nationalism primarily because he created a discourse which upheld the voice of the colonized; it was a voice which created an instantaneous bond among the socioculturally disparate Indians in adverse circumstances. Furthermore, though the voice that he articulated had certainly had contextual roots, it gradually became transcendental due to its global emotional appeal, as it helped the oppressed create a legitimate space for their instinctive battle against deprivation and denial.

This is one side of the exercise that he undertook in *Hind Swaraj*. The other equally important side of the story concerns with the fundamental precepts of what later became Gandhism. The three important themes that recur not only in his writings but also in his deeds are *Swaraj*, *Swadeshi* and *Satya*.[41] *Swaraj* was self-rule of the self by the self. It was, therefore, more than a political idea for it meant to the Mahatma India's spiritual liberation through a fundamental change in each individual's perception. This could hardly be achieved through political liberation. What it required was a continuous process of self-churning leading to self-actualization in its fullest possible form. Similarly, *Swadeshi*, which meant self-respect, self-realization and self-reliance, was not merely glorification of traditional and indigenous methods of production but a creative application of the available means meaningful to the people in consideration. He was not critical

[40] M. K. Gandhi, *Localizing Governance in India*, Chap. 2 (Oxford: Routledge, 2017), 69–104.

[41] A detailed exposition of these concepts is available in the section on major trends in Gandhian social and political thought. Hence, to deal with them again is redundant. These concepts—*Swaraj, Swadeshi* and *Satya*—remain the fundamental tenets of Gandhism though Gandhi redefined them in response to the circumstances keeping intact their basic thrust and spirit.

of mechanization per se, as he argued, 'mechanization is good when the hands are too few for the work to be intended to be accomplished. It is an evil', he argued, 'when there are more hands than required for the work, as is the case in India. … Spinning and weaving mills have deprived the villagers of a substantial means of livelihood'.[42] So, Gandhi felt that the technology that was appropriate for India should meet the needs of the masses. Modern technology failed to fulfil this because historically it tended to reward the skilled and the powerful and to marginalize the poor and the weak. So, his debate is not on 'whether India needs technology'; his debate is on 'the kind of technology that India needs'.[43]

Similarly, *Satya* is another basic pillar in Gandhian thought. *Satya* is truth-force and only *Ahimsa*, according to Gandhi, could make the quest for such truth viable. Together with *Ahimsa*, *Satya* constituted Satyagraha. Although Satyagraha appeared to be primarily a political strategy, it was 'basically a method of dialogue that would bring two disagreeing parties not just into mutual agreement, but into the realization of a deeper truth together'.[44] Based on *atmabal* (soul force) and not *sharirbal* (physical force), Satyagraha seeks to reach a higher mental plane where soul is able to exercise control over mind. And, the success of 'the ethic of non-violence depends on the state of the soul, the mind and the passions—in one word, on self-rule'.[45] What was distinctive about Gandhi was his ability to transform Satyagraha into a political strategy as well. It was 'a method of securing rights by personal suffering'.[46] Clearly, Gandhi's Satyagraha was an indigenous combination of reason, morality and politics; it appealed to the opponent's head, heart and interests'.[47]

42 Gandhi, 'Village Industries', reproduced in *CWMG*, Vol. 59, p. 356.

43 Parel, Introduction to the *Hind Swaraj*, lvii.

44 Rudolph C. Heredia, 'Interpreting Gandhi's Hind Swaraj,' *Economic and Political Weekly* 34, no. 24 (12 June 1999): 1499.

45 Parel, ed., *Hind Swaraj and Other Writings*; Parel, Introduction to the *Hind Swaraj*, lvi.

46 Parel, ed., *Hind Swaraj and Other Writings*, 90.

47 Parekh, *Gandhi's Political Philosophy*, 156.

Now, we are in a position to comprehend Gandhi's mental universe in a proper perspective within the available literature. Gandhi was a political activist responding creatively to the socio-political and economic circumstances in which he was located. As evident, drawn on practice, he evolved a theory of and about practice. Hence it would be safe to argue that Gandhi was an activist–theoretician in the sense that he was a theoretician who was simultaneously a practitioner. *Swaraj* was an ideal that needed to put into practice through human deeds. Hence self-rule without self-transformation is not Gandhian. *Swaraj* was not a utopia, as Gandhi himself argued that 'do not consider this swaraj to be a dream. There is no idea of sitting still'.[48] *Swaraj* is a complex unfolding simultaneously of a blueprint of future socio-political orders and also a method of how to organize human actions in accordance with *Ahimsa* and *Satya*.

Gandhi Being an Activist–Theoretician

What is distinctive about Gandhi was his constant endeavour to learn from the practice. His model of non-violent struggle had both indigenous and exogenous roots: it was a product of his own assessment of Indian socio-historical discourses, including the epics and also what he learnt from the Western philosophical discourses. In Gandhi's words, besides the Indian socio-economic context, 'three moderns have left a deep impress on [his] life and captivated [him]: Raychandbhai by his living contact; [Leo] Tolstoy by his book, *The Kingdom of God Is within You* and [John D] Ruskin by his *Unto This Last*'.[49] It is, therefore, fair to suggest that Gandhi's ideas evolved out of a serious engagement with multiple strands of thought; it was a creative blending of views that the Mahatma represented in course of the nationalist struggle that he spearheaded after his arrival on the Indian scene. An activist, guided by his ideological commitment to non-violence, the Mahatma also created a new genre of thinking in which the Enlightenment values of care, concern and empathy

[48] Parel, ed., *Hind Swaraj and Other Writings*, 73. 'Swaraj is', Gandhi further argued, 'when we learn to rule ourselves'.

[49] Gandhi, *An Autobiography*, 83.

remained fundamental. Like his colleagues who shared his views, Gandhi built his model of resistance against the British rule by being drawn on non-violence which was not only a source of inspiration but was an empowering device for the unprivileged and disfranchised segments of humanity. He rose as a messiah for those who always remained peripheral in socio-economic and political terms, which means that he gave a powerful voice to those who, so far, had hardly had a say in the shaping of their present and also future. That Gandhi was different from his erstwhile nationalist colleagues was evident when he launched his Satyagraha movement in remote areas of Champaran, Kheda and Ahmedabad, instead of presidency town that so far remained the hub of the nationalist activities. His political strategies brought about radical changes in the Congress that now expanded its sphere of influences even in the villages. As J. B. Kripalani, one of Gandhi's trusted lieutenants during the nationalist struggle, admitted,

> In those days, such was our nationalism that we did not know what was really happening in the villages. We, the educated, lived more or less an isolated life. Our world was confined to the cities and to our fraternity of the educated. Our contact with the masses was confined to our servants, and yet we talked of the masses and were anxious to free the country from foreign yoke.[50]

Kripalani's candid confession of the nationalist movement being 'a movement of the few' is illustrative of the argument that before Gandhi emerged, the politico-ideological campaign against the British rule had neither a popular base nor an appeal to the people beyond the metropolitan cities of Calcutta and Bombay. It was Gandhi who radically altered the texture of Indian nationalism by involving those politically marginalized sections of society who did not appear to have evinced interests in the struggle for freedom for a complex set of interconnected reasons. In other words, by spreading out the tentacles of the nationalist campaign to the small towns and villages, not only did the Mahatma develop a new mode of resistance but also expanded the constituencies of nationalism. Having been struck by Gandhi's mass

[50] J. B. Kripalani, *Gandhi: His Life and Thought* (New Delhi: Ministry of Information and Broadcasting, Government of India, 1970), 61.

appeal, Jawaharlal Nehru thus expressed his feelings after his visit to Pratapgarh (in Uttar Pradesh) by saying that

> The visit was a revelation to me. … [Though] I had often passed through villages, stopped there and talked to the peasants, … I had not fully realized what they were and what they meant to India. Like most of us, I took them for granted. This realization came to me during these Pratapgarh visits and ever since then my mental picture of India always contains this naked, hungry mass. Perhaps there was some kind of electricity in the air, perhaps I was in a receptive frame of mind and the pictures I saw and the impressions I gathered were indelibly impressed on my mind.[51]

This was not surprising because the earlier generation of the nationalist leaders appear to have been less concerned with those at the grassroots. For them, the nationalist constituencies did not go beyond the two major metropolitan cities of Calcutta and Bombay. Before Gandhi's rise on the Indian scene, neither the Moderate nor the Revolutionary Nationalist (Extremist in the conventional parlance) activists had ever thought of involving the peripheral masses in their campaign against the British.[52]

Articulation of Non-violent Protests

Gandhi is globally known for the three pan-Indian campaigns that he had launched between 1921 and 1942.[53] In conceptualizing Gandhi as an activist–theoretician, equally important were those campaigns that he led before he embarked on the Non-cooperation movement in 1921. There are three non-violent campaigns in which the Gandhian mode of nationalist resistance was tested: first, it was in Champaran in Bihar, followed by Kheda in Gujarat and finally in Ahmedabad also in Gujarat.

[51] Jawaharlal Nehru, *An Autobiography* (London: John Lane the Bodley Head, 1941), 57.

[52] For details, see Amales Tripathi, *The Extremist Challenge* (Delhi: Orient Longmans, 1967); Daniel Argov, *Moderates and Extremists in the Indian Nationalist Movement, 1883–1920, with Special Reference to Surendranath Banerjee and Lajpat Rai* (London: Asian Publishing House, 1968).

[53] A detailed discussion of these pan-Indian campaigns shall follow soon.

At Champaran in Bihar, peasants raised their voice against the European planters for forcing them to produce indigo under the *tinkathia* system (that imposed the production of indigo in three-twentieth part of their land). The movement that began in the 1860s gained momentum even before the arrival of Gandhi on the scene. Led by the local middle and rich peasant leaders, the pre-Gandhian efforts, however, failed to involve the actual cultivators. This is where Gandhi's intervention was most effective. A unique political action, the 1917 Champaran Satyagraha was first of this kind in India which Gandhi led in accordance with his plan and ideology. Gandhi's presence in Champaran represented hope for the raiyats of the plantations. His act of civil disobedience and determination to endure prison convinced the peasants that the Mahatma was their saviour. His extreme simplicity had brought him closer to them than all the erstwhile leaders. How he struck a chord with the peasants was surprising. Even Rajendra Prasad who accompanied him during the Champaran movement expressed that 'it is a matter of mystery to me how these people seemed to develop the confidence that their deliverer had come'.[54] Not only his co-workers, his arrival in Bettiah in the Champaran region also caught the British sub-divisional officer by surprise as evident in his following report:

> We may look on Mr. Gandhi as an idealist, a fanatic or a revolutionary according to our particular opinions. But to the raiyats, he is their liberator, and they credit him with extraordinary powers. He moves about in the villages, asking them to lay their grievance before him, and he is daily transfiguring the imagination of masses of ignorant men with visions of an early millennium.[55]

Gandhi, to the masses, meant a resurrection of hope. In his historical novel, *Kanthapura*, Raja Rao depicted how Gandhi became 'a symbol of hope' to the people despite police atrocities. Mahatma was not there in Kanthapura, and yet, he galvanized the masses into action against the British police. On one occasion,

[54] Rajendra Prasad, *At the Feet of Mahatma Gandhi* (New Delhi: Prabhat Prakashan, 1961), 7.

[55] A report of the Sub Divisional Officer, Bettiah on 23 September 1917, quoted in Jacques Pouchepadass, *Champaran and Gandhi: Planters, Peasants and Gandhian Politics* (New Delhi: Oxford University Press, 1999), 217–18.

> Rachanna, [a sincere Gandhi supporter], cries out, "*Mahatma Gandhi ki jai*" [victory to Mahatma Gandhi], the policeman rushes at the crowd and bangs them with his *lathi* [canes] and Rachanna quavers out the louder, "*Gandhi Mahatma ki jai*" and other policemen come and bang them too, and the women raise such a clamour and cry that the crows and bats set up an obsequial wail, and the sparrows join them from the roofs and eaves and the cattle rise up in the byre and the creaking of their bones is heard. ... There is again such a clamour—Mahatma Gandhi ki jai—the police inspector shouts "disperse the crowd" ... policemen beat the crowd this side that side, and groans and moans and cries and coughs and oaths and bangs and kicks are heard, and more shouts of "*Mahatma Gandhi ki jai! Mahatma Gandhi ki jai!*".[56]

His non-violent resistance provided a viable alternative in the struggle against colonialism where force had become both illegitimate and ineffective. The Champaran Satyagraha forced the government to adopt the 1918 Champaran Agricultural Act, whereby those compelled to let their land for indigo cultivation were given some relief. What Gandhi left was carried forward by local peasants and Champaran became a strong base for non-violent political mobilization, though the Congress leadership never allowed them to organize protests against the indigenous landlords. Despite the failure of the peasants to lead movements against the vested interests, the Champaran Satyagraha articulated the neglected voice of protests. Gandhi emerged as the supreme leader and non-violence gained salience. This was not a subaltern protest, but one in which the subalterns were inducted into the process of political mobilization. In other words, the Champaran Satyagraha represented 'a battle in which many different levels of consciousness coexisted [presumably because of] the complex perspective of the participants'.[57] Apart from projecting Gandhi as a perfect mobilizer, this 1917 Satyagraha also contributed to a unique multi-class political platform combining the clearly antagonistic classes for the battle against the foreign rule. Not only did Gandhi succeed in containing the class wrath within a specific limit, but he also created a situation in which the struggle against the exploiters coincided with the challenge against colonialism. So, Gandhian non-violence, as the Champaran

[56] Raja Rao, *Kanthapura* (New York: New Directions, 1967), 83–5.

[57] Pouchepadass, *Champaran and Gandhi*, 234.

Satyagraha demonstrates, provided a potent means for a legitimate and effective resistance within the new political dispensation in which the Congress was gaining in importance. The Champaran movement was a watershed in Gandhi's political life not only in terms of conceptualizing Satyagraha as a device but also in terms of its application to build a political platform regardless of classes.

Similar to the Champaran experiment, the 1918 Kheda Satyagraha was a Gandhi-led no-revenue campaign.[58] Hard-hit by economic hardships due to destruction of crops by rains, rise in agricultural wages, high rate of inflation and the outbreak of bubonic plague, the Patidar peasants organized a movement against the government's decision not to waive land revenue. Launched by Mohanlal Pandya and Shankarlal Parikh of a small town of Kathlal in the district of Kheda of Gujarat, the movement gained momentum as the Gujarat Sabha, an organization under the aegis of the Congress, extended support. Once approached by the Gujrat Sabha, Gandhi arrived in Kheda in March 1918 to launch a Satyagraha campaign against the government decision to confiscate properties of the defaulters. The campaign lasted for four months and in June the government of Bombay decided not to implement the order and peasants who failed to pay the revenue were spared. Like the Champaran Satyagraha, the movement, spearheaded by the local Congress activists, continued with local support. Gandhi's presence was more symbolical than anything else. Even his lieutenants, Vallabhbhai and Vitthalbhai Patel, remained insignificant in the entire movement in which the local leaders became most important. As a cementing factor, Gandhi brought the Satyagrahees together for the movement that had an agenda, set by the local leaders in their own terms. In other words, Gandhi was important in the Kheda Satyagraha so long as he agreed to support the demands of local leaders. This was evident when the villagers refused when Gandhi urged them to join the British army during the First World War.[59]

[58] For a detailed account of the Kheda Satyagraha, David Hardiman, *Peasant Nationalists of Gujarat: Kheda District, 1917–1934* (New Delhi: Oxford University Press, 1981).

[59] Hardiman, *Peasant Nationalists of Gujarat*, 85–113.

During the Kheda Satyagraha, Gandhi also participated in Ahmedabad textile mill strike of February–March 1918.[60] This was a different kind of experiment involving the workers. The successful campaign in Champaran catapulted Gandhi to the centre-stage. When the workers in Ahmedabad became restive, Gandhi was invited by Anasuya Sarabhai, a social worker who happened to be the sister of Ambalal Sarabhai, the president of the Ahmedabad Mill Owner's Association, to intervene and resolve the crisis. What triggered off the strike was the withdrawal of 'plague-bonus' to the workers, equivalent in some cases to 80 per cent of the wages that was paid to dissuade the workers from fleeing the plague-ravaged towns. Once the epidemic was over, the mill owners decided to discontinue the practice. For the workers, this decision hit the workers adversely, simply because of the spiralling price rise due to the outbreak of the War.

Drawn on his belief that there was no major contradiction between capital and labour, Gandhi sought to defuse the crisis through dialogues with the mill owners. The mill owners appeared to be adamant and characterized Gandhi's intervention as 'unwarranted'. On 22 February 1918, the mill owners locked out the weavers despite Gandhi's repeated requests. With the closure, Gandhi decided to champion the workers' demand, though he asked them to tone down their earlier demand of 50 per cent wage increase to 35 per cent hike. Although the workers agreed to Gandhi's suggestion, the mill owners did not relent and workers seemed to have lost morale. It was at this juncture, Gandhi began the 'first' of his 17 'fasts unto death' on 15 March 1918. This fast that lasted for three days appeared to have forced the mill owners who deeply respected Gandhi to come to an agreement with the striking workers. As per the Agreement, suggested by the arbitration board, the workers demand was partially fulfilled because they got 27.5 per cent wage hike instead of their original demand for 35 per cent increase. So, the compromise formula 'looked like a face-saving formula and a tactical defeat for

[60] The only comprehensive account of this strike is available in M. V. Kamath and V. B. Kher, *The Story of Militant But Non-violent Trade Unionism: A Biographical and Historical Study* (Ahmedabad: Navajivan Trust, 1993) (reprint).

Gandhi'[61] though he forced the mill owners to accept the principle of arbitration in which workers' representatives along with their employers had a say.

A unique event in Gandhi's political life, the Ahmedabad strike, added a new chapter to Indian nationalist movement. Although critical of Gandhi's 'obsession' with 'passive resistance', *The Bombay Chronicle* appreciated the principle of arbitration as 'a turning point in labour–employer relations in Ahmedabad' in particular and a unique system of 'resolving industrial disputes' in general.[62] Similarly, *The Times* criticized Gandhi for 'blackmailing' the mill owners who happened to be his 'admirers' by his 'fast unto death', though it hailed his role in articulating 'arbitration' as 'an effective device' to break the *impasse* between the workers and industrialists.[63]

These three movements projected Gandhi as an emerging leader with different kinds of mobilizing tactics. What was common in all these movements was the fact that (a) they were organized around local issues and (b) in mobilizing the people for the movements, the importance of the local leaders cannot be underestimated. There is no doubt that Gandhi's appearance on the scene gave a fillip to these movements. Yet, if we carefully chart the movements, we will discover that Gandhi was invited to lead when support was adequately mobilized by the local organizers. By his involvement with these movements at a stage when they struck roots in the concerned localities, Gandhi projected a specific kind of leadership: he was not a primary but a secondary organizer. There is no doubt that the movements gained different heights with his intervention. The masses interpreted Gandhi's message in their own terms and 'rumours surrounding the powers of this messianic leader served to break the barriers of fear involved in confronting formidable enemies'.[64] As evident in Champaran and

[61] B. R. Nanda, *In Search of Gandhi: Essays and Reflections* (New Delhi: Oxford University Press, 2004), 199.

[62] *The Bombay Chronicle*, 20 March 1918.

[63] *The Times*, London, 8 April 1918.

[64] Sekhar Bandyopadhyay, *From Plassey to Partition: A History of Modern India* (New Delhi: Orient Longman, 2004), 295.

Kheda, Gandhian intervention in elite-nationalist politics established for the first time that an authentic nationalist movement could be built upon the organized support of the peasantry, though its political object was not what Gandhi endorsed. The peasants were meant to become 'willing participants in a struggle wholly conceived and directed by others'. Gandhi provided 'a national framework of politics in which peasants are mobilized but do not participate' in its formulation.[65] This was also true of the Ahmedabad strike where Gandhi accommodated the interests of the mill owners even at the cost of the workers since their demand was partially conceded. Based on his belief that capital and labour were not contradictory to each other, Gandhi agreed to the negotiated settlements as probably the best solution under the circumstances. Workers failed to get what they had asked for. Yet Gandhi's role was most significant in articulating a form of political mobilization in which the workers were also decisive. Just like the Champaran and Kehda Satyagrahas that extended the constituencies of nationalist politics by incorporating the peasantry, the Ahmedabad Textile Strike was a watershed for it accorded a legitimate space to the workers in what was conceptualized as nationalism.

These three movements constitute a milestone in what Gandhi articulated as nationalist politics. A leader emerged to radically alter the complexion of India's struggle for freedom. With his involvement in mass movements in Champaran, Kheda and Ahmedabad, Gandhi 'forged a new language of protests for India by both building on older forms of resistance while at the same time accepting the colonial censure of all forms of violent protest'.[66] Two complementary processes seemed to have worked: at one level, local issues had obviously a significant role in mobilizing masses for protest movements in the localities; at another, the presence of Gandhi at a critical juncture helped sustain these movements that perhaps lost momentum due to the growing frustration of the local organizers. So, Gandhi was a missing link that not only galvanized the masses into action but also contributed immensely to the successful conclusion of these

[65] Chatterjee, *Nationalist Thought and the Colonial World*, 124–25.

[66] David Hardiman, *Gandhi in His Time and Ours* (New Delhi: Permanent Black, 2003), 51.

protest movements in Champaran, Kheda and Ahmedabad involving completely different constituencies of nationalist politics, namely, peasantry and labour. These movements appeared to have set the tone and tenor of the future movements which Gandhi was to lead in which people at large participated in response to his call for political action. Although he was a secondary organizer in all these movements, he appeared to have carried with him 'a magic wand' that not only activated those who remained peripheral but also sustained the momentum of the movements despite odds. He emerged as a mass leader who felt the pulse of the people perhaps most accurately than anybody else during the freedom struggle. And the consequence was obvious because it was Gandhi who transformed the struggle for freedom to a wider nationalist campaign involving various categories of people including those who remained detached. As Jawaharlal Nehru most eloquently put,

> [Gandhiji] attracted people. They did not agree with his philosophy of life, or even with many of his ideals. Often they did not understand him, But the action that he proposed was something tangible which could be understood and appreciated intellectually. Any action would have been welcome after the long tradition of inaction which our spineless politics had nurtured; brave and effective action with an ethical halo about it had an irresistible appeal, both to the intellect and emotions. Step by step he convinced us of the rightness of the action, and we went with him, although we did not accept his philosophy. ... Gandhiji, being essentially a man of action and very sensitive to changing conditions ... the road he was following was the right one thus far, and if the future meant a parting it would be folly to anticipate it.
>
> All this shows that we were by no means clear or certain in our minds. Always we had the feeling that while we might be more logical, Gandhiji knew India far better than we did, and a man who could command such tremendous devotion and loyalty must have something in him that corresponded to the needs and aspirations of the masses.[67]

This is perhaps the most apt description of the activist Gandhi who, by being integrally connected with those at the grassroots, became an icon for the masses fighting to do away with foreign rule. It was

[67] Nehru, *An Autobiography*, 254–55.

possible for him to become a messiah to the people largely due to the consolidation of his image of being one of them. Neither his predecessors nor any of his colleagues had had an appeal to the masses that he had. As the available literature shows, Gandhi was unmistakably a pan-Indian leader who stood out as the anti-British non-violent campaign progressed.

The Rise of Gandhi as a Pan-Indian Leader: The Non-cooperation and Civil Disobedience Movements

Gandhi inaugurated a new era in India's freedom struggle involving various social strata. He was also instrumental in transforming the Indian National Congress from an urban-based loose organization dominated by lawyers mainly from the metropolitan cities of Calcutta and Bombay into a political party with its organizational network even in villages. The structural core of Gandhi's democratization of the Congress lay 'in the proliferation of units capable of attracting and channelling a mass membership base'. The Congress that was just a platform for ventilation of grievances became a mass organization to challenge the British government. There is no doubt that it was only at the aegis of Gandhi that the Congress metamorphosed into a giant organization with its tentacles all over the country. As Jawaharlal Nehru most eloquently put,

> [t]he whole look of the Congress changed; European clothes vanished and soon only *khadi* was to be seen; a new class of delegate, chiefly drawn from the lower middle classes became the type of Congressmen; the language used became increasingly Hindustan, or sometimes the language of the province where the session was held, as many of the delegates did not understand English, and there was also a growing prejudice against using a foreign language in national work; and a new life and enthusiasm and earnestness became evident in Congress gatherings.[68]

The freedom struggle thus acquired a mass base in an unprecedented way. Furthermore, despite internal ideological divisions within the

[68] Ibid, 65–6.

Congress, its nationalist goal was never compromised. Gandhi became the supreme leader and Satyagraha had emerged as an effective mode of nationalist protest. With the inauguration of the Non-cooperation movement in 1921, the claim of Gandhi being in command of the nationalist campaign was conclusively substantiated.

The Non-cooperation Movement: Consolidation of Gandhi

What alarmed the administration was the impact of the boycott slogan on the government institutions as a whole; almost 80% of them were seriously affected between 1919 and 1921. While explaining this phenomenon, an official report thus admitted,

> There was something in the movement that appealed to most diverse types of minds. ... Imagination has been fired and a spiritual uplift initiated. Something that had been wanting in our college life had been supplied. ... the situation presented possibilities of romance and adventure that irradiated [otherwise sterile] student life. Picketing and procession were [therefore] as irresistible to such minds as a bump supper and a 'rag' to Oxford undergraduates. [Students] became for the first time conscious that they were wasting time over a kind of education not suited to their needs and leading them to an office stool.[69]

Compared with the erstwhile Congress campaign, the Non-cooperation movement demonstrated that the old closed shop of limited politics had been thrown wide open. Far greater numbers than before were participating in an overt political campaign, using a far wider range of techniques than earlier politicians had ever used simultaneously and participants came from all parts of India. The political nation was thus expanded to accommodate various kinds of interests that remained peripheral in the past.

An important dimension of the nationalist politics unfolded with the incorporation of the working-class struggle in its fold. In 1921, there were 396 strikes involving 600,351 workers and a loss of

[69] P. C. Bamford, *Histories of the Non-Cooperation and Khilafat Movements* (Delhi: Government of India, 1925), 102–103.

6,994,426 man days. What provoked strikes was the recession in the post-war period which forced the factory owners to cut production with a four-day week. The C. R. Das-led Bengal Congress immediately took up the cause of the workers to sharpen its attack on the colonial state. The chain of strikes in Bengal that followed the Chandpur firing was partly attributable to the involvement of the leading Congressmen like C. R. Das and J. M. Sengupta and partly due to a spontaneous rising of the entire population, especially the lower classes who expressed through the strikes their acute sense of economic exploitation and racial abasement under white rule. A disturbed Ronaldshay who appeared panic-stricken in view of the widespread nature of the strike thus wrote,

> The most disquieting feature is the extent of the hold which events have shown they have already acquired over large classes of people. They have been able to call strikes in the inland steamer lines and the Assam-Bengal Railway, and they have been able to call *hartals* in a number of east Bengal towns simultaneously.[70]

The 'strike fever', as it was characterized in the official discourse, was endemic and affected primarily the industries of eastern India. Part of the reason lay in the fact that the leadership succeeded in attributing workers' misery principally to the European–American ownership that with its association with the colonial state was naturally insensitive to the grievances of the Indians. Besides, the role of the local Congress leadership appeared crucial in organizing the disparate workers for a cause by providing an ideological direction as well as material help. For leaders, like C. R. Das and J. M. Sengupta, labour was increasingly becoming an important constituency of the nationalist politics, recognized later in the 1922 Gaya Congress; and thus by championing the workers' cause, they initiated a process which, though signalled and articulated various contradictions in the Gandhi-led movement, widened the social base of the freedom struggle. Because strikes 'do not fall within the plan of non-violent non-cooperation' Gandhi while condemning the strike fever thus argued,

[70] IOR, Mss. Eur. D 609(2), Zetland Collection, Ronaldshay to Monatague, 15 June 1921.

> In India we want no political strikes. ... we must gain control over the unruly and disturbing elements. ... we seek not to destroy capital or capitalists, but to regulate the relations between capital and labour. We want to harness capital to our side. *It would be folly to encourage sympathetic strikes.* (emphasis added)[71]

The Non-cooperation movement also brought the peasants to the forefront of the nationalist politics. By according priority to village reconstruction through self-help, Gandhi articulated his plan for an economic revival 'through spinning wheel and hand-woven cloth (*charkha* and *khadi*) panchayats or arbitration courts, national schools and campaign for Hindu–Muslim unity and against the evils of liquor and untouchability'. Although these programmes may not have been uniformly effective as strategies for political mobilization, they nonetheless unfolded a new process by involving the hitherto neglected section of society in a struggle which despite its pronounced political content was equally a battle against the well-entrenched vested interests in the localities. It was not, therefore, surprising that peasants of Kanika in Orissa challenged the local zamindars for having demanded an extra rent. Drawing upon Gandhi, the militant section of the Orissa Congress leaders organized 'the peasants for the establishment of Gandhi raj when no one would have to pay rent'; so convinced were the peasants that they 'boycotted and intimidated', on occasions, 'those who were inclined to pay rents to the zamindars'. The movement, though led by the Orissa Congress, did not receive Gandhi's approval, and was later unconditionally revoked. Gandhi was, however, inclined to encourage a no-revenue campaign in a *ryotwari* settlement area, like Bardoil, and not in any zamindari region where it would inevitably involve 'no rent'. By trying to contain 'no rent' campaigns, Gandhi projected a specific type of leadership which mobilized peasants exclusively in its terms and conditions. Peasants were organized and mobilized on the so-called unifying issues which transcend even the well-defined boundaries among the antagonistic classes. So, it was logical when Gandhi 'deprecated all attempts to

[71] Gandhi, 'The Lesson of Assam,' *Young India*, 15 June 1921. Gandhi reiterated his argument in a meeting in Calcutta on 11 September 1921 by condemning the strike fever which tended to disrupt unnecessarily the amicable relationship between the industrialists and the workers. *The Statesman*, 22 September 1921.

create a discord between landlords and tenants and advised the tenants to suffer rather than fight for they had to join all forces for fighting the most powerful *zamindar*, namely the Government'.

The Civil Disobedience Movement, 1930–1932

Gandhi launched the Civil Disobedience in 1930 to challenge both the British rule which appeared to him 'a perfect personification of violence' and also the growing hatred towards the agents of this rule which took the form of 'causal assassination'. 'The call of 1920', he further wrote, 'was a call for preparation. The call in 1930 is for engaging in the final conflict'.[72] Gandhi launched the Civil Disobedience Movement by sending a charter of demands to the Viceroy on 2 March 1930 which were as follows:

> (1) total prohibition; (2) reduction of the rupee ration to Is 4d; (3) reduction of land revenue by at least 50% and making it subject to legislative control; (4) abolition of the salt tax; (5) reduction of the military expenditure by at least 50%; (6) reduction of the salaries of the highest grade service to one half or less so as to suit the reduced revenue; (7) imposition of protective tariff on foreign cloth; (8) passage of the Coastal Tariff Reservation Bill; (9) discharge of all political prisoners save those condemned for murder, withdrawal of all political prosecutions and abrogation of Section 124-A, Regulation III of 1818 and the like and permission of all Indian exiles to return; (10) abolition of the CID or its popular control; and (11) issue of licenses to use firearms for self-defence, subject to popular control.

Gandhi's 11-point ultimatum to the Viceroy, however, disappointed many leading Congressmen including Nehru since it contained no demand for any change in the political structure, not even the dominion status. 'Bewildered' at Gandhi's charter of demands which ultimately boiled down to a campaign for salt preparation, Nehru thought that it was a sad climb-down from the *Purna Swaraj* resolution. As Nehru argued, '[s]alt suddenly became a mysterious word, a word of power. The Salt Tax was to be attacked; the salt laws were to be broken. We were bewildered and could not quite fit in a national

[72] *Young India*, 11 March 1930; *CWMG*, Vol. 43, p. 117.

struggle'.[73] Irwin, the viceroy, was not perturbed at all: in a letter to the secretary of state, Wedgewood Benn, he thus wrote, 'at present the prospect of a salt campaign does not keep me awake at night'.

Gandhi's 11 points incorporated demands of almost every section of Indian society. By choosing salt as the central issue, he strove to organize an anti-British campaign in which the participation of a majority of the people was ensured since salt was essential for everyday survival. The boycott of foreign cloth was also included as a strategy because of its effectiveness in the earlier Congress campaigns. Hence the Civil Disobedience Movement revolved primarily around attacks on the government salt monopoly and the boycott of foreign cloth.

On 12 March 1930, the Salt Satyagraha began with a carefully organized month-long march covering 240 miles which Gandhi undertook from Sabarmati Ashram in Ahmedabad to Dandi on the west coast of Gujarat. There were 78 chosen volunteers who accompanied Gandhi in the Dandi March (12 March–5 April) which inaugurated the Salt Satyagraha. It was a campaign for freedom because the 1929 Lahore Congress adopted the complete independence resolution and authorized the All India Congress Committee to launch Civil Disobedience. For the government, by deciding to breach the Salt Act, Gandhi became 'a laughing stock involved in kindergarten stage of political revolution'. Salt could never become, as the government was emphatic, 'an issue of concern'. The most that could happen was that small quantities of inferior salt would be sporadically produced in some coastal areas and consumed locally—which would neither threaten the government nor affect the price of salt adversely. Nevertheless, the movement gained momentum. As Subhas Chandra Bose commented, 'at every step the Mahatma received an unexpectedly warm welcome and that made the Government realize that the coming campaign would be a much more serious affair than they had thought at first'. Gandhi reached Dandi on 5 April. With 'the consummate showmanship of a great political artist', he picked up a palmful of salt in open defiance of the government and signalled his opposition to the unlawful Salt Act. In order 'to cope with the emergency', the government finally

[73] Nehru, *An Autobiography*, 210.

arrested Gandhi on 5 May under the archaic Bombay Regulation xxv of 1827 that legalized detention without trial. Instead of dampening the enthusiasm of the participants, the arrest of Mahatma seemed to have stimulated the resistance against the government. The Congress Working Committee left with the local leadership to decide the course of action once the Mahatma was interned. In order to sustain the spirit of Civil Disobedience, the *Young India* thus exhorted,

> Each town, each village may have ... to become its own battle field. The strategy of the battle must then come to be determined by local circumstances and change with them from day to day. The sooner the workers prepare for this state of things, the earlier shall we reach the goal. They should need little guidance from outside. They know that there must be no deviation from the principles of civil disobedience as laid down by Mahatma Gandhi or from the main programme of action as fixed by the Congress.[74]

Hence, it is argued that there was no 'all India blueprint for civil disobedience in 1930–1931' as there had been in 1920–1922 Non-cooperation and Khilafat movements, and as a result, the movement in practice became 'a series of loosely coordinated local conflicts'. There is no doubt that the success of the Civil Disobedience campaign was largely due to the importance of salt as an emotive issue. Once the scope of the movement was extended to the breach of forest laws, the non-payment of taxes to *ryotwari* areas, and the boycott of foreign clothes, banks, shipping and insurance companies, it took the form of a well-orchestrated campaign against the British rule. No part of British India escaped, though the intensity differed widely in proportion to which the campaign addressed the local grievances.

Although the 1930 Civil Disobedience Movement began with the breach of salt laws, civil resistance spread to other fields. Simultaneously with Mahatma's march in villages, an intense propaganda was carried on by those involved in the campaign asking the people to give up service under the British government and to prepare for non-payment of tax as well. It was not, therefore, surprising that violation of Salt Act soon became just one activity and resistance to the government took various forms. Jawaharlal Nehru attributed this to

[74] *Young India*, 17 July 1930; *CWMG*, Vol. 43, p. 358.

> the promulgation of various ordinances by the Viceroy prohibiting a number of activities. As these ordinances and prohibitions grew, the opportunities for breaking them also grew and civil resistance took the form of doing the very thing that the ordinance was intended to stop.[75]

At every village where Gandhi stopped, he spoke briefly. On one occasion, while reiterating the famous 11 points, he attacked the Salt Act by saying that

> Who can help liking this poor man's battle? The cruel tax is not respecter of persons. It is, therefore, as much the interest of the Mussalmans as of the Hindu to secure its abolition. This is a fight undertaken in the name of God and for the sake of millions of paupers of this country.[76]

Besides highlighting the inhuman nature of the British government, Gandhi in his speeches always couched his argument with issues relevant to the village life, on *khadi*, cow protection, hygiene and untouchability. He also appealed to those serving the government. By the time the Dandi March came to an end, about one-third of 760 village headmen resigned. This might not have seriously affected the alien administration, though it was symbolically significant when the governmental authority did not seem to be weak.

As a strategist, Gandhi succeeded in infusing popular misery with a political content by attributing it to the oppressive nature of the *Raj*. Astonished by the immense popularity of the Civil Disobedience campaign, the moderate Tejbahadur Sapru thus candidly admitted,

> The Congress has undoubtedly acquired a great hold on popular imaginations. On the roadside stations where until a few months ago I could hardly have suspected that people had any politics. I have seen with my eyes demonstrations and heard with my ears the usual Congress slogans. The popular feeling is one of excitement. It is fed from day to day by continuous and persistent propaganda on the part of the Congressmen—by lectures, delivered by their volunteers in running trains and similar activities ... there is no doubt whatever in my mind that *there is the most intense distrust of the*

[75] Nehru, *An Autobiography*, 215.

[76] Gandhi's speech at Broach, 26 March 1930; *Young India*, 4 April 1930; *CWMG*, Vol. 23, p. 127.

> *Government and its professions.* Indeed I have little doubt in my mind that racial feeling has been fanned to a very dangerous extent ... it seems to me that the Congress is really fighting for its own supremacy in the country (emphasis added).[77]

With a gradual expansion of its organizational network, the Congress certainly became stronger than before. For Gandhi, 'the violation of salt law was the last throw of a gambler', insisting that even 'the risk of violence was worth it'. The movement appeared inevitable given the government intransigence to concede the most humane demand which was unfortunate, as Gandhi himself articulated, because 'on bended knees I asked for bread and received stones instead'.[78] Hence, he repudiated the salt law and regarded it as his 'sacred duty to break the mournful mandatory of compulsory peace that is choking the heart of the Nation for want of free vent'.[79] The Salt Satyagraha was a momentous campaign, in the sense that it galvanized the Indian masses on an issue which was so dear to all of them. Here lies the credit of Gandhi who evolved a strategy that gave him maximum dividends, and the state was unable to contain the campaign simply because it had a mass base that was beyond its comprehension.

The August Revolution: A Radical Movement

The August Movement was probably most radical both in its attitude towards the British and in terms of methods employed. Gandhi's 'Do or Die' slogan was an ultimatum to the British leaving no space for negotiation at all. Such an attitude was not there in either the Non-cooperation or Civil Disobedience Movements when the Congress leadership was always keen to settle the disputes through some kind of compromise. Gandhi too agreed to accept this even at the cost of undermining the cause he fought for; its consequences were far-reaching: On the one hand, masses who took part in the anti-British

[77] IOR, Halifax Papers, Mss. Eur. C 152(25), Tejbahadur Sapru to Irwin, 19 September 1930.

[78] Gandhi's interview to Associated Press of India, 5 January 1933; *CWMG*, Vol. 52, p. 374.

[79] Gandhi's statement to the press, 7 January 1933; *CWMG*, Vol. 52, p. 379.

campaign felt betrayed—which was likely to adversely affect the future Congress mobilization. Just as Gandhi opposed radical social movements which tended to disrupt social equilibrium, he was identified as a conservative political activist who declined to disturb the alien rule. On the other hand, the failure of the past Congress movements, led by Gandhi or his success in containing them at his will, strengthened the Raj in two ways: (a) in its drive to challenge effectively the Congress campaign, the British had in Gandhi a friend who, due to his commitment to non-violence, steered the political agitation in such a way as not to cause severe disruption in the British rule; and (b) once the major organized political force was thus neutralized, the British administration could concentrate on controlling other radical socio-political movements challenging its continuity. So, despite the apparent threat to the Raj, both the Non-cooperation and the Civil Disobedience Movements let lose a political process, conducive to the prevalent rule which shaped, to a large extent, the anti-imperial movement before the onset of the open rebellion.

Whatever the implications of the past Congress-launched political movements, their significance cannot be denied especially in gradually radicalizing the Congress which loomed large in the August Revolution. The Congress had anticipated that the nature of the movement would be different and, hence, it was not surprising that the instructions to the Congress workers were tuned to capture the heightened mass radicalism in the wake of the open rebellion, which was radical for the Congress volunteers who resorted to open violence in a number of cases. It is debatable whether Gandhi would have allowed such a movement to continue in view of his strong antipathy to violence. The movement became violent gradually and British provocation had played a significant role. In fact, this also introduces another dimension to the structure of politics during the open rebellion. The movement's deviation from a true Gandhian path shows the autonomy of the unorganized level where political articulation and mobilization were being carried on through different idioms which were meaningful only in the context of a completely different ideological perception. This supports the argument highlighting the autonomy of unorganized politics following a unique pattern and demonstrating new dimensions of the structure of grassroots politics.

The argument seems convincing in the light of the 8 August revolution and the transformation of the movement after the incarceration of the top Congress leadership.

Concluding Observations

Gandhi can be conceptualized in three interrelated ways: first, he was a wave, a wave of thoughts and views which did not seem to have had an appeal to the masses before they were popularized by the Mahatma. These ideas were not entirely foreign but were never thought of being effective in political mobilization for a cause. Second, the ideas that the Mahatma propounded were an endeavour, couched in a voice that was never believed to have been persuasive in creating a nationalist constituency; in other words, the voice drawn on non-violence remained peripheral in a context when the Moderates and their counterparts the Extremists were involved in the struggle against the British masters. Although this phase of Indian nationalist resistance was short-lived, it is fair to argue that Gandhian arguments for non-violence had hardly had an appeal then. Finally, Gandhi was a journey because non-violence continues to remain a source of inspiration even after his brutal assassination in 1948. He was fiercely critiqued by M. A. Jinnah, V. D. Savarkar and B. R. Ambedkar, among others, since his ideas were at variance with them. Nonetheless, there is no doubt that the non-violent mode of political mobilization that Gandhi evolved and refined in the context India's freedom struggle remains, even in the 21st century, a fruitful design for politico-ideological campaign, as illustrated by examples.

The South African experience was remarkable in transforming Gandhi from a loyalist to a rebel. Once he returned to India, his strategy was different. In Champaran and Kheda, he championed the peasant causes. Supported by the local leaders, Gandhi mobilized the affected peasants against revenue remission. Similarly, in Kheda, he supported the movement of those peasants affected by the decision of the Bombay government to confiscate their property for their failure to pay tax. The Ahmedabad textile strike provided Gandhi with an opportunity to deal with the workers who were struggling for 'plague bonus'. Here the adversaries were the Gujarati mill owners who happened to be close to him. He was in a dilemma for obvious reason. The strategist Gandhi persuaded the workers to slash down their demand for increase of bonus and convinced the mill owners to accept the increase. Thus, strike came to an end and Gandhi gained tremendous nationwide popularity.

The Non-cooperation and Civil Disobedience Movements confirmed the growing popularity of the technique and also the acceptability of its author, Gandhi. So far confined to the educated middle class, the freedom struggle percolated down to the villages during the Non-cooperation movement and Gandhi remained its supreme leader. In the evolution of Gandhi, the period, 1920–1932, is most significant for a variety of obvious reasons. He became the Mahatma who rose to prominence not merely as a nationalist leader but also as 'a great soul' of India. Drawn on civilizational resources, his ideology of ahimsa infused fresh life into the nationalist movement that was fractured due to ideological rivalries among those participating in the anti-colonial struggle. So, the emergence of Gandhi as the undisputed leader of the Congress marked a radical break with the past.

At one level, Gandhi was an enigma since his mode of political mobilization was simply inconceivable when it was conceptualized by him at the outset of his political campaign in India. The Champaran Satyagraha was an eye-opener for his colleagues and also those who remained dominant in the Indian political scene before he arrived. That non-violence was a potent mobilizing device was firmly established when it was applied to the Kheda and Ahmedabad Satyagrahas. His grip over the pan-Indian nationalist campaigns was unquestionable, although all of them were not truly non-violent as the nature of the 1942 open rebellion or the Quit India Movement demonstrates. Nonetheless, the claim that Gandhi was truly a non-violent campaigner can hardly be disputed given his unflinching commitment to non-violence despite serious provocations.

The aforementioned narrative helps us build the argument that Gandhi remained a dominant politico-ideological force during India's nationalist campaign in the 20th century. There were other streams of thought as well, but they seem to have evolved either as an endorsement or as a critique of what the Mahatma stood for. In other words, it was Gandhi who created a conceptual universe that appears to have influenced, if not shaped, the other thought processes during the struggle for freedom. For instance, Jinnah's insistence on Hindus and Muslims being two nations was justified in contrast with the views that the Mahatma held vis-a-vis two major religious communities in India. Similarly, the arguments that Babasaheb advanced to defend Dalits' rights as citizens had an imprint of Gandhi's design of inclusive growth of communities. That he was not completely persuaded by Ambedkar's demand for separate electorate for the Dalits was politically contrived, since the Mahatma did not want to divide Hindus further in a situation when the Muslims had already been segregated. In the same fashion, V. D. Savarkar's the Hindutva project was a response to Gandhi's conception of syncretic nationalism. It is a tragedy that despite being a devout Hindu, a Sanatani Hindu, Mahatma was one of those few nationalists who relentlessly fought against divisive designs, meant to compartmentalize communities around the religious axis.

There is one final point. In view of the campaign that Gandhi had spearheaded along with his like-minded colleagues across India, it can fairly be said that he put forward a model of political mobilization in which socioculturally disparate Indians found a voice. It means, in other words, that the Mahatma aimed at organizing people at large regardless of one's religious affiliation of socio-economic location. For instance, the 1921–1922 Non-cooperation movement with its merger with Khilafat movement is illustrative of an endeavour showing that Gandhi was not in favour of championing sectional interests, but those of the multitude. It is true that it was primarily a political design since Muslims joined not for the nationalist cause but for the British decision to disband Caliph for the Muslim world. Nonetheless, it shows Gandhi as an astute strategist. In the campaigns that followed the Non-cooperation movement also reveals that he left no stone unturned to unite socioculturally separate communities for a common cause. This argument does not hold water in case of either Savarkar or Jinnah or Ambedkar. As evidence shows, they privileged the sectional interests over the national interests since, for them, the idea of India being a nation differed radically from one another. On the basis of the two-nation-theory, Jinnah offered an argument defending the claim of Muslims being an exclusive community given their religious identity; by his staunch critique of Gandhi being soft towards Muslims, Savarkar also revealed his stance vis-a-vis Muslims; it was again an exclusive design for the majority community, the Hindus. Ambedkar's critique was a critique within a critique since he found Gandhi's defence for caste system as supportive to social hierarchy which was prejudicial to the Dalits because of the accident of birth. Here too, Babasaheb took up the cudgels for justice for an exclusive community, the Dalits. The discussion remains incomplete if we stop here. It is true that Gandhi was a major referent in the nationalist context and the multiple ideas that thrived were conceptually linked with what he had evolved. This is part of the story; the other equally important part is articulated when one makes the point that Gandhi would not have become so all-inclusive had he not had the privilege of interacting with his detractors. In fact, it will not be an exaggeration to argue that Gandhi would have been less appealing had he not drawn on the ideas that his detractors had articulated. In that sense, Jinnah's concern for Muslims, Babasaheb's idea of Dalit empowerment and Savarkar's design for Hindu exclusivity had had their critical role in finally shaping what Gandhi stood for. The idea is simple: Gandhi's distinct thought processes thus dialectically evolved out of his interaction with his colleagues in a context in which the Enlightenment values were no less insignificant.

V. D. Savarkar (1883–1966)

Re-articulation of the Nationalist Voice

2

This chapter deals with the sociopolitical ideas of V. D. Savarkar (1883–1966) who, both during the nationalist phase and its aftermath, pursued, in a sustained manner, the Hindutva objectives regardless of consequences. Persuaded by his belief that only by creating a Hindu compact on the basis of 'Hinduness' shared by the Hindus in general, building of *Akhand Bharat* (united India) was possible. It was thus not surprising that he was introduced to Indian nationalism by the revolutionary nationalists of Maharashtra (where he was born and raised) and Bengal, which was the nursery of violent nationalism. It was also not surprising that he was inspired by the Italian nationalist Giuseppe Mazzini, who developed an ideological framework to galvanize the Italian youth while he was engaged in a battle for unification of Italy. Supportive of the motto *Dio e Popolo* (God and people), he thus regarded patriotism as a duty and love for the country as divine because this would create a template of linking the Italians on the basis of common religion, history and language. Opposed to Protestantism because it further subdivided the Christians by generating an anarchy of beliefs, he developed a concept of 'thought and action' suggesting the former made no sense unless complemented by the latter and vice versa. Like his intellectual mentor, Mazzini, Savarkar conceptualized a model of action on the basis of an ideological framework and a political philosophy seeking to create a homogeneous nationalist compact as perhaps the only means left for the nation to gain independence. It was a definite politico-ideological design based on nation's cultural pride and self-esteem which, he felt, was the need of the hour. For him, a unified India remained elusive so long as Hindus were divided around sociocultural axes. Hence his mission was to create an ambience in which nation was privileged over individual priorities. The task was not difficult to accomplish because of the obvious cultural compatibility among the Hindus by being together in a territory supportive of identical sociocultural values and mores.

Unlike M. A. Jinnah and B. R. Ambedkar who interacted with Gandhi on many occasions, Savarkar had not had many opportunities in this regard. It is true that he met the Mahatma in 1909 in London when he was a student. It is also true that Gandhi responded to some of his criticisms in his *Hind Swaraj* where he mentioned that this text was written in response to the views that he confronted when he had interactions with the Indian students. That Savarkar was not persuaded by Gandhian non-violence is too explicit to require reiteration. He was interned for his involvement in revolutionary nationalist activities, which means that his approach to nationalism was at variance with the Mahatma. So, the difference between him and Savarkar was primarily ideational in character. It is evident if one goes through the texts that he left; by being appreciative of the 1857 rebellion in which the rebels resorted to violence to do away with the British rule, Savarkar explicitly stated what he had in mind. The arguments in favour of violence were persuasively made in his *The Indian War of Independence of 1857*. In two respects, the text is remarkable: on the one hand, he, in unequivocal terms, admired the soldiers and the leadership for having made the supreme sacrifice and also resorted to military means, just like their bete noire, to violently combat the colonizers. This is also an effort, on the other, to unambiguously endorse violence, which was contrary to Gandhi's faith. Interestingly, Gandhi's *Hind Swaraj* which upheld non-violence and Savarkar's *The Indian War of Independence of 1857* were published in 1909. It may have been coincidental; nonetheless, at the ideational level, by defending violent means, Savarkar can be said to have made a persuasive point which his colleagues raised later in strengthening their arguments against Gandhi's defence for non-violence. The same Savarkar seems to have changed his approach when he accepted the constitutional path for freedom. During his stint as the Hindu Mahasabha President, he, despite being severely critical to Gandhi, neither did argue for violent means nor resorted to campaigns for generating support for violent struggle for freedom. The aim of this chapter is to delve into these aspects which projected Savarkar as one of the most powerful crusaders who was keen to explore other possibilities. As argued above, there are not many occasions of communication between Gandhi and Savarkar. The discussion that follows shall focus primarily on the ideational differences between them. Like the other detractors, Ambedkar and Jinnah, he too did not fall for Gandhi's mystical charm and common man appearance. Based on the assumption that the Mahatma was receptive to the responses that his nationalist colleagues offered, the chapter also reiterates the point that Gandhi became Gandhi out of the intellectual interactions that he had with his colleagues who did not, at all, acquiesce with his views. By arguing that both Savarkar and Gandhi drew on each other, the chapter also reinforces the point that their ideas evolved dialectically in a context in which their nationalist concerns had prevailed over other considerations. In a nutshell, the point that is being made here relates to one of the fundamental premises on which the entire text rests, namely, the ideas are the product of interactions based on specific socio-ideological priorities in specific socio-economic circumstances. Savarkar and Gandhi occupied the same socio-economic milieu in which some of the politico-ideological responses were privileged partly due to the colonial context in which Enlightenment values were espoused at the cost of both indigenous and other European philosophical discourses. Nonetheless, the contrarian ideas flourished, as India's nationalist history amply shows, which informed some of the ideological endeavours in adverse circumstances. Savarkar and his colleagues championing violence and militancy represented a trend which neither the Congress nationalists nor Gandhi had ever approved of. By highlighting the arguments that Savarkar put forward in his support, the chapter is also an elaboration of the processes to seek to explain the evolution and also consolidation of adversarial views in the nationalist context in which nationalism was hardly monochromatic in either perception or articulation.

Arrival on the Political Scene

V. D. Savarkar is generally credited with the conceptualization of Hindutva in which he defended the construction of a compact of

Hindus as a well-knit nation. A nationalist to the core, he got involved in revolutionary activities while he was a student in India and later in England when he joined India House, a platform for Indian students in London. During his stay in London he founded Abhinava Bharat Society and Free India Society to organize protest campaigns there by involving the Indian students and also their colleagues from other countries. In May 1907, he organized a meeting in London to commemorate the 1857 rebels as Indian martyrs on its 50th anniversary which attracted police attention in both India and England. A glimpse of the political activities that he undertook as a student shows that he was inspired to participate in the nationalist onslaught against the British, irrespective of the consequences. Characterizing V. D. Savarkar as a far more dangerous political activist who could be a threat to the Empire, a judicial dispatch from London underlined that he while staying in London was

> a very active member of the group of Indian revolutionaries residing in [the city]; ... he translated into Marathi the life of Mazzini with an introduction in which he point out how Mazzini relied upon the youth of the country to win freedom; he was also the author of the revolutionary book Indian War of Independence in praise of the rebels who rose in revolt against the Crown and distributed copies at a meeting organized by him ... in celebration.[1]

It was Mazzini, confirmed by the above dispatch, who, as his intellectual mentor, kindled in him the urge for participation in the campaign for freedom from the British rule. Being an ardent supporter of revolutionary nationalism, Savarkar appeared inclined to endorse the means that drew on the overthrowing of the British regime by violence. He was thus kept under surveillance which resulted in his arrest in 1910 for his alleged involvement in anti-British political activities along with those revolutionaries who were associated with the India House Group. He was incarcerated in the Cellular Jail in Andaman and Nicobar Islands for more than a decade, and was released in 1921 after he appealed to the British ruler for clemency. Savarkar's revolutionary self and request for mercy seem to be neither compatible nor

[1] http://anurupacinar.net/wp-content/uploads/2013/09/British-Secret-Files-on-Savarkar-1911-21.pdf, Judicial dispatch from London, 4 June 1919, 3.

easily comprehensible presumably because of the stark contradiction between the two. This needs elaboration. As evidence shows, Savarkar had written on 30 March 1920 to the Chief Commissioner of Andaman and Nicobar Islands for clemency in response to the Royal Declaration for clemency for all political prisoners. The decision was executed and many political prisoners, jailed in various prisons in India, were released. By making an appeal for clemency, Savarkar followed his other revolutionary colleagues. It is also logical that one needs to be extra careful while articulating the clemency appeal. Savarkar was no exception. Justifying why he had a case for clemency, he couched his appeal in such a way as to convince the decision-makers which was clear when he stated that he believed neither in the

> militant school of Bakunin nor the philosophical anarchism of Kropotkin or Tolstoy [but was committed to] the constitution ... and is ready to contribute to the orderly constitutional development in India. ... I am sincere in expressing my earnest intention of treading the constitutional path and trying my humble best to render the hands of the British dominions a Bond of Love and Respect and of mutual help and such an empire as is foreshadowed in the Proclamation with my hearty adherence.[2]

There is no doubt that Savarkar expressed his willingness to abide by the constitution if amnesty was guaranteed. As clemency for all was a policy decision, this individual letter was not an exception. For him, it was a matter of right and the decision was taken accordingly. It could also have been a strategy to seek for release from prison which would allow him to work further for independence. This was perhaps the reason for his appeal for amnesty as he reminisced later that 'it was not an amnesty but a political ploy of the ruling authority to demean the sacrifice of the revolutionaries [because it is likely to be] construed to the outside world as the reward of obedience and of abstention from [the nationalist] activities'.[3] So, Savarkar was aware of the consequences of the general clemency that the British government offered to quell the nationalist upsurges. That it had far-reaching

[2] http://anurupacinar.net/wp-content/uploads/2013/09/British-Secret-Files-on-Savarkar-1911-21.pdf, V. D. Savarkar's clemency appeal, 30 March 1920, 12.

[3] V. D. Savarkar, *My Transportation for Life* (New Delhi: Abhishek Publications, 2007), 310.

consequences was made clear when he stated that amnesty in exchange of a commitment for being obedient to British constitutionalism 'will react detrimentally on the freedom-fighters ... and other nationally-minded individuals; it will [ultimately] weaken the nationalists who may not feel so strongly for national independence [if those in prison] accept clemency for their freedom from jail'.[4] Despite his hard work, his appeal was turned down by the Viceroy in his letter of 12 July 1920. Although Savarkar did not succeed in securing amnesty for him that he asked for clemency gave a fillip to his detractors both during his life time and its aftermath.

Rise of a Nationalist

As per the available evidence, since his youth Savarkar was involved in the nationalist campaign in various forms. When he was just 16 years old, he, with support from his friends, founded Rashtrabhakta Samuha (Patriots' Society) which, in 1901, became Mitra Mela (Society of Friends). In the regular meeting of the Mela, besides seeking to develop togetherness among those willing to be associated with the endeavour, discussions were directed to rouse people to anti-colonial sentiments. In this sense, the Mitra Mela was a 'consciousness-raising design'[5] which was sought to be accomplished by series of lectures, organized at regular intervals. Before his departure for London in 1906, he was involved in the activities of the Mela which gradually spread its influences in the city of Nashik of Bombay presidency. It was a source of irritation to the government because Mela created a platform for the nationalists to come together for a cause. By insisting on reading the biographies of Mazzini, Garibaldi, Napoleon Bonaparte, among others, by the participants in the regular discussion, his purpose was to instil a sense of belongingness to the nation. The aim was to develop the Indianness which, Savarkar felt, was sadly missing. The lectures that the Mela organized focussed primarily on how the colonizers devised and executed devices to brutally exploit Indians which

[4] Ibid.

[5] Janaki Bakhle, 'Savarkar (1883–1966), Sedition and Surveillance: The Rule of Law in a Colonial Situation,' *Social History* 35, no. 1 (February 2019): 56.

could only be countered once the Indians were organized to combat the rulers and their supporters. This was a unique effort designed to mobilize the colonized by reference to 'history and historical memories'[6] highlighting that India became a prey largely due to the failure of the Indians to rise in unison against the intruders. Besides seeking to mobilize the nationalists, Savarkar, in his innumerable speeches in the Mela meetings, also insisted on being self-reliant, a vision that corresponded with Swadeshi campaign for making India economically self-dependent. It was clearly stated in one of his addresses when he categorically stated that

> [t]he reason why our country has reached the most wretched condition is that we have given up our religion, our industries and our trade, which has been taken up by others. [The British] … have monopolized our trade and hence their country is rich and ours is going down. … Let us bear this fully in mind and fight with them with weapons, that is, we must abide by our religion and we carry on our trade, which has gone into the hands of others. It means [that] we must use goods produced in our country, that Swadeshi sugar, cloth and other Swadeshi articles. … Hence, instead of sweet words let there be fire in your heart, let it blaze here.[7]

The speech is revealing in a number of ways. Prominent among them was the concern that Savarkar had expressed for India's decadence; it was an outcome of our failure, he stated clearly, to be respectful to our nation; as a result, we allowed the foreigners to build their fortune on our wealth and other resources. Besides being economically powerful, one of the reasons for the colonizers to prevail over the colonized was their success in weakening them culturally by taking away the civilizational values on which Indians thrived in the past. Here he had in mind the Vedic and Upanishadic wisdom that, he firmly believed, was of the source of India's emotional strength. It was therefore not surprising that he specifically mentioned the importance of religion which, later on, became an important pillar of his widely circulated notion of Hindutva. Interestingly, these two aspects reverberated in Gandhi's explanation of why India was colonized. In his 1909 tract,

[6] Ibid.

[7] India Office Records, London, L/PJ/6/1069, File No. 78, Savarkar Speeches, delivered during 1910–1911.

The Hind Swaraj, the Mahatma's views had an uncanny similarity with those of Savarkar, which is evident when he stated that

> The English have not taken India; we have given it to them. … We assisted them. If I am in the habit of drinking *bhang* [intoxicating narcotic substance, extracted out of the leaves and flower top of the cannabis] and a seller thereof sells it to me, am I to blame him or myself? By blaming the seller, shall I be able to avoid the habit? … [Furthermore], the Hindus and Mahomedans were at daggers drawn. This too gave the [British] an opportunity to control India. Hence it is truer to say that we gave India to the English than that India was lost.[8]

Implicit here are two fundamental points which are useful to pursue the argument that there are conceptual compatibilities between Gandhi and Savarkar. On the one hand, it is beyond doubt that both of them were nationalists par excellence, in the sense that they expressed identical concerns when they suggested that India's socio-economic degeneration was primarily due to colonialism; their main objective was therefore to create an ambience in which the argument attributing India's downfall to the British rule gained credibility. Along with this, they also firmly argued, on the other, that Indians needed to be self-reliant to effectively challenge the British. Here too, the ideas that both of them further elaborated in due course of their political career were presented in their rudimentary forms. Savarkar, in his two avatars, revolutionary nationalist and the president of Hindu Mahasabha, had undertaken appropriate steps to politically mobilize the nationalists for the cause; the aim of the Mahatma was similar; he too, organized the Satyagrahis for non-violent resistance in circumstances in which multiple ideological priorities jostled for space. What is sought to be highlighted here is the point that, in a significant way, they appear to have coalesced insofar as their theoretical understanding of how India was colonized and how to reverse the circumstances was concerned.

Once in London in 1907, he continued with what he had begun in India. At the aegis of Abhinava Bharat, an organization that he founded in London, gathered the Indian students, in May 1907 on the

[8] M. K. Gandhi, *The Hind Swaraj or Indian Hone Rule* (Ahmedabad: Navajivan Publishing House, 2005) (reprint), 34–35.

occasion of the golden jubilee celebration of the 1857 rebellion which he christened as the First War of Independence.[9] According to him, it was a first serious challenge in India to shake off colonial shackles. Inspired ideologically by nationalism, he argued that the 1857 rebellion had 'reflected the unified (Hindu and Muslim) nationalist desire of India to free herself from the oppressive yoke of British rule'.[10] On this occasion, he circulated an extremely patriotic pamphlet appreciating the sacrifice of the rebels by exhorting that

> we take up your cry, we revere your flag, we are determined to continue that fiery mission of "away with foreigners", which you uttered amidst the prophetic thundering of the Revolutionary war. Yes, it was a revolutionary war. For the War of 1857 shall not cease till the revolution arrives, striking slavery into dust, elevating liberty to the throne.[11]

That Savarkar was unequivocal in his admiration for those who laid their life for the nationalist cause was clearly stated in this pamphlet. He also saw a new beginning in the endeavour that the Indian soldiers undertook in their desire to get rid of the colonizers. It was obvious that he would be kept under observation by the police. Soon, he was incarcerated for life in Cellular Jail in Andaman and Nicobar Islands. It was a torturous phase in his life which he codified in his *My Transportation for Life*; the text which was originally written in Marathi with the title *Majhi Janmathep* in 1946. A biography of his days in the Cellular Jail, *My Transportation*, can be said to have some of his ideas of Hindutva in a rudimentary form. The book has one running theme, namely the brutality of the jail administrators and the unbearable sufferings of the jail inmates. For instance, at the beginning while narrating the inhuman ordeal of the prisoners, Savarkar wrote that

[9] An Indian Nationalist, *The Indian War of Independence of 1857* (London, 1909). This book was written by V. D. Savarkar, but to avoid the government attention, the authorship was attributed to An Indian Nationalist.

[10] Bakhle, 'Savarkar (1883–1966), Sedition and Surveillance, 57.

[11] V. D. Savarkar, Oh Martyrs' (London, 1908)—cited in Julia Kelley-Swift, 'A Misunderstood Legacy: V. D. Savarkar and the Creation of Hindutva' (dissertation for the degree of Bachelor of Arts, Wesleyan University, 2015), 52–53.

> none was spared, among political prisoners, from the rack of that inhuman toil. Most of them were unaccustomed to any kind of physical labour; the best part of them were college youths; some of them had not turned sixteen; they were tender in age and body. But they were forced, for months on end, to toil hard even when they suffer from fever or other ailments.[12]

There were protests and Savarkar was in the lead in organizing the first strike in 1913 in the Cellular Jail. It was not an easy task because the inmates were divided between two groups: one that was close to the jail authority was reluctant and the other group felt impelled to join the strike. In Savarkar's words, they were 'those who, suppressed and downcast by all the vigours of their prison life, were now out to fight it out to the finish, and never submit at the cost of self-respect and honour'.[13] It was a strike on a small scale. Nonetheless, the very act was a testimony of how political mobilization could work even in adverse circumstances; it was a reconfirmation of Savarkar's faith in human spirit which was a tremendous source of strength if it was tapped for a legitimate cause. The strike was a baby step, felt Savarkar, which was not only 'a threatening challenge to the prison authority [it also] created a stir and excitement in the prison-world the like of which had not witnessed before'.[14] In response to the strike, the prison authority resorted to stern actions to quell the situation. Consequently, the political prisoners on strike were subjected to all kinds of punishments, including handcuffs shackles, solitary confinement and other torturous forms of punishment. Under normal circumstances, these punishments lasted only for a week, as per jail manuals, but in this case, it went on beyond 10 days. Savarkar, being one of the victims, raised his voice against the violation of the well-established rules in this regard, which finally forced the jail authority to stick to the time-period of seven days. It was a grand success proving again how an organized protest yielded results.

In the Cellular Jail, Savarkar also realized the importance of education to combat superstitions and also voluntary acceptance of the

[12] Savarkar, *My Transportation for Life*, 76.

[13] Ibid, 82.

[14] Ibid.

torture in jail as being fated. He felt the need of a travelling library in the prison; the prison library had books which mainly dealt with the British history and the glorious role that the Empire had played in contributing to human civilization. Most of the ordinary prisoners were not allowed to read books; instead they were encouraged to chew tobacco and indulge openly in any vices affecting health. It was a conspiratorial design which provoked Savarkar to raise voice, though he did not succeed completely in allowing the ordinary prisoners access to the library. He took another route. From the secret funds that he generated, he procured books on economics, history, fiction and novel to make them available for the ordinary prisoners. How did he get books? It was an ingenious technique that he evolved. As he said, '[w]e ordered [books] on the address of Hindu officers outside the jail. We did not stock them in one place and we circulated them among the intending readers'.[15] This was an innovative design whereby ordinary prisoners had an opportunity to be baptized in the nationalist mission because most of the books that were procured dealt with India's ancient past and also the achievements of the kings and queens. Besides being acquainted with what India was in the past, the reading of books also brought them closer to Hinduism as an empowering religion which helped them question the Christian priests who visited the jail for proselytizing the prisoners to Christianity, Savarkar argued. This was certainly a deterrent to conversion, although the rate of conversion considerably dwindled following the 1857 rebellion. Savarkar thus mentioned that

> till 1857, both in prisons and in the army, the ruling authorities had encouraged the spread of Christianity [which was stopped, to a considerable extent] after the terrible catastrophe of the War of Independence [when] the British authorities seldom interfered with religion and did not encourage conversion.[16]

Conversion was halted, though the prison authority devised newer mechanisms to prevent the prisoners from embarking on activities seeking to undermine the Empire. In wards of Hindu prisoners,

[15] Ibid, 184.

[16] Ibid, 185.

majority of the jamadars (junior staff in the prison who were incharge of the wards) were Pathans simply because they

> were notorious for their fanatical hatred of the Hindus. The Pathans, the Sindhis and the Baluchi Muslims ... were, one and all, cruel and unscrupulous persons, and were full of fanatical hatred for the Hindus. The officers had pampered them to serve their own ends.[17]

This does not seem to be odd in any context of nationalist agitation. It is therefore not an exaggeration to make the point that British government remained invincible largely due to its ability to generate and also sustain communal animosity between two major communities, Hindus and Muslims. This is not the space to dwell on the adverse consequences of the communal divide; there is no dearth of literature. What is important here is the point that Savarkar's deportation in Andaman and Nicobar Islands created in him a future leader who devised a different path of nationalist mobilization drawing on Hindutva.

Unfolding of an Ideology

As argued above, Savarkar's internment in the Cellular Jail was not simply a phase of his incarceration but also a phase of learning which helped him build his ideological priorities when he appeared on the national scene. Besides nurturing the nationalist zeal and also creating a nationalist compact out of the prisoners along with the like-minded prison inmates, Savarkar also displayed his politico-ideological priorities during his incarceration in the Cellular Jail. The death of B. G. Tilak, the firebrand Marathi leader, in August 1920 gave him probably the first opportunity to infuse the nationalist zeal among the fellow prisoners. Savarkar planned a day-long fast to mourn the loss. It was difficult to observe fast since it was to be construed as 'treason, and may lead to trial, and punishment for the offence'.[18] Notwithstanding the adverse consequences, 'at the dinner time, it was found that every one of them had refused to take food, from the inmates of Silver Jail to

[17] Ibid, 88.

[18] Ibid, 330.

inhabitants on the far-off island of Ras'.[19] For Savarkar, it was a matter of great satisfaction for two reasons: first, it was clear that nationalism was an empowering ideology capable of inspiring the Indians regardless of consequences; and, also, the sustained effort towards organizing prisoners generating the nationalistic fervour yielded positive results which were inconceivable in the prison context. Furthermore, it was also a matter of learning to Savarkar because in just two hours' notice the whole prison world of Andaman and Nicobar Islands went on absolute fast in honour of Tilak; it was surprising that even the prisoners toiling on hard labour happily agreed to undertake fast as they were inspired too. For Savarkar, it was not a miracle but an outcome of hard work by the nationalists to create a nationalist compact by adequately generating the concern for the motherland. The nine-year hard work, claimed Savarkar,

> brought tremendous awakening and unity among the prisoners and free men throughout the settlement [which was evident] when in just two hours the news could be carried all over the place and thousands of prisoners could observe fast regarding the day as a day of national mourning.[20]

This was the beginning of a realization for Savarkar that only by inculcating concern for the nation his nationalist mission was certain to be fulfilled. Here too, he always drew on the Hindu imageries while being engaged in mobilizing the prison inmates. For instance, serving the nation was also a service to *Bharat Mata*, according to Savarkar. In his conceptual universe, Tilak perfectly fits in presumably because it was Tilak who nurtured the nationalist zeal in Maharashtra by drawing upon the heroic deeds of Shivaji or by popularizing Ganapati festival; he was also one of the few nationalist leaders who opposed the 1893 Age of Consent Bill since it was a foreign intervention in an exclusive spiritual domain of the Hindus, and was thus unwarranted. Fundamental here is the point that Savarkar was in the process of building his conceptual politico-ideological framework around these ideas which are integrally connected with the Hindu mindset. Second, the prison days also helped him build his political arguments

[19] Ibid.

[20] Ibid.

vis-a-vis other nationalist events. He was not, at all, comfortable with the merger of the Gandhi-led Non-cooperation movement with the Khilafat movement. Persuaded to believe that it would not have been possible had there been Tilak on the national scene, he thus argued that 'the exit from the Indian world of a powerful personality like Lokmanya Tilak ushered in the mad intoxication of Khilafat agitation conspiring with the cult of the *Charkha* as a way to Swaraj in one year'.[21] His opposition to the campaign was based on two important considerations: on the one hand, he believed that the fight for the Muslims for restoring *Khalif* was suicidal since it was not exactly nationalistic because it was directed to fulfil an exclusive Muslim demand. With this objective, it would be difficult, if not impossible, to persuade the Hindus to join hands with the Muslims for a cause which was to protect their exclusive interests. Hence, Savarkar denounced the Khilafat campaign because it was, in his views, 'an *afat* or menace to the country'.[22] Furthermore, those who joined Khilafat campaign had double faces, humanitarian for the wider public and sectarian for the Hindus. To illustrate his point, he referred to an incident in the Cellular Jail when a Khilafat campaigner abused a Hindu untouchable for taking water from a vessel of water for the Muslims with the plea that his touch would make the water unholy for prayer (*Namaz*).[23] In addition to condemning the Khilafat agitation as harmful to nation's interests, he questioned, on the other, Gandhi's Non-cooperation movement which drew, as he characterized, on 'the perverse doctrine of non-violence and truth'. He thus strongly felt that

> the Noncooperation movement for Swaraj based on these twin principles was a movement without power and was bound to destroy the power of the country; it is an illusion, a hallucination, not unlike the hurricane that sweeps over a land only to destroy it; it is a disease of insanity, an epidemic and megalomania.[24]

[21] Ibid, 343.

[22] Ibid.

[23] Ibid, 362.

[24] Ibid, 343.

What is explicitly stated here is Savarkar's unambivalent stance vis-a-vis Gandhian mode of conceptualizing the campaign for freedom. Being an ardent supporter of Tilak and a strong believer in militant nationalism, it does not seem odd; in fact, it is obvious that Savarkar, being baptized in an ideology in which violence was privileged, would never have approved the Gandhian principle of ahimsa or non-violence as capable of winning independence for India. Gandhi too was not persuaded. In a significant comment on *Hind Swaraj* that he wrote in 1909, he thus explained that this text was

> written ... in answer to the Indian school of violence and its prototype in South Africa. I came in contact with every known Indian anarchist in London. Their bravery impressed me, but I feel that their zeal was misguided. I felt that violence was no remedy for India's ills, and that her civilization required the use of a different and higher weapon for self-protection.[25]

So, the battle line was drawn. Contrary to what the Mahatma held, Savarkar with his faith in militant nationalism found Gandhi's non-violent struggle hollow and non-functional in the Indian context. Savarkar and Gandhi differed from each other not merely over their chosen mode of conceptualizing nationalism, but over their ideological predilections which were strikingly different. As will be shown below, as days passed on, there was hardly a space between them which allowed them to come together presumably (except perhaps their commitment to political freedom) because they drew sustenance from completely contrasting ideological persuasions.

Articulating a Nationalist Voice

In conventional historiography, the 1857 rebel is known as the Sepoy Mutiny. For Savarkar, it was a distortion of history seeking to demean the heroic sacrifice of the Indians regardless of religion, region and economic barriers. The campaign against the East India Company was confined neither to any specific region nor to a select

[25] *Collected Works of Mahatma Gandhi*, Vol. 25 (27 October 1921–22 January 1922); Gandhi notes on the *Hind Swaraj*, 14 December 1921, 243.

group of kings and rulers, but spread out to a wider section of the population which was a testimony of how it became a nationalist offensive against colonialism. Those who led the attack succeeded in bringing people from different strata and also religious groups for a united venture against the ruling authority. As a conscious nationalist, Savarkar felt persuaded to highlight the glorious effort that the Indians in the context of the 1857 rebel had undertaken. It was moral responsibility to bring back the memory of martyrdom as a source of 'fiery inspiration'[26] and also to reinforce the point that 'a nation must develop its capacity of claiming a past but also of knowing how to use it for the furtherance of its future'.[27] What was striking for him was the ability of the rebels to create a platform in which Hindus, Muslims and other religious groups joined hands in their opposition to the British rule. According to Savarkar, it was not a matter of surprise because 'the feeling of hatred against the Mohammedans was just and necessary in the times of Shivaji, but, such a feeling would be unjust and foolish if nursed now simply because it was the dominant feeling of the Hindus then'.[28] A perceptive comment with a contextual significance, this assessment will help us understand his approach to communal issues which loomed large in the context of the nationalist movement following the consolidation of the Muslims around M. A. Jinnah's two-nation theory.

As an author who believed in the dialectical interconnection between text and context, Savarkar did not endorse the widely publicized theory of the fear, by the sepoys, of cutting in their teeth of greased cartridges (with cow and pig fat) and the annexation of Oudh as singularly responsible for this outrage. In fact, there were many factors which finally ignited the feelings of hatred among the

[26] Savarkar relied on these texts highlighting 'the mutiny': Charles Bell, *The History of the Indian Mutiny*, 2 Vols.; Alexander Duff, *The Indian Rebellion: Its Causes and Results* (1858); John William Kay, *A History of the Sepoy War in India*, 3 Vols. (1864–1876); George Bruce Malleson, *Red Pamphlet* (1858); John William Kay and George Bruce Malleson, *History of the Indian Mutiny*, 6 Vols. and George Trevelyan, *Cawnpore* (1865).

[27] An Indian Nationalist, *The Indian War of Independence of 1857*, vii.

[28] Ibid, vii–viii.

participants. To explain his point further, he drew on the 1789 French Revolution which was not merely the outcome of demeaning comments of the Queen, but a series of happenings just before the mass eruptions, leading to the overthrow of the regime. The kidnapping of Sita, he further argued 'was only the incidental cause of the fight between Rama and Ravana [while] the real causes were deeper and more inward'.[29] This is a fair point directing our attention to argument that in case of mass upsurges, one needs to be sensitive to the processes and also triggering factors; while the latter can be grievances of the soldiers as they were forced to do what their religion forbade, the former is about the growing hatred of the Indian rulers and people due to torturous colonial governance. One of the factors that created an instantaneous bond among the rebels was, as per Savarkar, the tyrannical administration that flourished under the stewardship of Lord Dalhousie. It was not, at all, his brainchild; he put in practice what he was asked to, Savarkar mentioned. In his words,

> as long as the general policy is dictated from Home, ... it would certainly be unjust to hold Dalhousie responsible for all those combined acts and deeds which had to flow directly from the situation created for him by his masters in England and his assistants in India; he merely reaped that harvest of political robbery, the seeds of which had been sedulously sown for a hundred years by his predecessors.[30]

Dalhousie did the final act in a context when his predecessors, moved by unholy designs, had prepared the ground, stated Savarkar. There are two points that deserve attention. First, the rebel was an attack on the inhuman governance that flourished in India in the wake of the East India Company rule; it was an administration that hardly addressed the genuine concerns of the governed which ultimately led to the rise in 1857. Second, it was also an event that needed to be celebrated simply because the 1857 revolt was an example of communal harmony that appeared to have dwindled in later days.

[29] Ibid, 7.

[30] Ibid, 35.

There is substance in the argument that greased cartridges caused immediate outbursts. That it was blasphemous needs to be seen in the historical context when the Christian priests were engaged wildly in proselytizing Hindus and Muslims. The reasons are not difficult to seek given the fact that

> the minds of the Feringhi (Englishman) was filled with such contempt and such hatred for the Hindu and Muslim faith, the two principal religions of India, that very prominent writers, forgetting even ordinary conventionalities, constantly heaped shameful abuse on the two religions whenever they got a chance.[31]

There was a design here. By conversion to Christianity, the East India Company intended to purge India of both Hindus and Muslims. With the disappearance of Hinduism and Islam, there would hardly be a template of togetherness among those practising those faiths. As a result, 'the national feeling would die, individuality would die and it is infinitely easier to rule a nation whose individuality is dead than to rule one which had a clearly marked individuality'.[32] To reinforce his point, Savarkar quoted one Reverend Kennedy who was specifically sent from England to India for this task. As he elaborated, according to Kennedy, the holiest task was to

> propagate Christianity in the Empire, from Cape Comorin [Kanyakumari of today] to the Himalayas [and] ... for this work all the efforts we can and use all the power and all the authority in our hands; and continuous and unceasing efforts must be kept on until India becomes a magnificent nation, the bulwark of Christianity in the East.[33]

As a strategy, it was resorted to earlier by the Moghol ruler, Aurangzeb who felt, Savarkar highlighted, that 'the destruction of the religion of the conquered race makes the problem of retaining it in perpetual slavery much easier'[34] which the English utilized for sustaining the Empire. There were also instances of Koran and Vedas being defiled

[31] Ibid, 47.

[32] Ibid.

[33] Ibid.

[34] Ibid.

by the English officers, which, if challenged by the sepoys, resulted in the denial of food to those who retaliated.[35]

In light of the above empirical details with the purpose of providing an explanatory framework, Savarkar was now in a position to account for the outbreak in conceptual terms. In his schema, the two great principles of *Swadharma* (own religious identity) and *Swaraj* (freedom) will help us plausibly explain the apparently sudden outbursts of the sepoys against the authority. 'The seed of the Revolution of 1857 is', argued Savarkar, 'in this holy and inspiring idea, clear and explicit, propounded form the throne of Delhi'.[36] Drawing on his intellectual mentor, Mazzini, he further stated that Swadharma and Swaraj were the both sides of the same coin; just like Mazzini who argued that there was no barrier between heaven and earth, but were interconnected, as the former was inconceivable without the latter. 'Our idea of Swadharma too, is', adumbrated Savarkar,

> not contradictory to that of Swaraj. The two are connected as means and end. Swaraj without *Swadharma* is despicable and *Swadharma* without Swaraj is powerless. The sword of material power, Swaraj, should always be readily drawn for our object, our safety in the other world, *Swadharma*. This trend of the Eastern mind will often be found in its history. The reason why, in the East, all revolutions take a religious form, way more, the reason why Eastern history knows of no revolutions unconnected with religion, lies in the all-embracing meaning of Dharma has. That this dual principle of *Swadharma* and Swaraj, always seen in the history of India, appeared also in the Revolution of 1857, should [therefore] be a matter of no surprise.[37]

A perceptive explanatory scheme, the twin principle of Swadharma and Swaraj, was a source of inspiration for the rebels who rose in one voice against the British authority regardless of adverse consequences. For Savarkar, it was not, at all, surprising because the urge for protecting one's religion and country was instinctive of conscious human beings. The quarrel over the greased cartridges was but the chance spark flung in among all the combustible material. If that spark

[35] Ibid, 50.

[36] Ibid, 8.

[37] Ibid, 9–10.

had not triggered the rebel, some other would have done it, believed Savarkar. In other words, the participants had found a leader, a flag and a cause which was adequate, as examples from elsewhere show, to transform a mutiny into a revolutionary war. The milieu generated an atmosphere in which the sepoys believed that 'the first step towards Dharma is to be a free man of a free country'[38] and thus were 'determined that, whether they had to use these cartridges or not, they would not rest quiet until they had destroyed this political slavery and this dependence which was at the root of all this trouble'.[39] This was a charged atmosphere in which the determined rebels put across the point that so long as foreign domination continued Swaraj and Swadharma remained elusive. Those who 'lifted their swords for Swadharma and Swaraj and courted death, if not for victory, at least for duty' were hailed as heroes who continued to inspire, Savarkar underlined, the generations to come.

What was the lesson? Savarkar himself stated that despite being abortive, '[t]he Revolution of 1857 was a test to see how far India had come towards unity, independence and popular power'.[40] The rebellion failed to oust the Company rule due to 'the idle, effeminate, selfish and treacherous men who ruined it'.[41] Nonetheless, there was a silver lining since the rebellion created an environment in which Brahmans and Sudras, Hindus and Muslims were united for protecting Swadharma and Swaraj. As he mentioned,

> Not [only] one individual, not [only] one class, alone had been moved deeply by seeing the sufferings of their country. Hindu and Mohamedan, Brahmin and Sudra, Kshatriya and Vaisya, prince and pauper, men and women, Pandits and Moulvies, Sepoys and the police, townsmen and villagers, merchants and farmers—men of different religions, men of different castes, people following widely different profession—not able any longer

[38] Ibid, 55.

[39] Ibid.

[40] Ibid, 443.

[41] Ibid. According to Savarkar, 'the defeat was chiefly due to the treachery of those men who failed to understand that the English power was more harmful than the former kind of Swaraj ever could be, and of those who had not the honesty and patriotism to refuse to give help to the foreigner against their own countrymen'.

> to bear the sight of persecution of Bharat Mata, brought about the avenging Revolution in an incredibly short time.[42]

By highlighting this aspect of the rebellion, Savarkar appears to have endeavoured to build a conceptual framework for Hindu–Muslim unity. There are reasons to believe that in reaching such a conclusion, he was influenced, to a significant extent, by the developments in Bengal in the context of the campaign for the revocation of the 1905 first partition of the province.[43] Although the plan for separating the Muslim preponderant east Bengal from the Hindu-majority west Bengal was withdrawn, the nationalist campaign revealed how the social distance between the Hindus and Muslims caused dissension within the rank and file of the campaigners. The rise of India as a national compact was not possible without Hindus joining hands with their Muslim brethren and *vice versa*, warned Savarkar.

The Indian War of Independence of 1857 is a powerful statement and a well-organized endeavour: a powerful statement of rise of nation as a united entity, supported by an all-round endeavour at mobilizing the nation regardless of social, economic and political barriers. Till the publication of Savarkar's tract in 1909, the historical accounts of the events of 1857 that were available were those of the British officers and their agents. It was, for the first time, Savarkar, while characterizing the 1857 rebellion as the First War of Independence, generated interests in what was distorted as a mere rebellion of the disgruntled sepoys. With his persuasive arguments, he defended his nationalist project by drawing upon India's past, highlighting how the nation as a whole rose in revolt in opposition to a ruthless colonial regime. By reinterpreting the causes of the rebellion and also why it failed, Savarkar discharged a historical role in the early part of the 20th century when the nation was in doldrums due to schisms around multiple socio-economic and political axes. Besides being a product of the nationalist concern that Savarkar evinced, the text can be said to have raised some of the pertinent issues regarding caste, class and religion that would soon

[42] An Indian Nationalist, *The Indian War of Independence of 1857*, 227.

[43] Rabindranath Tagore graphically illustrated this issue in his 1916 novel, *Ghare-Baire* (Home and the World).

attract nationalists' attention with the growing involvement of so far peripheral sections of society.

Hindutva Project

It was V. D. Savarkar who designed a model of Hindu nationalism by emphasizing the critical importance of cultural unity in creating a solid nationhood. In his widely acclaimed text *Hindutva*, which was published in 1923, Savarkar thus argued a Hindu was one

> who looks upon the land that extends from Sindu to Sindu—from the Indus to the seas—as the land of his forefathers—his fatherland who inherits the blood of that race whose first discernible source could be traced to the Vedic Saptasindhus and which on its onward march, assimilating much that was incorporated ... has come to be known as the Hindu people, who has inherited and claims as his own the culture of that race as expressed chiefly in their common cultural language, Sanskrit and represented by a common history, a common literature, art and architecture, law and jurisprudence, rites and rituals, ceremonies and sacraments, fairs and festivals; and who, above all, addresses this land, this Sindustan as his holy land, as the land of his prophets and seers, of his godmen and gurus, the land of piety and pilgrimage.[44]

There are three important elements that Savarkar had in mind while articulating his alternative mode of conceptualization: (a) demarcation of a group of people, located in a specific geographical space, (b) the idea of fatherland being espoused to suggest the racial compatibility of those settled in Hindustan and (c) the insistence on holy land for those who remain closeted in the area between Sindu (the river) to Sindu (the ocean). This was clearly stated when he further developed his argument by saying that

> these are the essentials of Hindutva—a common nation (Rashtra), a common jati (race) and a common civilization (Sanskriti). All these essentials could best be summed by stating in brief that he is a Hindu to whom Sindhustan is not only a fatherland but also a holyland. For the first two essentials of Hindutva—nation and jati—are clearly denoted and connoted by the word fatherland while the third essential culture is

[44] V. D. Savarkar, *Hindutva: Who is a Hindu* (Delhi: Bharti Sahitya Sadan, 1923), 115–16.

> pre-eminently implied in the word holy land, as it is precisely Sanskriti, including sanskaras, i.e., rituals, ceremonies and sacraments that makes a land a holy land.[45]

Savarkar's construction of Hindu identity is *territorial* (the land between Indus and the Indian Ocean), *genealogical* (fatherland) and *religious* (holyland). The *Hindu Rashtra* is therefore more of a territorial than a religious nationalism because Hindus represented a cultural and civilizational synthesis which is more 'a secular-rationalist than a religio-fundamentalist construction'. This is further reinforced when he reconfirmed by saying that

> what is needed is to take lessons from history, recognize the vitality and resilience of India, the power of its world view and utilize its strength, which drove it to glorious heights and analyse its weaknesses, which led to her abysmal fall. Pick up the thread from the points where the continuum of our civilizational consciousness was lost and reorient the policy in consonance with those strong points of Indian psyche which will be the engine of our future glory.[46]

This particular conceptualization was also an outcome of a specific politico-ideological debate that unfolded with the propagation of Muslims being a separate nation which got a concrete shape in the 1940 Lahore Resolution when Pakistan was formally conceptualized and demanded. So, by highlighting the cultural aspect of Hindu Rashtra, Savarkar, one of the first pioneers of Hindu nationalism, strove to provide a persuasive alternative to the Muslim League's insistence on Muslims being socioculturally different from their Hindu counterparts. This was the beginning of the institutionalization of Hindu nationalism or Hindutva on the basis of what Savarkar construed as the essence of Hindu culture.

With the above summary, let us get into the details of Hindutva which Savarkar elaborated in detail in a 1923 publication, entitled Hindutva.[47] This is both a conceptual and a historical tract:

[45] Ibid.

[46] Ibid, 39–40.

[47] V. D. Savarkar, *Hindutva: Who is a Hindu* (New Delhi: Bharati Sahitya Sadan, 1989) (reprint), originally published in 1923.

historical because it was an outcome of the contextual compulsions that he confronted, and conceptual since it helped build an alternative model in a context when constitutional liberalism was generally privileged. Hindutva was also a protestant conceptual parameter that drew on the Hindu nationalists' concern for a culturally unified India which was not possible perhaps due to the nationalists' failure to adequately generate nationalist fervour among the Hindus. There are two points that deserve attention: first, as a political activist, it was natural for him to seek to suggest ways and means for nationalist political mobilization drawing on the typical Hindu nationalist design. That he fulfilled his historical role is beyond question; that he was interned in the Cellular Jail for more than a decade is a testimony to the claim. Second, his endeavour made him stand out for two reasons: on the one hand, it represented a great challenge to the mainstream nationalist ideology drawing on the derivative intellectual discourse of the West; it also brought, on the other, those ideas in the public which remained peripheral, if not entirely absent. Just like B. R. Ambedkar who forcefully argued for giving adequate social and political space to the marginalized social groups, Savarkar created an ambience in which the Hindu nationalist ideas seem to have received importance which was sadly missing in the past.

Hindutva is about a search for a space and a reliable constituency. The task was not an easy one, given the hegemonic influence of the ideological values linked with constitutional liberalism that emerged organically in India presumably because of British colonialism. At the outset, he made it very clear that Hinduism and Hindutva were not identical in connotations. While the latter is an ideological response, the former means

> the ism of Hindu, [and] as the word Hindu has been derived from the word Sindhu, the Indus, meaning primarily all the people who reside in the land that extends from Sindhu to Sindhu [which reemphasized that] Hinduism must necessarily mean the religion or religions that are peculiar and native to this land and these people.[48]

[48] Ibid, 104.

So, Hinduism was not adequate to conceptually explain Hindutva presumably because of its ideological appeal; Hinduism remained integrally connected with Hindutva, though it was not enough in the latter's constitution. There was something else which he captured, in an ingenious fashion, by couching the idea in a cultural format which was a smart move because the nation sustains its continuity on the basis of its cultural ingenuity. As he argued,

> Hindutva is not a word, but a history. Not only the spiritual or religious history of our people as at times it is mistaken to be by being confounded with the other cognate term, Hinduism, but a history in full. Hinduism is only derivative, a fraction, a part of Hindutva. ... Hindutva embraces all the departments of thought and activity of the whole Being of our Hindu race.[49]

Savarkar's principal concern was to explain how Hindus remained together despite being inherently diverse for multiple sociocultural reasons. Despite being socioculturally different, what sustained them as a compact were the cultural resources that they inherit by being located in a specific territory.[50] For him, the most important cementing factor was the idea of being a Hindu, which exercised 'an imperial sway over the hearts of millions of mankind and won a loving allegiance from the bravest and best of them'.[51] The argument hinges on the contention that, as per Savarkar, Hindus

> are bound together ... by the dearest ties, most sacred and enduring bonds of a common Fatherland and common Holy land. ... All tests whatever of a common country, race, religion, language that to entitle a people to form a nation, entitle the Hindus with a greater emphasis to that claim.[52]

To this was added the regular foreign invasion which automatically connected the Hindus for self-defence. Savarkar defended the point by stating that

[49] Ibid, 3–4.

[50] Thomas Blom Hansen, *The Saffron Wave: Democracy and Hindu Nationalism in Modern India* (New Delhi: Oxford University Press, 1999), 77–80.

[51] Savarkar, *Hindutva*, 4.

[52] Dhananjay Keer, *Veer Savarkar* (Bombay: Popular Prakashan, 1966), 265.

> [n]othing can weld people into a nation and nations into a state as the pressure of common foe. Hatred separates as well unites. Never had Sindhusthan a better chance and more powerful stimulus to be herself forged into an indivisible whole as on that dire day, when the great iconoclast [Alexander] crossed the Indus.[53]

Instead of judging the historical authenticity of the claim, suffice it to say here that Savarkar's main concern was to consolidate Hindus as a well-knit sociocultural group, for which, the idea of common enemy was certain to generate a sense of belonging among those in the opposition camp. Here too, he followed the Western criterion of how the battle against a common enemy brought people together under one flag. Nonetheless, by highlighting the importance of a common cause for nationalist compatibility, he put forward a factor which was potentially effective as history has shown. At one level, the argument does not seem to be novel; but if we expand the concept at a wider psychological level, it will have another persuasive characteristic, namely, the capacity of Hindutva to evolve a sense of compatibility among the Hindus regardless of their physical location. As Savarkar explained,

> this one word, Hindutva, ran like a vital spinal cord through our whole body politic and made the Nayyars of Malabar weep over the sufferings of the Brahmins of Kashmir. Our bards bewailed the fall of Hindus, our seers roused the feelings of Hindus, our heroes fought the battle of Hindus, our saints blessed the efforts of Hindus, our statesmen moulded the fate of Hindus, our mothers wept over the wounds and shared the joy over the triumphs of Hindus.[54]

An unequivocal statement, this contention underlines how a nation is formed by drawing on common memories of both suffering and joyfulness. It is also an argument in defence of the point that despite being strikingly different, on occasions, Hindus always remained a solid community largely due to the undercurrent of commonality that ran through them regardless of their location in different parts of the country. To argue further, he referred to Shivaji, the Maratha King, who, by defeating Aurangzeb, the Muslim emperor of Delhi,

[53] Savarkar, *Hindutva*, 43.

[54] Ibid, 46.

'had electrified', claimed Savarkar, 'the Hindu mind all over India [and] the oppressed looked upon him as an Avatar and Saviour'.[55] That Shivaji was a messiah for the Hindus was not only a source of inspiration but helped spread the idea that Hindus were physically strong enough 'to acquire new kingdoms by [their] power and that bread [they] eat'.[56] So, Hindus were, historically speaking, a powerful entity in human civilization not because they held an identical religious faith but because they retained an identity, the root of which was traced back to the glorious period of Hindu hegemony under the tutelage of Shivaji, who Savarkar characterized as 'a great Hindu king'.[57]

With his own conceptual framework of how Hindus became a strong unit, Savarkar proceeded to explain the essentials of Hindutva. Intrigued by the fact that while the Indian Jains described themselves as Hindus, the Mohammedans maintained their sociocultural identity as distinct from the rest of Indians, which he explained by referring to the Mohammedans being 'intransigent'.[58] According to him, this was absolutely a temporary phase of history that at some future date,

> the word Hindu may come to indicate a citizen of Hindusthan and nothing else; that day can only rise when all cultural and religious bigotry has disbanded its forces pledged to aggressive egoism, and religions cease to be "isms" and become merely the common fund of eternal principles that lie at the root of all [with the concern for building] a common foundation on which the Human State majestically and firmly rests.[59]

Savarkar further problematized the idea by saying that in principle one could easily become a citizen of India, but one was not incorporated in the Hindu fold until one adopted the culture that remained critical

[55] Ibid, 58.

[56] Ibid, 56.

[57] Ibid, 58.

[58] Ibid, 83.

[59] Ibid.

to Hindutva. Besides accepting the rights of a citizen, which does not seem to be odd if it is conceptualized juridically,

> one has to come to look upon our land not only as the land of one's love but even of his worship [for] ... although the first requisite of Hindutva is that he be a citizen of Hindusthan either by himself or through his forefathers, yet it is not the only requisite qualification of it as the term Hindu has come to mean much more than its geographical significance.[60]

So, being together in a common land does not qualify one to be part of Hindutva; one being a citizen is not enough; one needs to be incorporated in the Hindutva sociocultural fold, as per Savarkar. This is the first implication; the second implication is the importance of the bond of common blood that brings the Hindus in one fold. Hinduness is consolidated on the basis of being united by blood connections among those who are part of the same demographic entity. In other words, Hindus are part of Hindutva fold not by a design but by a natural bond of blood relations linking one with another within the same community. As Savarkar argued,

> [t]he Hindus are not merely the citizens of the Indian state because they are united not only by the bonds of love they bear to a common motherland, but also by the bonds of common blood [which made them] not only a Nation, but also a race-jati.[61]

Whether Hindus were a race is debatable and Savarkar was aware of this, as the elaboration of his argument amply proves. Hindus were certainly a *jati* which is derived from (a) common origin, (b) common brotherhood and (c) bond of common blood. On the basis of this clarification, Savarkar now claimed that '[a]ll Hindus ... have in their veins the blood of the mighty race incorporated with and descended from the Vedic fathers, the Sindhus'.[62] From this argument, he now developed the point that Hindustan was not a transitional entity, but a

[60] Ibid, 84.

[61] Ibid.

[62] Ibid, 85.

permanent sociocultural formation being supported by those upholding the distinct Hindutva values. It was a civilization articulating 'the expression of the mind of a man, ... an account of what man had made of the matte'.[63] By dint of their being truly connected with their distinctive civilizational ethos, Hindus 'have succeeded in preserving their history, riding through earthquakes, bridging over deluges'. It was not merely a chronicle of events, it was also a narrative that had begun with

> the Vedas which are the first extant chapter of the story of our race; the first cradle songs that every Hindu girl listens are the songs of Sita [the mythical character of Ramayana]; some of us worship Rama as an incarnation, some admire him as a hero and a warrior, and all love him as the most illustrious representative monarch of our race.[64]

The third essential component of Hindutva was Sanskrit, a mother language that contributed to other Indian languages. It is true, as Savarkar admitted that Sanskrit is not being spoken now. Nonetheless, as he further argued, it is 'the tongue in which the mothers of our race spoke ... and which has given birth to all our present tongues'.[65] Sanskrit was always held in high esteem, he further stated, since '[o]ur Gods spoke in Sanskrit, our Sages thought in Sanskrit, our poets wrote in Sanskrit; all that is best in us, the best thought, best ideas, best lines—seeks instinctively to clothe itself in Sanskrit'.[66]Hindustan's civilizational voice was thus articulated in Sanskrit, which thus remained integrally connected with Hindutva. This was a connecting language because this was also an ideational platform which helped Hindustan build her intellectual prowess and rigour. Justifying that Sanskrit was a source of intellectual nourishment to the Hindus, Savarkar further defended his point by saying that

> [T]o millions, it is still the language of their Gods; to others it is the language of their ancestors; to all it is the language par excellence; a common

[63] Ibid, 92.

[64] Ibid, 93–94.

[65] Ibid, 95.

[66] Ibid.

> inheritance, a common treasure that enriches all the family of major sister languages, Gujarati, Gurmukhi, Sindhi, Hindi, among others.[67]

Primary here is the insistence that since Sanskrit was the mother language which was derivative of Vedas, the Hindu past remained the first and formidable reference point. Not only was Sanskrit the integral part of our glorious heritage which was not to be ignored, it also helped us develop 'Hindu *sanskriti* [culture], represented in a common history, common heroes, a common literature, common art, a common law and common jurisprudence, common fairs and festivals, rites and rituals, ceremonies and sacraments'.[68] This was an argument justifying the necessity of building a common cultural bond on the basis of those sociocultural practices and mores which automatically merged the Hindus underplaying those which were divisive. By emphasizing the points of uniformity rather than schism, Savarkar provided a persuasive model of Hindu nationalism which, despite being context-driven, had also features of transcendental character. It was therefore both a clarion call to the mainstream nationalists in the Gandhian phase of India's freedom struggle and an instructive design for political mobilization in its aftermath on the basis of indigenous knowledge and wisdom and past heritage.

Redesigning of the Nationalist Project

As against the discourse of social justice whose ramifications at times ranged to the extent of attempts for separating the oppressed classes from the fold of Hinduism, the idea of Hindutva was propounded by V. D. Savarkar to act as the overbearing basis of Indian nationalism. Hindutva, as a political philosophy, not only reflected the firm conviction of Savarkar in the veracity and practicability of religious-cultural ethos of Hindus to be the infallible basis of conceptualizing India as a Hindu Rashtra, but also the response of a Hindu nationalist to the prevailing circumstances of the time.

[67] Ibid, 95–96.

[68] Ibid, 100.

> As a spokesman of the majority interests, V.D. Savarkar formulated an ideology which could demolish the claims of national parity made by the Muslims, negate the territorial concept of nationhood propagated by the Congress, blunt the edge of the demands made by the Depressed Classes and prevent further atomization of the Hindu community.[69]

Still, above all, it was an ideological construct to provide for the consolidation of the Hindus in India.[70] It was, in fact, the full-blown articulation of the subtle idea which was simmering in the mind of Savarkar since his childhood given his apparent upbringing in the intellectual ambience where the cure to the ills of the Hindu society was construed to lay in the establishment of the Hindu Rashtra in India.

Savarkar began his conceptualization of the idea of Hindutva by seeking answer to the question whether what could be considered as a Hindu. He tersely proclaims that a Hindu could be anyone who considered this land of *Bharatvarsha*, from the Indus to the Seas, as his Fatherland as well as his Holy land, which would be the cradle land of his religion. Further he envisaged three fundamental bonds that would conjoin the Hindus as a common entity, namely, *rashtra* (territory), *jati* (race) and *sanskriti* (culture). Thus, territorially, a Hindu is one who feels being attached to the geographical tract extending between the rivers Sindhu (Indus) and Brahmaputra, on the one hand, and from Himalayas to the Cape Comorin, on the other. This geographical specification, indeed, becomes identical to what has traditionally been considered to the land of India for centuries.

Racially, Savarkar considered a Hindu as the one 'whose first and discernible source could be traced to the Himalayan altitudes of the Vedic *Saptasindhu*'. Such a racial demarcation of the Hindus was seemingly not meant to claim any sort of superiority of the Hindus in comparison to the other races in the world but to distinguish them

[69] Prabha Dixit, 'The Ideology of Hindu Nationalism', in *Political Thought in Modern India*, eds. Thomas Pantham and Kenneth L. Deutsch (New Delhi: SAGE Publications, 1986), 131.

[70] Suresh Sharma, 'Savarkar's Quest for a Modern Hindu Consolidation,' *Studies in Humanities and Social Sciences* II, no. 2 (1996): 190.

from others. Moreover, Savarkar pronounced that the trait of Hindutva encompassing the life of the inhabitants of this part of land would remain indelible as the impulse of his Hindu blood would make him feel the pride of being a Hindu. As he writes,

> A Hindu believing in any theoretical or philosophical or social system, orthodox or heterodox, provided it is unquestionably indigenous and founded by a Hindu, may lose his sect but not his Hindutva—his Hinduness—because the most important and essential which determines it is the inheritance of the Hindu blood. Therefore, all those who love the land that stretches from Sindhu to Sindhu, from Indus to Seas, as their fatherland and consequently claim to inherit the blood of the race that has evolved, by incorporation and adaptation, from the ancient Saptasindhu, can be said to possess tow of the most essential requisites of Hindutva.[71]

Culturally, Savarkar maintains that a Hindu must feel the pride and commonality of his cultural roots with the other people of the Hindustan. As he explains,

> Hindus are bound together not only by the tie of the love we bear to a common fatherland and by the common blood that courses throughout veins and keeps our hearts throbbing and out affection warm, but also by the tie of the common homage we pay to our great civilization—our Hindu culture, which could not be better rendered than by the word Sanskriti, suggestive as it is of that language, Sanskrit, which has been the chosen means of expression and preservation of that culture, of all that was best and worth preserving in the history of our race. We are one because we are a nation, a race and own a common Sanskriti (civilization).[72]

Savarkar, thus, provides for a complex criterion to ordain a distinct identity and character to the Hindus in the Indian society.

To forcefully articulate the political connotations of the notion of Hindutva as against the religious meaning of the term Hinduism, Savarkar emphasized the inherent differences between the two seemingly synonymous terms. 'Hinduism', to Savarkar,

[71] Savarkar, *Hindutva*, 90–91.

[72] Ibid., 91–92

> means the 'ism' of the Hindus: and as the word Hindu has been derived from the word Sindhu, the Indus, meaning primarily all those who reside in the land that extends from Sindhu to Sindhu, Hinduism must necessarily mean the religion or the religions that are peculiar and native to this land and to these people.[73]

However, a mischievous parochial construction of the idea of Hinduism confines it as the religion of the majority people, leaving aside a vast number of people outside the fold of Hindu religion.

> And thus we find that while millions of our Sikhs, Jains, Lingayats, several Samajis and others would deeply resent to be told that they—whose fathers' fathers up to the tenth generation had the blood of Hindus in their veins—had suddenly ceased to be Hindu![74]

But Savarkar points out that they, indeed, are the part and parcel of the Hinduism as they, despite following numerous shades and schools, consider this land of Hindus as their fatherland and holyland. 'So to every Hindu from the Santal to the Sadhu, this Bharat bhumi, this Sindhusthan is at once a *pitribhu* and a *punyabhu*—fatherland and a holy land.' [75] Applying this canon, therefore, Savarkar asserts that the converts to Christianity and Islam could not be considered as Hindus despite sharing common culture and lifestyle due to the fact that though they regard Hindustan as their fatherland, they do not regard it as their holyland.

By delineating the twin criteria of who could be a Hindu and who could not be so, Savarkar appeared to be advancing his interrelated agenda of bringing about a broad-based Hindu *Sangathan* on the one hand, and preclude the believers in the other religions from such a Sangathan, on the other. He, therefore, was categorical in pointing out the identicalness between the notions of Hindutva and Indianness. As he declared,

> A Hindu patriot worth the name cannot but be an Indian patriot as well. To the Hindus, Hindustan being fatherland and holy land, the love they

[73] Ibid, 104.

[74] Ibid, 106.

[75] Ibid, 113.

> bear to Hindustan is boundless. What is called nationalism can be defined as in fact the national communalism of the majority community. Thus, in Hindustan it is the Hindus, professing Hindu religion and being in the overwhelming majority, that constitutes the national community and create and formulate the nationalism of the nation.[76]

In substance, the ideology of Hindutva, as propounded by Savarkar, was rooted in the vision of Hindu solidarity. Hindutva is not thus the same as Hinduism; it was 'only a derivative or, a fraction, a part of Hindutva'[77] A careful reading of Savarkar's conceptualization of Hindutva suggests that while Hinduism, as a religion, comprises a set of religious beliefs and doctrine, Hindutva was in fact a political construct whose antecedents lay in the cultural ethos of the Hindus. It therefore transcends 'the internal sectarian disputes among the Hindus comprising both the believers and non-believers'.[78] He maintained that despite having numerous external differentiations, internally, Hindus are bound together by certain distinct cultural, historical, religious, social and linguistic commonalities which have been brought about by centuries of assimilation and association with each other. To Savarkar, in the making of the Hindu Rashtra, what counted more than anything else was the cultural, racial and religious unity of the people. In his perception, a nation would have been a political formation having people living in a contiguous and adequate landscape with a common national identity, marked by the internal cohesion brought about by subtle cultural and racial affinities. As the Hindus consisted of all these characteristics, they undoubtedly constituted a nation in the nature of a Hindu Rashtra. This was most succinctly stated by him when he argued that

> [w]e Hindus, in spite of thousand and one differences within out fold or bound by such religious, cultural, historical, racial, linguistic and other affinities in common as to stand out as a definitely homogenous people as soon as we are placed in contrast with any other non-Hindu people, say the English or Japanese or even the Indian Muslims. That is the reason why

[76] Quoted in, Prabha Dixit, 'The Ideology of Hindu Nationalism', 132–33.

[77] Savarkar, Hindutva, 3.

[78] Anthony J. Parel, *Pax Gandhiana: The Political Philosophy of Mahatma Gandhi* (New Delhi: Oxford University Press, 2016), 151.

> today we the Hindus from Kashmir to Madras and Sindh to Assam [are] to be a nation by themselves, while the Indian Muslims are on the whole more inclined to identify themselves and their interests with Muslim outside India than Hindus who lived next door.[79]

There is a powerful argument here. For Savarkar, Hindus were a nation since the bond based on being sensitive to an identical civilizational concern brought the disparate Indians together and also sustained unity on that basis. Hindus were thus a homogeneous people. In order to clarify his position, he further argued that given the civilizational togetherness Hindus always remained one since time immemorial which was not the case with regard to non-Hindus, since they came together purposely at a particular juncture of history as a matter of convenience. The argument is reinforced by him when he argued that due to the innate and unbridgeable gulf between the Hindus and Muslims, the efforts for bringing them together were bound to fail. By couching the argument in the Hindutva mould, Savarkar consistently argued against the Gandhi's design of communal amity involving the Hindus and Muslims on the basis of his model of *Sarva Dharma Samabhava* (equal respect to all religions) in view of the Indian Muslims not being appreciative of the well-entrenched civilizational bond. By 1937, he thus came out most starkly with his views in favour of a scheme permanently separating the two communities. While seeking to emotionally prepare his followers to accept that the differences between Hindus and Muslims were too ingrained to be rooted out so easily, he thus argued that 'we need to be ready to bravely face unpleasant facts as they are. India cannot assume today to be a unitarian and homogeneous nation, but, on the contrary, there are two nations in the main: the Hindus and the Muslims, in India'.[80] Given the obvious sociocultural schism between these two demographically preponderant communities, Savarkar was persuaded to appreciate the arguments defending

[79] V. D. Savarkar, *Hindu Rashtra Darpan* (Poona: Maharashtra Prantik Hindusabha, n. d.), 44—cited in Swapan Dasgupta, *Awakening Bharat Mata: The Political Beliefs of the Indian Right* (Gurgaon: Penguin Random House, 2019), 83.

[80] Savarkar address to the delegates of the Nineteenth annual session of Hindu Mahasabha, held at Ahmadabad in 1937, reproduced in Savarkar, *Hindu Rashtra Darshan* (Bombay: Veer Savarkar Prakashan, 1962) (reprint), 24.

Hindu–Muslim segmented existence; yet, he was not in favour of creating a Hindustan independent of the Muslims since he also believed that there was a scope for them to be socioculturally united with the rest of the communities. In his proposed *rashtra*, Savarkar offered the minorities the same degree of freedom and right to participation in the affairs of the state, provided they accept a position of non-aggression to the interests and the rights of the Hindus. As he clarifies,

> We shall ever guarantee protection to the religion, culture and language of the minorities for themselves, but we shall no longer tolerate any aggression on their part on the equal liberty of the Hindus to guard their religion, culture and language as well. If non-Hindu minorities are to be protected, then surely the Hindu majority also must be protected against any aggressive minority in India.[81]

He, therefore, opposed the demand of the Muslims for the grant of separate electorate in India. He claimed that being bestowed with such preferential treatment, the Muslims would probably be handed down the right of

> exercising the political veto on the legitimate rights and privileges of the majority and call it *Swarajya.* The Hindus do not want a change of masters, are not going to … fight and die only to replace an Edward by an Aurangzeb simply because the latter happens to be born within the Indian borders, but they want henceforth to be masters themselves in their own house, in their own land.[82]

Thus, on the question of minority rights, the approach of Savarkar was in consonance with his broad conceptualization of the philosophy of Hindutva.

An Innovatively Designed Ideational Intervention

As mentioned above, Savarkar expressed his ideological differences when he met Gandhi in London in 1907. It was a disagreement on

[81] V. D. Savarkar, *Hindu Rashtra Darshan (Collection of Presidential addresses to the sessions of Hindu Mahasabha)*, 3rd ed. (Veer Savarkar Prakashan, Bombay, 1992), 46.

[82] Ibid, 41.

the means that the nationalist needed to deploy for fulfilling politico-ideological objectives. Being an architect of non-violent resistance, Gandhi naturally differed from the young colleague who favoured resorting to violence as justified. Both of them were important voices in the nationalist struggle. During his revolutionary nationalist phase, Savarkar was determined not to abdicate violence which led to his internment in Cellular Jail for almost a decade. Even after his release from prison in 1924, he never endorsed non-violence because, as he felt, it was a clearly a crafty design for avoiding face-to-face confrontation with the colonizers. On being elected the president of Hindu Mahasabha in 1937, he further elaborated his viewpoints to sharply make his points in favour of an alternative mode of conceptualizing the nationalist counter-attack. During his five-year-stint when he held the saddle of the Mahasabha, he persuasively defended the argument which, if read with his another text entitled *Hindutva* of 1923 publication, shall help us understand how his ideas evolved dialectically while seeking to expose the inherent limitations of Gandhi's model of non-violent resistance. Broadly speaking, Savarkar and Gandhi differed from each other mainly on how they conceived India as a nation and how the nationalist struggle needed to be organized. As shown above, Gandhi was hardly persuaded by Savarkar's conceptualization of India being an exclusive civilization as per his ideational parameter of Hindutva; the Mahatma further believed that Hindus needed to be accommodative of the Muslims' interests for the sake of creating strong anti-colonial pan-Indian nationalist sentiments. Besides bringing different religio-social groups together, the aim was also to cement a solid bond among the regional-linguistic communities. It was an all-inclusive platform regardless of socio-religious and socio-economic separating one community from another. For Savarkar, two ideas seem important which are critical to comprehend his peculiarly innovative design of Hindutva. In contrast with argument that Hindutva was similar to Hinduism, Savarkar insisted on defining Hindutva as an attempt to build a civilizational code based on the age-old sociocultural traits that were distinctive to India, not as a territorial segment but as an emotional entity developing and also strengthening a permanent bond among those located in India. Following this logic, India was more than a mere geographical unit given the emotional quotient binding those living together for ages.

One of the first instances showing clear differences of opinion was how Gandhi and Savarkar viewed the 1920–1922 Non-Cooperation and Khilafat merger. Savarkar was terribly rankled because it gave the Muslims 'unnecessary importance in the nationalist campaign with which they remain completely dissociated'.[83] He was unhappy because 'by linking the Non-Cooperation movement to an overtly religious agenda [was] taking things beyond acceptable limits'.[84] Being persuaded by B. G. Tilak's characterization of the merger as 'a strategic blunder',[85] Savarkar found an intellectual in the former who, he accepted, as his political mentor. In no uncertain terms, he thus condemned the merger because it meant 'a commitment of the Congress [justifying] a purely communal, religious and extra-territorial Khilafat agitation to placate the Moslem and himself … insisting on the point that the question of Swaraj itself should be subordinated to the Khilafat issue;—nay, he said [that] it was the religious duty of the Hindus to help the Khalifa!'.[86] In politico-ideological terms, the appreciation of the Khilafat cause seemed 'bizarre, especially as no other nation, including the Islamic ones, was showing any interests in saving the [Caliph] and the Turkish people were in fact fed up with his misrule'.[87] Hence, for Savarkar, this was no Khilafat, but simply 'an *afat*'[88] which meant serious trouble.

In order to develop a sharp critique of Gandhi, Savarkar clearly formulated his ideas which drew on the Muslims being opposed to the creation of India as a collective compact based on her civilizational values and ethos. It was explicitly stated in his 1937 Ahmedabad speech in the annual session of the Hindu Mahasabha:

> The Hindus as a nation are willing to discharge their duty to a common Indian state on equal footing. But if our Moslem countrymen thrust on a

[83] Ibid, 46.

[84] Vaibhav Purandare, *Savarkar: The True Story of the Father Hindutva* (New Delhi: Juggernaut, 2019), 190.

[85] Savarkar, *Hindu Rashtra Darshan*, 3rd ed., 46.

[86] Ibid, 98.

[87] Purandare, *Savarkar*, 190.

[88] Savarkar, *My Transportation for Life*, 151.

> communal strife on the Hindus and cherish anti-Indian and extra-territorial designs of establishing a Mohammedan rule or supremacy in India then let the Hindus look to themselves and stand on their legs and fight single-handed as best as they can for the liberation of India from any non-Hindu yoke, be in English or Moslem or otherwise.[89]

By conceptualizing the Muslims as the perceived enemy, Savarkar appears to have built his argument to translate into reality his distinct nationalist approach. For him, it was a battle which needed to be waged to contain the possibility of one community being privileged over others, since it was contrary to Mahatma's concern for India being an inclusive nation. Savarkar hinted at this when he stated that 'for a real and justifiable Indian Nationalism must be equitable to all communities that compose Indian Nation'.[90] Gandhi's endorsement of the Khilafat campaign encouraged the Muslims to retain their identity as a separate community, which was a deterrent for the Indians to rise as one collectivity. Here too, Savarkar was very categorical in condemning the Muslim desire not to fight together for the nationalist cause which was evident when he said that by insisting on the separate communal existence, 'the Moslem alone are communalists in an unjustifiable anti-national and treacherous sense of the term [which also confirms that] they want to usurp to themselves all that belongs to others'.[91] The idea is crystal clear: if they are deviant from the pan-Indian nationalist concerns, the Muslims needed to be excluded and, if required, the nationalist Hindus were to be emotionally prepared to combat them just like any other enemy seeking to weaken the foundation of India as a nation state. It was further elaborated in his 1939 speech before the Hindu Mahasabha delegates attending the 21st annual session when he exhorted that

> the anti-National and aggressive designs on the part of the Moslem minority constitute a danger to all non-Moslem Indians in India and not only to the Hindus alone. It is too clear a point to require any further elaboration here. It is the anti-National attitude of the Moslem minority alone which is

[89] Savarkar, *Hindu Rashtra Darshan*, 3rd ed., 24.

[90] Ibid, 54.

[91] Ibid.

> giving a handle to the British government to obstruct further political and constitutional progress in Hindusthan. But in order to camouflage their own special responsibility for this guilt the Moslems always try to drag in other minorities also in support of their attitude and want the world to believe that all non-Hindu minorities are as determinedly uncompromising in the anti-National demands advanced by the Moslem League.[92]

Here too, he reiterated his belief that in order to create a nation, Indians regardless of religion needed to be weaved together for a common cause which Gandhi was not willing to concede presumably because of his misconception of the Muslims being a part of the nation. On the basis of a threadbare analysis of how Muslims retained their separate existence to the extent of dividing the national platform which helped the British effectively deploy the *divide et impera* (divide and rule) strategy, Savarkar drew this conclusion. Being true to his ideological belief, he reinforced the point in the same speech that he delivered in 1939 by stating that

> let it proclaim once for all that it stands by these principles alone: firstly it recognizes no Moslem as a Moslem, or Christian as a Christian or Hindu as a Hindu; but look upon them all and deal with all as Indians only; and, therefore, will have nothing to do with any special, communal, religious or racial interests as apart from the fundamental interests guaranteed to all citizens alike. Secondly, it does not acknowledge any other constitutional principle with regard to electorates than the rule 'one-man one-vote' and public services to go by merit alone. Only one alternative it may condescend to subscribe in view of the peculiar situation in India to the effect that if communal representation is to be restored to at all then it must strictly be in relations to the numerical strength of the constituents and in the public services too that relations may be observed—by only in so far as it is consistent with merit.[93]

A careful decoding of the above claim reveals that Savarkar pursued an argument to build an inclusive India where the division around the religious axes was discarded in categorical terms. India was for Indians and not for any specific religious community is the main theme

[92] Ibid, 96.

[93] Ibid, 105.

that runs through his contention. Espousing liberal constitutionalism supporting political equality, he did not seem to be radically different from the Mahatma who also acquiesced with the view that for India to remain united the principle of 'one-man one-vote' was perhaps the best one capable of cementing a solid bond among the Indians. Similarly, regarding public jobs, he evolved a model in which the numerical strength and merit received equal importance.

So far, the discussion hovered around Savarkar's very definite views on nationalism with reference to his well-argued positions defending why independent communal existence of minorities was an anathema to even Gandhi's design of inclusive nationalism. There is another powerful design which he developed and sharpened to further deviate from the widely accepted non-violent mode of nationalist counter-attack at the behest of Gandhi. Despite being appreciative of constitutional liberal means, Savarkar did not seem to have completely revised his stance vis-a-vis violence and militancy. As he believed, 'the belief in absolute non-violence condemning all armed resistance even to aggression evinces no mahatmatic (sic) saintliness but a monomaniacal senselessness!'[94] According to him, Mahatma's unflinching faith in non-violence was hardly an effective device to attain his political freedom since the colonizers remained fully armed to resist an attempt harming their interests. It was evident when he stated that

> [w]hat held good in man's struggle with the brute world continued to be true throughout his social struggle, the struggle of clan against clan, race against race, nation against nation. The lesson is branded on every page of human history down to the latest page that nations, which, other things being equal, are superior in military strength are bound to survive, flourish and dominate while those which are militarily weak shall be politically subjected or cease to exist at all.[95]

It was not possible for the Indians to explore the possibility of organizing an armed struggle against the British given Gandhi's strong

[94] Ibid, 153.

[95] Ibid, 152.

resistance, as Savarkar believed. Unable to appreciate that non-violence was an adequately equipped means to politically liberate India, he further castigated the Mahatma by saying that

> [o]wing to the Gandhist lead the Congress had neglected the question of fostering military strength of our people, to such an extent that even the wordy resolution which the Congress used to pass while it was under the lead of the Moderates [who believed in prayer, petition and peaceful protest] were ... more extremists and far-sighted than this spineless school of Gandhist non-resisters.[96]

A sharp condemnation of Gandhi, the above statement reconfirms some of the arguments that he put forward during his revolutionary nationalist phase. There are two interrelated aspects here that merit attention: on the one hand, that he was persuaded to believe that violent challenge was far more effective especially when the British Raj was, being adequately armed, not hesitant to coercively contain the nationalist attack. By being supportive to the British, not only did the Muslims, on the other, weaken the nationalist mobilization but also demoralized those fighting for freedom by caring 'a fig to any non-violent, non-resisting, non-cooperation nonsense in which the Congress kept indulging under Gandhiji's pressure'.[97] This was, to Savarkar, ridiculous to believe that non-violence was an empowering device for a subjugated nation. An 'eccentric Mahatmaic' construct, non-violence was 'an insane temerity to preach in all seriousness to the Indian public that "even the taking up of lathi" is sinful'.[98] As the British ruler pursued a brutal policy to sustain its political dominance, Savarkar was convinced that non-violence was of no use in these circumstances. He thus further argued that

> the Gandhist Satyagraha which demands freedom to preach this immoral principle of absolute nonviolence condemning all armed resistance even to alien aggression [is] ... highly detrimental to our national interests. The

[96] Ibid, 155.

[97] Ibid, 155–56.

[98] Ibid, 153.

> claim that the best means of freeing Indian from the foreign yoke is spinning wheel is a crafty design that Gandhi evolved to keep "the true nationalists" away from the nationalist struggle. … Crafty as the British policy makers have ever been, [they] … like that someone should always be preaching to the nationalist fighters that the spinning qualities are more spiritual than the fighting ones and that the highest human virtue consists in getting killed by any invading aggressors than killing them in self-defense.[99]

Here is a sharp critique that Savarkar had mounted against 'the Gandhist Satyagraha' since it was not, at all, adequate to do away with the foreign rule. There is also a conspiratorial angle here because peaceful resistance appears, to him, to be a means, deliberately designed by Gandhi not to harm the British interests. In a nutshell, he was opposed to Gandhi for two reasons: in his views, non-violent counter to the alien administration was, on the one hand, a ploy to control the nationalist wrath in such a way as not to undermine the foundation of the British rule. By being fiercely critical of Satyagraha, he also exposed, on the other, the inherent limitations of Gandhi's unconditional appreciation for spinning wheel as a device for effectively challenging the colonizers. It was, according to Savarkar, a quid pro quo strategy which he articulated when he said that 'I shall not be surprised if the Government allows the Gandhists to preach the doctrine of non-violence provided they do not attack the Government and its policies'[100] He also referred to instances where the non-violent Satyagrahis were spared of imprisonment to argue that this was 'a trophy' that Gandhi managed to get in exchange of his assurance of not harming the British interests. Although it is debatable and is also not supported by conclusive evidence that the British government exercised restraint in punishing the Gandhian nationalists, the available evidence suggests that the Hindu Mahasabha hardly figured in any of the deliberations over India's political future, just like the communists. This could have been a source of his concern since by not recognizing the Mahasabha as a critical player in Indian nationalist politics the view that it could easily be ignored was established. The developments leading to India's freedom confirmed what Savarkar

[99] Ibid, 154.

[100] Ibid, 154–55

had apprehended: Hindu Mahasabha remained at the periphery in the discussions over India's independence, although the arguments that it strongly made opposing partition received huge public support. Illustrative here is the sustained campaign that Hindu Mahasabha launched in Bengal for partition under the leadership of a very popular leader Syma Prasad Mookherjee challenging the campaign that some of the Congress leaders like Sarat Bose, Kiran Sankar Roy, among others, spearheaded for a united Bengal which was later realized as a ploy to create a greater Pakistan.[101]

Savarkar–Gandhi interaction is a relatively unknown chapter of India's nationalist history. As the above discussion shows, being couched in the well-entrenched argumentative tradition, the dialogical interaction between the two is illustrative of an endeavour to articulate two contrasting viewpoints with more or less same politico-ideological mission, namely India's liberation from foreign rule. There is, however, a general misconception that Savarkar was in favour of a Hindu Pakistan which obviously had its root in his widely-circulated model of Hindutva. On the basis of the above discussion, it is argued here that his views were distorted since the conceptualization of Hindutva is clearly an areligious formulation seeking to create a multitude by reference to the civilizational–cultural code of communities living together separately for generations. Hindutva is, in no circumstances, an endeavour, let alone an attempt, at designing an independent India exclusively in religious format; it is purely a socio-anthropological conceptual construct being derivative of well-entrenched sociocultural behavioural traits that evolved dialectically over centuries. It is however true that insistence on Hindutva, specifically by M. S. Golwalkar in his *We or Our Nationhood Defined* (1939), was justified as a design to mobilize Hindus as a nation in opposition to Jinnah's politico-ideological design of Hindus and Muslims being two nations; otherwise, the claim that Hindutva is merely a sociocultural construct does not seem to have many detractors. In this sense, the dismissal

[101] Bidyut Chakrabarty, 'An Alternative to Partition: The United Bengal Scheme,' in *The Partition of Bengal and Assam: Contour of Freedom*, Chap. 4 (London and New York: Routledge, 2004), 132–53.

of Hindutva as an attempt to Hinduize India appears to be superfluous and is a politically contrived effort seeking to muzzle alternative voices. The surface reading of the idea shall lead us nowhere but to cloud our vision as clearly myopic.

As things stood, the debate between Gandhi and Savarkar, both implicit and explicit, directs our attention to an important aspect of Indian nationalist design which hardly came to the public domain presumably because of the hegemonic grip of Gandhian values and beliefs, derivative primarily of the philosophy of Enlightenment. Nonetheless, Savarkar persuasively made a case for Hindutva in a language which was anything but religious. Like Jinnah and Ambedkar, he too raised a voice, powerful enough to create a constituency of loyalists and supporters in circumstances in which the Mahatma was indisputably the most popular icon cutting across caste, class and ethnicity. Still, Savarkar was heard and his views gained credibility presumably because Gandhi's nationalist ideas did not seem to have halted the campaign for partition nor they helped contain the processes of Muslims being alienated from the mainstream anti-British onslaught. The freedom struggle that Gandhi led was thus partly successful because it culminated in India's political freedom; it was partly a failure since the joy for freedom was marred by the pangs of partition. Hindutva was, in these circumstances, an antithesis because it was meant to create a sociocultural compact in which the segmentation of people around religious axes was clearly an anathema. Gandhi's failure to successfully combat an exclusively religion-driven campaign appears to have created a milieu in which Savarkar's arguments for Hindutva seem to have generated support, rather automatically, presumably because they caught the sentiments of a significant section of the Indians cutting across the length and breadth of the country. A political argument made in a poetic register, Hindutva can thus be said to have made

> an argument with and against an unnamed Gandhi at an opportune moment when he seemed to have finished with politics. Hindutva was also a political cry [championing an alternative discourse to defend the point that] ... a sense of Hindu-ness ... could be the basis for a more genuine

> and, in the end, more effective nationalism than that of the Mahatma [by asserting] … that it was not religion that made Hindus Hindu.[102]

The idea is unambiguous. Savarkar, in his endeavour to evolve a persuasive politico-ideological alternative, resorted to a secular argument which is misconstrued easily since it drew on the distinctive characteristics of Hinduism being universally conceptualized primarily as a religion. For Savarkar, that was misleading because Hinduism was more than a religion; it represented, according to him, a historically evolved cultural code. Hence it is fairly argued that 'the fundamental contribution of Hindutva was to install a new term for nationalist discourse, one that was both modern and secular'.[103] In line with this argument, one can further add that Hindutva was not Gandhi's *Sarva Dharma Samabhava* (equal respect to all religions), but a well-argued design for a collectivity that remained united largely because of the prevalence of a cultural code that cemented and also sustained the bond regardless of sociocultural demarcation and regional differences. The argument that Hindutva was not constructed but evolved over centuries was made to put across the point that it was neither conceptually valid nor historically justified to characterize Hindutva merely as religious denomination ignoring completely the sociocultural features that Savarkar upheld in his well-thought-out viewpoints.

Concluding Observations

Savarkar and Gandhi can both be contrasted since their views on various issues were dissimilar; they can also be conceptualized in a single theoretical format because they were nationalists par excellence in the sense that they privileged their nationalist concerns over other considerations. What is most striking is the fact that while Savarkar, despite not being a devout Hindu, pursued his political objectives by being drawn to the distinctive character of the Hindus as a religio-cultural community. In other words, for political mobilization, he

102 Janaki Bakhle, 'Country First? Vinayak Damodar Savarkar (1883–1966) and the Writing of Essentials of Hindutva,' *Public Culture* 22, no. 1 (2010): 151.

103 Bakhle, 'Country First?, 185.

developed and sharpened his arguments by reference to the age-old sociocultural traditions that evolved with the Hindus despite challenges to their existence by rulers in various phases of Indian history. In contrast, Gandhi, a practising Hindu, never endeavoured to attain his politico-ideological goal by seeking to create an exclusively Hindu brigade. Despite being true to Hinduism, he was also careful to be equally protective of the religious minorities which, he felt, was necessary to unite the disparate Indians for the nationalist cause. And also, being appreciative of *Varnashrama* (justifying caste division), he was vigorously opposed to Shuddhi or reconversion. For uniting people of well-entrenched diversities, Gandhi was thus persuaded to evolve a model of inclusive nationalism. Contrarily, Savarkar was hardly a practising Hindu in the strict religious sense; he neither followed the rituals, as Gandhi did, nor was appreciative of socio-religious restrictions on one's choice of food though he, unlike the Mahatma, strongly believed in Shuddhi which, according to him, was the only option to retain Hindu identity and character in the face of what he saw as Islamic aggression and Gandhi's appeasement of the Muslims in the nationalist context. Even with the risk of digression, it also can be said that there also existed stark differences between Maulana Azad and M. A. Jinnah: while the former, being a conservative Muslim in his private life, never allowed his personal belief in Islam clouded his politico-ideological vision and activities. Jinnah's ideological plans and priorities present a completely contrasting picture; he was never a pious Muslim, and yet, he defended his two-nation-theory on the basis of Muslims being politico-culturally distinct from their Hindu counterparts. A probe into how their ideas developed will help us understand how it happened. Suffice it to say here that they held different approaches presumably because they felt that it was an appropriate strategy to fulfil their politico-ideological aims.

That V. D. Savarkar stood by himself in the pantheon of Hindu nationalism is now easily comprehensible. There were thinkers before him who provided him with enough conceptual inputs to defend his Hindu nationalist approach; what is distinctive about him was his capacity to persuasively conceptualize the alternative model which was an attempt to articulate an Indian response in a derivative Western mode. In other words, the concern for making Hindustan a homogeneous nation following the signing of the 1648 Westphalia Treaty appears to suggest that he drew on the derivative parameters. According to him, India's national identity had therefore to be 'singular, well-bounded and well-defined' which needed to be built by abstracting and combining other overlapping identities into 'a monolithic one'.[104] That he also took ample care in looking back to the Hindu glorious past he reaffirmed a nationalist drive in which India's past heritage and wisdom were privileged. Savarkar's model was a creative fusion of the Western mode of thinking with what was based on a quest for counter narratives from what appear to have been forgotten. It is illustrative when he strongly criticized 'hotchpotch nations based only on the shifting sands of the conception of territorial nationality, not cemented by any cultural, racial or historical affinities and consequently having no will to incorporate themselves into a nation'.[105] What he sought to put across is the idea that the effort towards conceptualizing the Hindus being a nation in derivative Western criteria was bound to be faulty because Hindus were not a nation in the narrow Western sense but 'an organic national being'.[106] Explicit here is the claim that Hindus always remained a nation since they were united in terms of certain instinctive socio-historical and emotional traits that were inconceivable vis-a-vis the Western nations which came into being out of an agreement (the Westphalia Treaty of 1648) among the warring states in Europe as perhaps the only option available to stop the long-drawn Thirty Years' War that devastated the region. Nations in Europe had emerged as a politically designed escape route. In other words, the idea of territorial nationality was a product of the circumstances in which efforts were made to cement togetherness by reference to those socioculturally meaningful devices, like religion, language, ethnicity,

[104] Aparna Devare, *History and the Making of a Modern Hindu Self* (New Delhi: Routledge, 2011), 201.

[105] Savarkar, *Hindu Rashtra Darpan*, n. d., 44—cited in Dasgupta, *Awakening Bharat Mata*, 83.

[106] Dasgupta, *Awakening Bharat Mata*, 83.

among others, which were readily acceptable. In case of the Hindus, the instinctive civilizational unity was too strong to be undermined so easily. Hence the fundamental basis of the argument in favour of not recognizing the Hindus as a nation seems to be neither persuasive nor logically drawn.

Savarkar's Hindu nationalist design can be said to have been largely contextually contrived for two reasons: on the one hand, he raised his voice in opposition to the nationalist mainstream in favour of a point of view that did not have the importance that it deserved. As history has shown, given the hegemony of constitutional liberalism which Gandhi and his colleagues in the freedom struggle had upheld, other alternative socio-ideological priorities had hardly had a presence. There was another reason, on the other, attributing the growing acceptance of Gandhi being the supreme commander left no chance for ideologues holding contrary views. This further gave a fillip to the mainstream nationalists largely undermining the endeavours, made by those who while challenging Gandhi and the Congress nationalists sought to evolve an alternative mode of conceptualizing nationalism. In such a context, it was not a mean achievement when not only did Savarkar articulate a persuasive set of ideas supportive of Hindu nationalism, but he also succeeded in creating an ambience in which it became a real nationalist alternative.

Hindu nationalism that Savarkar championed was a critique within a critique. The mainstream nationalism provided a critique of colonialism on the basis of Enlightenment philosophy, while the critics of Gandhian non-violence articulated a critique to pursue their alternative mode of political mobilization for freedom. Beginning with Dayananda Saraswati (1824–1883) who, in his *Satyarth Prakash* (1875), developed a model of Hindu mobilization by being true to the Vedas, it was a refreshing attempt in which India's indigenous tradition was privileged. Savarkar carried forward the ideas also in a context when the Muslims had emerged as a powerful segment of the nationalist struggle. It is true that his aim was to build a Hindu compact in which communities other than Hindus remained peripheral, if not entirely neglected. It is also true, as the above discussion confirms, that he also strove to build an Indian nationalist compact with the support of Muslims and Christians provided they were culturally sensitive enough to internalize the long-drawn Hindu values and mores. Claiming that Hindus were 'the bedrock on which an Indian independent state could be built', the views that Savarkar propounded helped his successors defend the fundamental tenets of Hindu nationalism. For him, it was therefore a foregone conclusion that the non-Hindus were welcome to the Hindu nationalist fold so long as they merged their sociocultural identity with the mainstream Hindus.

Conceptually speaking, what was M. A. Jinnah to Muslim League, Savarkar was to Hindu Mahasabha and later Hindu nationalist outfits. In other words, similar to Jinnah who applied a nationalist logic to defend India's partition, Savarkar provided exactly the same ideational format to develop a Hindu nationalist compact. It is true that his model has elements which make one argue that he was anti-Muslim. An oft-quoted, but not justified by contemporary evidence, incident is usually referred to while defending Savarkar being clearly opposed to the Muslims. According to a commentator, being terribly infuriated following the 1893 communal riot in Azamgarh in United Province in which Hindus were reported to have been killed by the Muslims, 'the boy Savarkar led a batch of his selected schoolmates in a march upon the village mosque. The battalion of these boys showered stones upon it, shattered its windows and tiles and returned victorious'.[107] One may draw on this unsubstantiated event to make a point on the basis of some of his statements which bordered on him being a rabid Hindu communal thinker. There is however substance in the argument that being a committed Hindu nationalist, it was natural for him to draw on the views which would support his ideological priorities. What he accepted as his assigned task was to build a nationalistic model for political mobilization and in his schema the Muslims did not appear to be compatriots which explains why they were never taken in the activities which he undertook to attain his aspired goal. Attributing the Hindu–Muslims chasm to the British *divide et impera*, Savarkar was keen to bring together both the communities to unitedly

[107] Keer, *Veer Savarkar*, 4.

fight the battle for freedom. It was a design to create 'a united Indian nation, a contingency likely to prove perhaps most dangerous to the British supremacy'. So, for the British, sustained attempts were made to encourage and help 'surreptitiously the fanatical hatred, enmity and distrust which the Moslems bore to the Hindus, thus rendering any efficient Indian national unity as delusive as a mirage'.[108] This is a statement showing that he was in favour of creating a national compact which was impossible without Hindu–Muslim amity. It is also true that his 1923 Hindutva tract was directed to evolve a compact of Hindus for the nationalist cause which appear to have been diluted when he was involved in mobilizing for the nation as a Hindu Mahasabha ideologue perhaps demonstrating how ideas get transformed in real politics.

[108] V. D. Savarkar's presidential address in the 1938 annual session of Hindu Mahasabha in Nagpur, reproduced in Savarkar, *Hindu Rashtra Darshan*, 3rd ed., 41.

B. R. Ambedkar (1891–1956)

3

A Combative Rebel with a Compassionate Heart

B. R. Ambedkar (1891–1956), popularly known as Babasaheb, is hailed as a Dalit messiah who fought relentlessly against caste atrocities by resorting to the fundamental ethos of political liberalism. In his perception, a liberal India was a perfect shield against exploitation of human beings by their fellow counterparts on the basis of an ideological framework, drawn on those Hindu socio-religious texts that were clearly prejudiced against the socially peripheral sections of society, now known as Dalits. Being ideologically baptized to liberalism in the USA by his teacher-cum-mentor, John Dewey while pursuing his PhD, he was persuaded to believe that a government, based on the philosophy of Enlightenment, needed to be established in India to realize his goal of creating an inclusive society. For him, liberalism was an empowering ideology which he experienced in the USA when he never felt threatened because of his Dalit identity. It was possible for the USA to avoid social discrimination, felt Ambedkar, simply because of the consolidation of liberal political values in governance. The scene in India was radically different; since the primary goal of the Gandhi-led anti-British campaign was political freedom, those social issues were generally put under the carpet which were potentially harmful for the multi-caste and multi-ethnic nationalist platform. So, a battleground had emerged where Ambedkar held liberalism as an empowering ideology in contrast with his other nationalist colleagues, including the Mahatma who also sharpened his critique against colonialism by drawing on basic liberal values, but did not push him adequately to upset the prevalent social balance by challenging the foundational basis of caste system. For the Mahatma, caste prejudices could be conclusively tackled by social reforms, while to Ambedkar, a liberal political system with individual being the basic unit of governance was the best protection available to the citizens. Representing two different perspectives of liberalism, Gandhi and Ambedkar played a critical role in introducing liberal constitutionalism in India once she became politically free. The aim of this chapter is to understand the trajectory of constitutional liberalism in India in the context of the nationalist movement and its immediate aftermath, especially during the making of the Constitution of India when Ambedkar's choice of individual being the basic unit of governance was preferred to Gandhi's village-centric constitutional structure of governance. The chapter argues that in view of their differential understanding of liberalism as a guiding ideology, they ended having appreciated two varied routes to constitutional democracy. Ambedkar became a hard-core liberal presumably because of the circumstances in which he underwent severe mental agony due to his birth as a Dalit and also the inspiration that he had derived from John Dewey's unflinching commitment to liberalism, while Gandhi sought to address social evils, like caste prejudices, by devising mechanisms within the acceptable parameters of Hinduism.

Ambedkar pursued a scathing critique against the dominant nationalist discourse that Gandhi shaped, to a significant extent. Unlike Gandhi who insisted on village Swaraj, Babasaheb preferred liberal democracy of the Western variety in which individual remained the basic unit of governance. What he established in the 1950 Constitution of India had its beginning in Ambedkar's witness before the 1919 Southborough Committee and 1930–1932 the Round Table Conference. This was a political battle that he had waged against the Mahatma to substantiate his arguments in favour of liberalism. There was also another battle that he was engaged in while challenging 'the archaic social values' supportive of caste discrimination. On the basis of his thorough research, he reinvented the idea of social justice in tune with his firm commitment to liberalism. True that he did not always succeed in his mission; nonetheless, the debate between the Mahatma and Babasaheb testifies several new dimensions of India's nationalist thought that did not, so far, receive adequate scholarly attention. By drawing on a rather neglected aspect of the nationalist debate, the chapter seeks to fill up in our understanding of the ideas of Gandhi and Ambedkar which were definitely context-driven. The chapter also makes the point that Ambedkar's ideas did not appear to be as significant as they later became in independent India, presumably because of the hegemonic influence of Gandhi in the nationalist universe probably due to contextual reasons.

Conceptualizing Liberalism

As argued earlier, Gandhi and Ambedkar had contrasting perspectives on liberalism; for Gandhi, it can flourish within 'the constraints' of Hindu society, while the latter was convinced that the basic thrust of liberalism remained elusive if discriminatory practices, nurtured by Hinduism, were not completely discarded.[1] Gandhi's liberalism was a unique interpretation of liberalism that drew its sustenance from well-defined moral parameters. In the context of non-violent civil resistance in South Africa, which gave him the first opportunity to fine-tune his strategy of Satyagraha, Gandhi always couched his argument within a moral mould. Hence the main thrust of his views on liberalism and constitutionalism has been nothing more than a critique of the theory for not being adequately moral; Gandhi thus sought to refurbish its fundamental foundation with moral justification. But such an assertion may appear superficial if one looks at the basic dichotomy between Gandhi's understanding of liberalism and that of other proponents, including B. R. Ambedkar. As an avowed supporter of equality, Ambedkar rejected the liberal amnesia about the dogma-based-birth-driven social segregation which, in his views, was contrary to the fundamental ethos of liberalism. He strongly felt that the social order of the caste was antithetical to the political institutions of democracy. Hence so long as the hierarchical social structure existed, equality, in its substantial sense, would remain elusive. This was undoubtedly a powerful theoretical critique of the Gandhi-led dominant nationalist discourse in which, because of the obvious political compulsions of the freedom struggle in diverse society like India, *varnashrama* was

[1] B. R. Ambedkar, *Social and Political Thought of Mahatma Gandhi*, chapter 3 (Oxford and New York: Routledge, 2006), 84–115.

defended possibly not to weaken the multicultural anti-British political platform. So Ambedkar fulfilled, as the article argues, a historical role, along with other Congress stalwarts, in creating a space for liberal constitutional values to strike roots in India long before 1946 when the Constituent Assembly met for the first time to produce the 1950 constitution for independent India.

Unlike the classical liberals, Ambedkar defended an interventionist state as perhaps the only tool to realize liberalism in its true form. He diverged, argued Chris Bayly, 'from classic liberalism ... in his concern to make the state work for the underprivileged'.[2] But wherever such pivotal role for the state is alluded to, it is 'based on the premise of a regime of rights that suggested the reasons and limits of state intervention'.[3] So, it was not an absolutist state that he favoured. He made this argument in conjunction with his suggestions for checks and balances for a majoritarian state with partisan goals. One discerns here his commitment to the institutional parameters of liberalism. Hence he qualified majoritarianism with 'strong grids of the rule of law, special privileges to minorities and the existence of a civil society which could nurture [equality regardless of class, caste and ethnicity] as a civic virtue'.[4] The description of Ambedkar being a radical liberal seems apt given the fact that he reinvented liberalism in a radical way by privileging the role of the state which was contrary to the basic liberal ethos. His main concern was to create a social environment in which 'discrimination which is feared shall not take place'.[5] And the state, which is sensitive to the conditions that he laid out, appeared to be the only available instrument for change.

Ambedkar was heavily influenced by his teacher at Columbia University, John Dewey, by believing that change was fundamental to

[2] C. A. Bayly, *Recovering Liberties: Indian Thought in the Age of Liberalism and Empire* (Cambridge: Cambridge University Press, 2012), 305.

[3] Valerian Rodrigues, *The Essential Writings of B. R. Ambedkar* (New Delhi: Oxford University Press, 2004), 22.

[4] Rodrigues, *The Essential Writings*, 22.

[5] B. R. Ambedkar, speech at the felicitation function at Wadi Bandar, Bombay, 4 March 1933, reproduced in Narendra Jadhav, *Ambedkar Speaks*, Vol. I (New Delhi: Konark Publishers Pvt. Ltd., 2013), 31.

life and there was nothing in life which was sacrosanct. Thus, he challenged the hegemonic ideas, supported by 'omnipresent providence' or 'manifest destiny' and also the deterministic conceptualization of Marxism. Second, their idea of democracy coalesced in the sense that both Dewey and Ambedkar agreed that democracy built not only 'a collegial atmosphere for deliberations', but also an 'associated living' which was free from social prejudices. Hence, in their perception, individuals were not 'atomistic or isolated individual of the Enlightenment thought, but always embedded in the social'.[6] Ambedkar imbibed John Dewey's spirit when he advised the caste Hindus to discard much of what they considered as their heritage since it 'dehumanizes a large section of their brethren'. As he stated, 'the Hindus must consider whether they should conserve the whole of their heritage or select what is helpful and transmit to future generations only that much and no more' (Ambedkar, 1936). He also questioned the tendencies towards worshipping the past as 'inherently retrogressive' since it blocked 'the visions for future' to strike roots. Following Dewey, he thus argued that

> an individual can live only in the present. The present is not just something which comes after the past; much less something produced by it. It is what life is in leaving the past behind it. The study of past products will not help us to understand the past. A knowledge of the past and its heritage is of great significance when it enters into the present, but not otherwise. And the mistake of making the records and remains of the past [a determinant of the present] it tends to make the past a rival of the present and the present a more or less futile imitation of the past.[7]

Hence, an uncritical dependence on the past 'makes the present … look empty and future distantly connected'. Instead of inculcating healthy practices, such an endeavour was 'inimical to progress and [was] a hindrance to a strong and a steady current of life'.[8] So what was the alternative that Ambedkar sought to build on the basis of his understanding of John Dewey's critique of the dependence on the past?

[6] Arun P. Mukherjee, 'B. R. Ambedkar, John Dewey and the Meaning of Democracy,' *New Literary History* 40, no. 2 (2009): 348.

[7] B. R. Ambedkar, *Annihilation of Caste* (New Delhi: Critical Quest, 2007) (reprint), 53.

[8] Ambedkar, *Annihilation of Caste*, 51.

Ambedkar's answer was to create space for social endosmosis to strike roots because he believed that without holding 'an attitude of respect and reverence towards fellowmen' substantial equality remained distant.[9] This sentiment was echoed in his address to the Constituent Assembly in 1948 when he said that

> it is for the majority to realize its duty not to discriminate against minorities. Whether the minorities will continue or will vanish must depend upon this habit of the majority. The moment the majority loses the habit of discriminating against the minority, the minorities can have no ground to exist. They will vanish.[10]

Here too, Ambedkar reverberated Dewey's understanding of democracy which, in Dewey's perception, was 'more than a form of government [because] it is primarily a mode of associated living, of conjoint communicated experience ... denoting a greater diversity of stimuli to which an individual has to respond'.[11] He reproduced the Dewey formulation *verbatim* in his defence by saying that 'democracy is not merely a form of government, [but also] a mode of associated living, of conjoint communicated experience ... [with] an attitude of respect and reverence towards fellowmen'.[12] This was not possible because 'Hindus and the Untouchables are divided by a fence of barbed wire [which] is actually a cordon sanitaire which the Untouchables have never been allowed to cross and can never hope to cross'.[13] So, there is no scope for social endosmosis to evolve simply because the social reality is 'alarmingly fragmented'.

[9] Ibid.

[10] *Constituent Assembly* (*CA* hereafter) *Debates*, Vol. VII, 4/11/1948–8/1/1949, the statement of B. R. Ambedkar, 4 November 1948, p. 39.

[11] John Dewey, *Democracy and Education: An Introduction to the Philosophy of Education* (Cambridge: Harvard University Press, 1916), 101.

[12] B. R. Ambedkar, speech before the Round Table Conference in Vasant Menon, ed., *Dr. Babasaheb Ambedkar's Writings and Speeches*, Vol. 2 (Bombay: Education Department, Government of Maharashtra, 1982), 81.

[13] Ibid, 187.

Situating Gandhi and Ambedkar as Contrasting-cum-Complementary Icons

A hardboiled rationalist, Ambedkar found in the liberal democratic rule of law a powerful argument to challenge the prevalent caste discrimination, especially between the caste Hindus and so-called untouchables. Thus, there are two complementary sources from which Ambedkar seemed to have derived his unbridled and firm commitment to fight against social segregation: first, his personal experience as an untouchable which he could not reconcile since it was based on artificial arguments and systems of discrimination; and second, his academic training in England and later in the USA enabled him to conceptualize equality which was being practised in the Western world in its true spirit. He thus led a relentless battle to purge the society of evil systems and practices at two levels: at one level, by exposing the vacuous principles defending the practices emanating from the scriptures, Ambedkar reinvented the idea of social justice by reiterating the fundamental cannons of liberalism; at another, by seeking to govern human behaviour through the well-defined constitutional values, he also contributed to a search for a political arrangement which was free from social discrimination, not only on the basis of primordial values but also on any other count. It was B. R. Ambedkar who is said to have given new impetus to the old Indian liberal project that was articulated differently by the early nationalists in their crusade against the colonial rule. Given his faith in constitutional democracy of the Western variety supporting liberty, equality and fraternity, Ambedkar while challenging the infallibility of the so-called sacred scriptures also created a new wave of thinking questioning some of the fundamental assumptions on which Hinduism was based. There were, of course, elements of continuity of liberal ideas even before Ambedkar emerged on India's political scene. In his own way, Jyotiba Phule, before Ambedkar, fought against social injustice, as it was contrary to the fundamental ethos of British liberalism. But what was unique in Ambedkar was to argue the case for the principle of constitutional and political discrimination of the underprivileged, disinherited and sociopolitically secluded untouchables in India as complementary to the growth of a truly liberal-democratic polity.

In the context of the Gandhi-led nationalist movement in India, B. R. Ambedkar did not seem to have played as critical a role as other mainstream nationalist leaders. What was, however, striking was his life-long endeavour to uproot the sources of injustice in hierarchical Hindu society for which he not only exposed the logical fallacy of the so-called holy texts but also developed a persuasive counter-model on the basis of his unflinching commitment to the issues of social justice. This is one side of his long-drawn battle; the other equally important aspect of his political challenge was reflected in his effort at constitutionalizing the polity in a liberal fashion which is a relatively little-known facet of his political career. There is no doubt that his arguments for social justice which he evolved while being engaged in challenging the Gandhi-led orthodox nationalist leadership. Equally significant was his defence for constitutional democracy drawing sustenance from a codified rule of law and complementary ethos and values. The aim of this chapter is therefore to focus on Ambedkar's distinct contribution to constitutionalizing India since his testifying before Southborough Committee, which finally prepared the 1919 Government of India Act. It was Ambedkar who forcefully argued for 'separate electorate and reservations' for untouchables and other religious communities before the Committee which though went in vain. On the basis of a thorough analysis of Ambedkar's idea of constitutionalism in a historical context, the chapter makes the argument that Ambedkar, true to his liberal faith, upheld constitutionalism as a shield against social discrimination, but as an avowed supporter of equality in its unalloyed form, he rejected the liberal amnesia about others' nationality because instead of being an outcome of common territory, common ethnicity or a common language, it evolved out of common memories and myths of origin and history. This was undoubtedly a powerful theoretical critique of the conventional nationalist discourse that Babasaheb never reconciled to presumably because of the irreconcilable contradictions in what was sought to be projected as a nation in the context of the nationalist offensive against colonialism.

A cursory look at the nationalist movement shows that with the rise of Gandhi, it became overwhelmingly Gandhian which means that it was Gandhi who appeared to have shaped the campaign for freedom in accordance with what he deemed appropriate. This is a part of the story since Gandhism is a creative blending of multiple ideological influences, of which the ideas of Ambedkar did not seem to be no less insignificant. Here is an argument that what Gandhi nurtured as his ideology evolved out of being interactive with his colleagues in the nationalist phase who conceptualized nationalism in different perspectives. There are two obvious implications of such an assumption: on the one hand, it implies that the nationalist ideology that evolved in the 20th century following the rise of Gandhi was not exclusively Gandhian, but was accommodative of ideas and claims which were not exactly derivative of the typical Gandhian ideological mould. For instance, it is now a matter of common knowledge that Gandhi owed a great deal to Rabindranath Tagore in realizing that the Western notion of nation was hardly applicable to India given the well-entrenched socio-economic and cultural diversity. In a similar vein, it can also be argued that had B. R. Ambedkar not presented his forceful arguments for social justice, Indian nationalist discourse of which Gandhi was the prime priest would have been handicapped to a significant extent. There is no denying that Gandhi conceptualized untouchability as inhuman, and he also led campaigns to eradicate such social practices justifying discrimination on the basis of the accident of birth. This was one of the significant components of the nationalist campaign that he had launched primarily for political freedom from British rule which implies that the struggle for social equality did not seem to be as critical as that of independence for the Indian National Congress. This was a serious lacuna, Ambedkar felt, of the Gandhi-led battle for freedom for it allowed the Mahatma to conceive freedom in its most restricted sense since political freedom without social freedom remained vacuous. Hence, for Babasaheb, while conceptualizing freedom in its most expansive sense, Indian nationalism was skewed with narrow politico-ideological vision which, instead of being liberating, contributed to circumstances in which the sociopolitical forces supportive of unfreedom of the socially peripheral segments of the population appeared to have received a moral boost. A challenging theoretical formulation nonetheless, it further problematized the nationalist discourse which no longer remained monochromatic but became multidimensional. In the light of Ambedkar's unflinching commitment for the downtrodden, supported by persuasive arguments, the ideological discourse that he developed immediately gained especially in the context of growing democratization of nationalist politics.

A new era of politics had ushered in with the acceptance of the Dalits as a critical player in the design of governance in which the role of Babasaheb remained most significant. It is true that he built on some of the arguments that Jotirao Phule made in the past to claim a legitimate space for the untouchables. The effort went on unabated. For example, in his presidential address at the second session of the Depressed Classes Conference, held at Madras in July 1911, G. A. Natesan drew attention to the agony that the Depressed Classes experienced in their quotidian life by exhorting that

> no fair-minded man can contemplate for a moment the present condition of the depressed classes, without being forced to admit that it is absolutely monstrous that a class of human beings with bodies similar to our own, with brains that can think and hearts that can feel, should be perpetually condemned to a low life of utter wretchedness, servitude and mental and moral degradation, and that permanent barriers should be placed in their way that it should be impossible for them to overcome them and improve their lot.[14]

For the Dalits, the British rule was a panacea, in the sense that it helped develop a voice against caste-driven discriminatory practices as nothing but an artificial design to protect partisan interests. Hence it was argued that

> the British rule and English education have roused … new aims, new aspirations, and all who are actively engaged in the great task of uplifting Indians are deeply alive to the fact that there can be no true uplift for the Indian nation until the so-called depressed classes rise with them.[15]

[14] G. K. Natesan, presidential address at the second session of the Depressed Classes Conference, Madras, 8 July 1911, reproduced in Sabyasachi Bhattacharya and Yagati Chinna Rao, eds., *The Past of the Outcaste: Readings in Dalit History* (Hyderabad: Orient Blackswan, 2017), 41.

[15] Ibid, 43.

In a milieu which was heavily tilted against the Dalits, the concern that their uplift was necessary for national well-being represented a new line of thinking that gained momentum soon. It was B. R. Ambedkar who took up the cudgels for the depressed classes which not only changed the language of nationalist politics but also transformed its texture by making the concern for social justice integral to its articulation. In so doing, Babasaheb partnered with the British for the initiatives that it had taken to create conditions for the growth of a liberal polity. What is, however, distinctive about Ambedkar was his capacity to persuade the British authority to constitutionally guarantee those rights and privileges for the Dalits which were admissible to the caste Hindus and other religious groups. Being a liberal, the idea came to him instantaneously, and thus it did seem odd when Babasaheb strongly argued for an all-pervasive state, capable of doing away with the archaic social practices which, he further felt, needed to be strengthened to completely eradicate their roots in Indian society. It was not an easy task though by launching a scathing attack on the prevalent system of caste segregation, Ambedkar set the ball rolling which was undoubtedly a stepping stone towards evolving a milieu in which Dalits were also taken as legitimate partners in nation building.

Nonetheless, there is no denying the fact that Gandhi set the universe of India's nationalist movement, to a significant extent, notwithstanding challenges and counter-challenges to his political ideology and also the style of leadership that he perfected during the course of his interactive endeavours with his colleagues, followers and, of course, the colonial rulers and detractors. Gandhi remained, in other words, a prime reference point for Ambedkar. Linked with this, there was another concern—the concern for democracy—that seems to have been dominant in the discourse that he crafted while challenging the prevalent nationalist conceptualization of freedom and also its supporters. It was a difficult task indeed. Nonetheless, Babasaheb made a definite stride in this regard by redrawing the conceptual contours of democracy which was neither exclusively Western nor clearly indigenous, but a creative blending of the traditions and ideas which were organic to the Indian socio-economic and political reality.

Conceptually speaking, Ambedkar and Gandhi were, at one level, diametrically opposite in their approach to human well-being, since the former's insistence on treating the Dalits as a separate political entity was never endorsed by the Mahatma to avoid further division among the Indians. The contrast was thus visible. At a far more perceptive level, they were complementary to each other for both of them believed in weeding out the roots of birth-driven hierarchy. Being humiliated for his Dalit identity, Babasaheb failed to comprehend Gandhi's support to the caste system which, he felt, was a deterrent towards the establishment of fair society; Gandhi, despite not being appreciative, decided not to disturb the social equilibrium which the caste hierarchy was believed to have sustained. For the Mahatma, it was a strategic design which he justified as appropriate in the context of the freedom struggle. There are reasons to accept the contention since he undertook several campaigns against caste prejudices which he always condemned as a malice for India. Gandhi abhorred caste system since it justified inequality and exploitation. Critical of those supporting the foul practice on the grounds of religion and cited scripture in their favour, Gandhi condemned them since they distorted the religious scriptures to fulfil their partisan aims. 'This religion', he thus argued, 'if it can be called such, stinks in my nostrils … [and] this cannot be the Hindu religion'.[16] Here, Gandhi and Ambedkar held identical views vis-a-vis caste system. Both of them were persuaded to accept that caste hierarchy was not, at all, justified by the scriptures, but came out of a peculiar interplay of socio-economic processes in which exploitation of human beings by human beings was defended to privilege one segment of society against the rest.

Debate Unfolds

Critical of the nationalist movement that upheld caste and untouchability at the behest of Gandhi, Ambedkar sought to articulate an alternative political ideology by challenging the very foundation of the 'Hinduized' nationalist movement. One of the most significant

[16] M. K. Gandhi, 'Where is Swaraj,' *Young India*, 26 January 1922, reproduced in M. K. Gandhi, *Collected Works of Mahatma Gandhi*, Vol. 22, p. 229.

arguments that Ambedkar made against Hinduism was that caste and untouchability struck at its foundation and hence it was inherently divisive. Gandhi by clinging to the basic philosophy of caste never seriously challenged, as Ambedkar accused, untouchability in Hinduism. According to him, Gandhism was 'a paradox' because 'it stands for freedom from foreign domination [and] at the same time it seeks to maintain intact a social structure which permits the domination of one class by another on a hereditary basis which means a perpetual domination of one class by another'.[17] To Ambedkar, Gandhi's loyalty to Hinduism amounted to supporting 'untouchability' because it also evolved as integrally linked with Hinduism and was thus justified. This assumption, however, stands in contradiction with what the Mahatma sincerely believed. According to him, 'untouchability is not a sanction of religion; it is a device of Satan. … There is neither nobility nor bravery in treating the great and uncomplaining scavengers of the nation as worse than dogs to be despised and spat upon'.[18]

He criticized Gandhi further for having eulogized the Indian villages as illustrative of a unique unit of social, economic and political equilibrium. Instead, Ambedkar argued, Indian villages

> represent a kind of colonialism of the Hindus designed to exploit the Untouchables. The Untouchables have no rights. They are there only to wait, serve and submit. They are there to do or to die. They have no rights because they are outside the village republic and because they are outside the so-called republic, they are outside the Hindu fold. This is a vicious circle. But this is a fact which cannot be gainsaid.[19]

For Gandhi, the village was the basis for building a republican society,[20] not polluted by colonialism, while for Ambedkar it was 'the black hole'

[17] B. R. Ambedkar, 'Gandhism', reproduced in Rodrigues, *The Essential Writings*, 165.

[18] *Young India*, 19 January 1921, reproduced in Mahatma Gandhi, *What Is Hinduism* (New Delhi: National Book Trust, 2001) (reprint), 115.

[19] B. R. Ambedkar, 'Outside the Fold'; Rodrigues, *The Essential Writings*, 331.

[20] Gandhi's idea of village *Swaraj* is that 'it is completely republic, independent of its neighbours for its own vital wants, and yet interdependent for many others in which dependence is a necessity. Thus every villager's first concern will be to grow its own food crops and cotton for its cloth. … The government of the village will be

of Indian civilization. Village, for Gandhi, was not merely a geographical location where people lived in small settlement drawn on land. For him, the essence it reflected was the essence of Indian civilization. The Indian village had a design, a way of life which had the potential of becoming 'an alternative to the city-based and technology-driven capitalist West'.[21] His conception of village was not anchored 'on the modern notion of development but on the post-modern perspective of quality life'.[22] And, yet for the Dalits 'the village … could never be an embodiment of justice [since] to remain in village meant remaining tied to the same humiliating occupation that had so far been their fate'.[23] So, for Ambedkar, the structure of village settlements reflected the basic tenets of Hinduism that never recognized Dalits as its integral part. In other words, village contributed and simultaneously sustained the divisive nature of the Hindu society where the untouchables always remained 'outside the fold'. As he most eloquently put,

> the Hindu society insists on segregation of the untouchables. The Hindu will not live in the quarters of the untouchables and will not allow the untouchables to live inside the Hindu quarters. … It is not a case of social separation, a mere stoppage of social intercourse for a temporary period. It is a case of territorial segregation and of a cordon sanitaire putting the impure people inside the barbed wire into a sort of a cage. Every Hindu village has a ghetto. The Hindus live in the village and the untouchables live in the ghetto.[24]

In contrast with Gandhi, Ambedkar conceptualized village as a model of the oppressive Hindu social organization, a microcosm of the

conducted by a panchayat of five persons, annually elected by the adult villagers, male and female, possessing minimum prescribed qualifications'. Gandhi, *Harijan*, 7 July 1942; Gandhi, *The Collected Works of Mahatma Gandhi*, LXXVII: 308–09.

[21] Surinder S. Jodhika, 'Nation and Village: Images of Rural India in Gandhi, Nehru and Ambedkar,' *Economic and Political Weekly*, 10 (August 2002): 3346.

[22] T. K. Oommen, 'Gandhi and Village: Towards a Critical Appraisal,' in *Economic and Social Principles of Mahatma Gandhi*, eds. Subrata Mukherjee and Sushila Ramaswamy (New Delhi: Deep & Deep, 1998), 226.

[23] Gauri Viswanathan, *Outside the Fold: Conversion, Modernity and Belief* (Delhi: Oxford University Press, 1998), 238.

[24] B. R. Ambedkar, *The Untouchables: Who Were They Why They Became Untouchables*? (New Delhi: Amrit Book Company, 1948), 21–22.

over-all demeaning circumstance in which Dalits were located. It was 'the working plant of the Hindu social order' where one could see the atrocious nature of Hinduism. Given the obvious role of the villages in sustaining the atrocious social circumstances of the Dalits, Ambedkar never, as evident, endorse Gandhi's eulogy for Indian villages because they represented an exclusive domain for the touchables at the cost of the untouchables who invariably were pushed into the ghetto.

The conflict between Gandhi and Ambedkar on the issue of the separate electorates for untouchables and the depressed classes was an articulation of two contrasting perspectives that fundamentally altered the nature of political participation by the Scheduled Castes and Tribes in the British India and its aftermath. What had begun in Ambedkar's own representation for Dalit rights in the 1919 Franchise Committee (also known as the Southborough Committee) was never lost in the long battle that Babasaheb had fought for political equality for the Dalits. For him, the British rule was a messiah. As he argued, 'the Depressed classes welcomed the British as their deliverers from age long tyranny and oppression by the orthodox Hindus. The British', he further added, 'assumed the role of trustees for the Depressed Classes'.[25] A firm believer of liberal democracy of the Western variety, he was thus persuaded to believe that a strong government, free from caste prejudices, was required to alter the prevalent Hindu mindset justifying oppression of Dalits by caste Hindus. Hence, he suggested that

> we must have a government in which men in power ... will not be afraid to amend social and economic code of life which the dictates of justice and expediency so urgently call for; ... it is possible only a Government, which is of the people, for the people and by the people.[26]

So long as the caste Hindus dominate the political scene, political equality remained a distant dream. In view of their well-entrenched prejudices against those identified as Dalits because of the accident of

[25] B. R. Ambedkar's speeches in the Round Table Conference, 20 September 1930, reproduced in B. R. Ambedkar, *Speeches at Round Table Conference* (New Delhi: Critical Quest, 2011), 4.

[26] Ibid, 5.

birth, it was difficult to reverse the political attitudes of the Congress so long the caste Hindus reigned supreme as leaders. Hence, the Depressed Classes were vehemently opposed to any constitutional arrangement which allowed the caste Hindus to remain supreme. They needed protection because they

> fear that the proposed [system of governance], constituted by the majority principle of democracy will be rule of the orthodox Hindus [and] there is a great danger of that majority rule with its orthodox Hindu beliefs and prejudices contravening the dictates of justice, equality and good conscience.[27]

Seeking to establish the claim of the Dalits as equals in India, Ambedkar fearlessly attacked Gandhi as well since the latter was never persuaded to accept what the former suggested. For the Mahatma, Ambedkar's assessment of the situation was perhaps correct, though it was not the right time to highlight them because that would adversely affect the freedom struggle. While arguing for Dalits' political rights, Ambedkar had to grapple with two issues: on the one hand, he had to offer strong arguments for constitutional protection of Dalit rights and also to counter, on the other, Gandhi's claim to be the leader of Dalits and to also to affirm that he represented them. A careful perusal of Gandhi–Ambedkar confrontation during the Round Table Conference (1930–1932) reveals that neither Gandhi nor Ambedkar was willing to compromise on the issue of Dalit representation. On 17 October 1931, Gandhi, for instance, issued a press statement underlining that 'I know it is thought in some quarters that [the Dalits] ought to have separate electorates and that I am not qualified to speak for them'.[28] That it was not acceptable to him was evident when he mentioned that 'I do not hesitate to say that, if the untouchables in all parts of India would record their votes, I should be their representative'.[29] He echoed the sentiments in a far more stronger language in his speech before the Quakers Society in London on 31 October 1931 when he attacked Babasaheb by saying that

27 Ibid, 17.

28 Gandhi, *The Collected Works of Mahatma Gandhi*, Vol. 54, p. 37.

29 Ibid.

> Dr. Ambedkar, able as he is, has unhappily lost his head over [the question of representation to the Dalits]. He sees blood wherever Hinduism is. If he was a real representative, I should have withdrawn. Today he cannot coherently think of the problem. I repudiate his claim to represent [the Dalits]. I am the representative of the depressed classes.[30]

Being fiercely opposed to separate electorate to the Dalits which he articulated by saying that 'with all the emphasis that I can command ... I would resist it with life'[31], Gandhi expressed that he was not, at all, favourable to Ambedkar being recognized as the representative of the Dalits. Ambedkar's diatribe against the Mahatma was no less attacking. As he wrote, the future of the Round Table Conference was bleak since

> the Congress chose a worse person like Gandhi to guide India's destiny. As a unifying force he was a failure. Mr. Gandhi presents himself as a man full of humility. But his behaviour at the Round Table Conference showed that in the flush of victory Mr. Gandhi can be very petty-minded. [Not only did he] treat the non-Congress delegates with contempt he also insulted them whenever an occasion furnished him with an excuse by openly telling them that they were nobodies and that he alone, as the delegate of the Congress, represented the country.[32]

A perusal of the aforementioned arguments and counter-arguments helps us make the point that insofar as the separate electorate for Dalits was concerned Gandhi and Ambedkar were poles apart: neither of them was willing to budge an inch from their respective points of view. The scene did not, however, remain the same, as soon the Muslims were constitutionally protected by the adoption of the 1932 Communal Award.[33]. Once the separate electorate was for the Muslims was conceded by the Congress while accepting the 1935 Government of India Act, Ambedkar argued, on behalf of the Dalits, that they must be allowed to constitute a separate electorate and elect their own representatives to the central and provincial

[30] Ibid, 117.

[31] Ibid, 119.

[32] Vasant Moon, ed., *Dr. Babasaheb Ambedkar Writings and Speeches*, Vol. 9 (New Delhi: Ministry of Social Justice and Empowerment, Government of India), 55.

[33] B. R. Ambedkar, 'The 1932 Communal Award and Its Implications in Bengal,' *Modern Asian Studies* 23, no. 3 (1989): 493–523.

legislatures. He further defended the claim by saying that since voting was severely restricted by property and educational qualifications, the geographically highly disparate depressed classes were unlikely to have any influence in the decision-making process. So, the solution lay in separate electorate for them. Ambedkar held the view that untouchables were absolutely separate from Hinduism and hence he tried 'to find a solution to their problem through political separatism'.[34] In order to substantiate, he further argued that the Hindus 'had much to lose by the abolition of untouchability, though they had nothing to fear from political reservation leading to this abolition'.[35] The matter was 'economic' rather than 'religious'. In an unambiguous way, Ambedkar brought out the economic dimension of untouchability by stating that

> the system of untouchability is a gold mine to the Hindus. In it the 240 millions of Hindus have 60 millions of Untouchables to serve as their retinue to enable the Hindus to maintain pomp and ceremony and to cultivate a feeling of pride and dignity befitting a master class, which cannot be fostered and sustained unless there is beneath it a servile class to look down upon. In it the 240 millions of Hindus have 60 millions of Untouchables to be used as forced labourers; ... in it the 240 millions of Hindus have 60 millions of Untouchables to do the dirty work of scavengers and sweepers which the Hindu is debarred by his religion to do and which must be done by non-Hindus who could be no other than Untouchables. In it the 240 millions of Hindus have 60 millions of Untouchables who can be kept to lower jobs. ... In it the 240 millions of Hindus have the 60 millions of Untouchables who can be used as shock-absorbers in slumps and deadweights in booms, for in slumps, it is the Untouchables who are fired first and the Hindu is fired last and in booms the Hindu is employed first and the Untouchables is employed last. [So, untouchability is not a religious] but an economic system which is worse than slavery.[36]

[34] Judith Brown, 'The Mahatma and Modern India,' *Modern Asian Studies* 3, no. 4 (1969): 331.

[35] Upendra Baxi, 'Emancipation as Justice: Babasaheb Ambedkar's Legacy and Vision.' Unpublished paper presented at the inaugural oration at the Babasaheb Ambedkar Centenary Celebration, University of Madras, 5 March 1991, p. 17.

[36] B. R. Ambedkar, *Mr. Gandhi and Emancipation of Untouchables* (Jullander: Bheem Patrika Publications, 1943), 196–97.

Unable to appreciate Ambedkar's demand, Gandhi declined to accept that the untouchables were a community separate from the Hindus and instead was prepared to have reserved seats for them in general constituencies. For him, the matter was highly 'religious', as he stated, 'for me the question of these classes is predominantly moral and religious. The political aspect, important though it is', he further added, 'dwindles into insignificance compared to the moral and religious issue'.[37] He reacted strongly when a charge was labelled that the upper-caste Congress leaders could never properly represent the untouchables. When his attention was drawn to the Congress acceptance of the 1932 Communal Award, Gandhi insisted that unlike the question of religious minorities, the issue of untouchability was a matter internal to Hinduism and had to be resolved within it. Underlining the adverse consequences of such division on the Hindus, the Mahatma thus emphatically argued that

> I cannot possibly tolerate what is in store for Hinduism if there are two division set forth in the villages. Those who speak of the political rights of Untouchables do not know their India, do not know how Indian society is today constructed, and therefore I want to say with all the emphasis that I can command that if I was the only person to resist this thing I would resist it with my life.[38]

Gandhi's protest against the extension of the separate electorate to the Dalits was double-edged: on the one hand, Gandhi sincerely believed that the separate electorate would also split them from the Hindu society and absolve the latter of its moral responsibility to fight against the practice of untouchability. There were clear political calculations that, as Bhikhu Parekh argues, governed Gandhi's mind for 'the separate electorate would have reduced the numerical strength of the Hindu majority, encouraged minority alliance against it, and fragmented the country yet further'.[39] So, the Gandhian intervention was, on the other, the result of skilful political strategy as well as of his passionate concern for Indian unity. Ambedkar was equally assertive and insisted

[37] Gandhi's Press Statement, *Harijan*, 10 June 1933.

[38] Gandhi to Tagore, 9 May 1933, reproduced in the *Amrita Bazar Patrika*, 10 May 1933.

[39] Bhikhu Parekh, *Gandhi* (Oxford: Oxford University Press, 1997), 18.

on separate electorate as the best device to protect the social, economic and political interests of the Dalits. As he stated,

> I trust [that] the Mahatma would not drive me to the necessity of making a choice between his life and the rights of my people. For I can never consent to deliver my people bound hand and foot to the caste Hindus for generations to come.[40]

No solution was visible. For Gandhi, the separate electorate for the untouchables was to divide the Hindu society further, perpetuating their inferiority. Ambedkar denounced this as a strategic argument for using the untouchables as 'weightage for the Hindus against the Muslims'.[41] When the British government endorsed the separate electorate in the Communal Award of August 1932, Ambedkar had an edge over his rival. Now, the only course of action open to Gandhi was to embark on a fast. He went on a fast rather than approving the demand of the separate electorate for the depressed classes. His decision to fast unto death on the issues of representation for Dalits 'threw the British India into disarray'[42] and the pressure was mounted on Ambedkar for conceding what the Mahatma had desired. Gandhi who was in Yerwada Jail in Poona began the fast on 20 September that ended only on 24 September once Ambedkar agreed to accept the reservation of seats for Dalits within the caste-Hindu constituencies. An agreement between Gandhi and Ambedkar, known as the Poona Pact, was signed in 1933[43] and the depressed classes were given a substantial number of reserved seats but within the Hindu electorate. As a biographer thus noted,

[40] C. B. Khairmode, *Dr. Bhimrao Ramji Ambedkar* (in Marathi), Vol. 4 (Pune: Sugava Prakashan, 1989), 42, quoted in M. S. Gore, *The Social Context of An Ideology: P Ambedkar's Political and Social Thought* (New Delhi: SAGE Publications, 1993), 137.

[41] Ainslie T. Embree, *Imagining India: Essays on Indian History* (Delhi: Oxford University Press, 1989), 171.

[42] Raja Sekhar Vundru, *Ambedkar, Gandhi and Patel: The Making of India's Electoral System* (New Delhi: Bloomsbury, 2018), 37.

[43] For details, see Ravinder Kumar, 'Ambedkar, Gandhi and the Poona Pact,' Occasional Paper on Society and History, No. 20 (New Delhi: Nehru Memorial Library and Museum, 1985); and also, Gore, *The Social Context of An Ideology*, 136–39.

> at Yerawada, the politician in Gandhi became successful and the Mahatma was defeated. So effective and crushing was the victory of Gandhi that he deprived Ambedkar of all his life-saving weapons and made him a powerless man as did Indra in the case of Karna.[44]

The Poona Pact represented a victory for the Mahatma in two ways: (a) it was accepted that untouchability was 'a social' and not 'a political problem' and (b) it was a problem of Hindu religion and not of the Hindu economy. Nonetheless, what was unique about the Pact that it, for the first time, placed the Backward Classes later classified as the Scheduled Castes in the 1935 Government of India Act on the centre stage of Indian politics with a separate identity. From now on, the Scheduled Castes invariably figured in any discussion on national identity. Although in Ambedkar, the Scheduled Castes found a powerful leader, they continued to remain a politically significant 'minority' with narrow social, economic and political goals. As a dissenter bent on dismantling an oppressive caste system, Ambedkar therefore 'fulfilled the historical role of dissent not only to question hateful religious dogma but also to unbuckle the consolidating ambitions of the secular state within which former religious orthodoxies are subsumed'.[45] What is striking is that despite having opposed Hindu orthodoxy, manifested in caste rigidity of which he was a victim, Babasaheb attempted to steer a steady course between a separatist, sectarian stance and unconditional citizenship function in which identity of untouchables would be subsumed within Hinduism.[46] It would, however, be wrong to suggest that Ambedkar believed that the problem of untouchability would be solved not through legislative feats but through institutionalized social measures. As he argued,

> any electoral arrangement, I believe, cannot be a solution of the larger social problems. It requires more than any political arrangement and I hope that it would be possible for you to go beyond this political arrangement that we are making today [of joint electorate] and devise ways and means

44 Dhananjay Keer, *Dr. Ambedkar: Life and Mission* (Bombay: Popular Prakashan, 1962), 215–16.

45 Gauri Viswanathan, *Outside the Fold: Conversion, Modernity and Belief* (Delhi: Oxford University Press, 1998), 213.

46 For an elaboration of this argument, see Viswanathan, *Outside the Fold*, 211–39.

> whereby it would be possible for the Depressed Classes not only to be part and parcel of the Hindu community but also to occupy an honourable position, a position of equality of status in the community.[47]

Despite Ambedkar's reservations, the 1932 Poona Pact is the first well-articulated arrangement in which the Scheduled Castes were identified as a separate group within Hinduism; their emergence with a distinct political identity significantly influenced the provincial elections that followed the 1935 Government of India Act. Apart from the Muslims who had already asserted their existence as a significant community, the ascendancy of the Scheduled Castes clearly indicated the complexity of the future course of Indian history, which, so far, glossed over the well-entrenched fragmented identities within both the Hindus and Muslims. In fact, the Pakistan demand that drew upon Jinnah's 'two nation theory' hinges on the exclusive identities of both the principal communities, Hindus and Muslims, despite sharing the same socio-economic and politico-cultural milieu. For the nationalists, the idea of separate Hindu and Muslim identity had no natural basis and also the two communities were politically separated through the manoeuvres of communal forces and imperial divide et impera. For Jinnah and the Muslim League, the demand for a sovereign and independent Muslim state was logical since Muslims constituted a separate nation with a different religious philosophy, social customs and literature. Hindus and Muslims belong to two completely different civilizations which drew on conflicting ideas and conceptions. The Hindu counterpart of this logic was articulated by V. D. Savarkar who argued strongly for a separate Hindu identity because of distinctive features separating Hindus from Muslims though its root can be traced back to the 18th century when the English writing on India clearly provided the Hindus with a distinct identity 'in racial, religious and linguistic terms'.[48] That Muslims constituted a self-determining political community was always emphasized to completely dissociate from the Hindus seeking

[47] Quoted in Bhagwan Das, 'Ambedkar's Journey to Mass Conversion,' in *B. R. Ambedkar*, ed. V. Grover (New Delhi: Deep & Deep Publications, 1993), 595.

[48] Sushil Srivastava, 'Constructing the Hindu Identity: European Moral and Intellectual Adventurism in 18th Century India,' *Economic and Political Weekly* 33, no. 20 (16 May 1998), 1186.

to establish 'a Hindu Raj'.[49] The Hindu–Muslim schism was not merely based on religious differences but also on certain fundamental principles guiding their respective lives. As Muslims drew upon completely different socio-cultural values, it was unthinkable that they could live as 'a mere minority in a Hindu-dominated India'. While explaining the Hindu–Muslim chasm in colonial India, Ambedkar thus argued that the Hindu–Muslim 'antagonism . . . is formed by causes which take their origin in historical, religious, cultural and social antipathy of which political antipathy is only a reflection'. These form, he further elaborated, 'one deep river of discontent which, being regularly fed by these sources, keeps on mounting to a head and overflowing its ordinary channels'.[50] So, Ambedkar held the Hindus equally responsible for the rise of Muslim separatism that was finally resolved in the emergence of Pakistan as a nation.

B. R. Ambedkar, in his *Pakistan or the Partition of India*, endorsed the claim for Pakistan in terms of realist politics. According to him, partition was possibly the best solution to resolve the constitutional impasse in India for two reasons. First, given the hostility of the Muslims to the idea of a single central government, inevitably dominated by the Hindu majority, it was certain that if there was no partition, the animosities and suspicion between the communities would remain: 'burying Pakistan is not the same thing as burying the ghost of Pakistan'.[51] Furthermore, given the demographic composition of what was proposed as Pakistan, there was no doubt that it would be a homogeneous state and hence free from communal bickering and mutual distrust. Second, Ambedkar felt that in united India where more than one-third of the population was Muslim, 'could Hindu dominance be a serious threat to the very existence of the polity'. In such a state, Muslims apprehending the tyranny of the Hindu majority were likely to organize themselves into 'a theocratic party' provoking in turn the rise of Hindu fundamentalist forces seeking to establish 'a Hindu raj'. Partition would radically alter the situation where Muslims

[49] *Star of India*, 24 March 1940.

[50] B. R. Ambedkar, 'Thoughts on Pakistan,' in *Inventing Boundaries: Gender, Politcs and Partition of India*, ed. Mushirul Hasan (Delhi: Oxford University Press, 2000), 48.

[51] B. R. Ambedkar, *Pakistan or the Partition of India*, 2nd ed. (Bombay, 1945), p. vii.

in Hindustan would be 'a small and widely scattered minority' joining different political parties in accordance with what they consider 'as most protective' of their socio-economic and political interests. As a result, a party like Hindu Mahasabha that drew on the principle of 'a Hindu raj' would gradually disappear. Persuaded by the logic of his argument, Ambedkar suggested that the lower of Hindu society should join hands with the Muslim minority to fight the Hindu high castes for their rights of citizenship and social dignity.[52]

As is argued earlier, Ambedkar's demand for equal citizenship is an outcome of being an unalloyed liberal which is a defensible position. The issue, however, gets terribly complicated once it gets integrated with his insistence on special constitutional protection for the Dalits. How did he grapple with this contradiction? According to him, the demands for equal citizenship and group-differentiated rights are neither conceptually contradictory nor empirically indefensible, for the latter prepares the ground for the former by creating a level-playing field in which socio-economic discriminations are completely erased. In his *Who Were the Shudras* (1946) and *The Untouchables* (1948), he, by analysing the historical roots of untouchability, argued that it was not integral to Hindu society but had evolved in a specific historical context when Buddhism declined and tendencies supportive of socio-economic discriminations gained wider acceptance. So, special constitutional protection to the untouchables, felt Ambedkar, would enable them 'to return to that primary equality that was the original historical condition' in which discrimination was an anathema.[53] Implicit here is also the assumption that discriminatory constitutional protection is purely an enabling device which will become defunct once the mindset supportive of equality, in its substantial sense, is well-entrenched in Hindu society. As a rebel-liberal who hardly conformed to the conventional way of thinking, the aim of Ambedkar

[52] Ibid, 352–58. For a detailed analytical discussion of Ambedkar's argument in favour of the claim for Pakistan, see Partha Chatterjee, 'The Nation in Heterogeneous Time,' *Indian Economic and Social History Review* 38, no. 4 (2001): 414–15.

[53] Partha Chatterjee pursues this argument in his *The Politics of the Governed: Reflections on Popular Politics in Most of the World* (New Delhi: Permanent Black, 2004), 13–15.

was, in other words, to resort to group-differentiated rights simply as a device to support his mission of creating a true liberal society based on equal citizenship.

Constitutional Liberalism and the Making of India's Constitution

B. R. Ambedkar was a liberal rebel who flourished and stuck to his gun despite the Gandhian hegemony in the nationalist thinking. A dissenter of Gandhi's views, he vehemently criticized Gandhi's argument for self-dependent village Swaraj since (a) it was inadequate to rejuvenate India as an independent polity and (b) it had obvious structural limitations in view of the well-entrenched caste prejudices in Indian villages. While denouncing the proposal to make the village the basic unit of governance, he argued that

> it is said that the new Constitution should have been drafted on the ancient Hindu model of a state and that instead of incorporating Western theories the new Constitution should have been raised and built upon village panchayats and district panchayats. ... They just want India to contain so many village governments. The love of the intellectual Indian for the village community is of course infinite if not pathetic. ... I hold that the village republics have been the ruination of India. I am therefore surprised that those who condemn provincialism and communalism should come forward as champions of the village. What is the village but a sink of localism, a den of ignorance, narrow mindedness and communalism? I am glad that the Draft Constitution has discarded the village and adopted the individual as its unit.[54]

As is evident, Ambedkar was opposed to the very idea of village being a focal point of governance because he strongly felt that it was a source of oppression. Persuaded by Ambedkar's argument, Nehru too came out openly in his support by stating that 'a village, normally speaking, is backward intellectually and culturally and no progress can be made from a backward environment. Narrow-minded people are much

[54] B. R. Ambedkar's statement in the Constituent Assembly, 4 November 1949; B. R. Ambedkar, *The Constituent Assembly Debates*, Vol. VII (New Delhi: Lok Sabha Secretariat, 2003), 38–39.

more likely to be untruthful and violent'.[55] Being supported by Nehru, Patel and other leading Congressmen in the Assembly, it was easier for Ambedkar to persuade the members. In contrast with Ambedkar's arguments in favour of individual-driven constitution, there were leading Gandhians who built their arguments around Gandhi's ideas. A wide spectrum of members supported the Gandhian argument in favour of a state constituted of self-sufficient village republics.

The perusal of the debates in the Assembly reveals that it was divided between Ambedkar and his supporters and those who held contrasting Gandhian views. The draft constitution had, A. C. Guha held, 'no trace of Congress outlook, no trace of Gandhian social and political outlook'.[56] Ambedkar was criticized as in his long speech in the Assembly, he had 'found not occasion to refer to Gandhiji or the Congress', as Arun Chandra Guha, one of the prominent members who came from West Bengal, strongly felt which he substantiated further by saying that 'the whole Constitution lacks in Congress ideal and Congress ideology particularly'.[57] Insisting that 'the future constitution of India should be a pyramidal structure based on the village panchayat', Guha further argues that since the idea of village panchayats was the Congress ideal, and it should be respected. For T. Prakasam, another member from Madras, it was expected of Ambedkar who 'had been attacking the whole system and programme of Gandhi and Congress all his life-time'.[58] In one stroke, [he], felt Prakasam,

> condemned the village panchayat [though] he has referred one great man of those old days of the British, Mr. Metcalfe, and the description given by him that the village panchayats existed and continued whatever may have been happening with regard to the Government at the top; whoever may have come and whoever may have gone, they did not concern themselves.

[55] Jawaharlal Nehru to Gandhi, 9 October 1945; *A Bunch of Old Letters (written mostly to Jawaharlal Nehru and some written by him)* (Delhi: Oxford University Press, 1988), 508.

[56] *Constituent Assembly* (*CA* hereafter) *Debates*, Vol. VII, 4/11/1948–8/1/1949, p. 255, the statement of Arun Chandra Guha, 6 November 1948.

[57] Ibid.

[58] Ibid, 259, the statement of T. Prakasam, 6 November 1948.

> It is not a matter which should have been treated by Dr. Ambedkar in that manner. That was a condition to which we have been reduced, after the village panchayats had been exhausted on account of the oppression of the various foreign rulers who had come over to this country. Still in spite of all that been done for their suppression, they survived. That is what Metcalfe wanted to explain to the world and to us who have been ignoring it. Therefore village panchayat is not to be condemned on that basis.[59]

While reiterating Prakasam's views, Guha further pursued the point by saying that the problems that appeared to have crippled villages were largely the creation of foreign rule which led to a condition whereby 'our villages have been starved; or villages have been strangled deliberately by the foreign government; and the townspeople have played a willing tool in this ignoble task'.[60] Hence he recommended that 'resuscitating of the villages … should be first task of the future free India … to create an India … according to the Gandhian outlook and the Congress outlook'[61] and village panchayats needed to be revitalized because, as he believed, 'if we can build the whole structure on the village panchayats, on the willing cooperation of the people then [he felt that] the centre would automatically become strong'.[62] In his opinion, India's salvation lay on 'a pyramidal structure [of governance] based on the village panchayats'.[63] Guha pursued the point forcefully by making two arguments in his favour: first, he felt the importance of the constituent units for a strong centre. As he argued,

> we cannot have a strong Centre without strong limbs. If we can build the whole structure on the village panchayats, on the willing cooperation of the people, then I feel the Centre would automatically become strong; [hence he urged the Assembly] to incorporate some clauses so that village panchayats may be allowed to play some effective part in the future administration of the country.[64]

59 Ibid, 257–58.

60 Ibid, 256, the statement of Arun Chandra Guha, 6 November 1948.

61 Ibid.

62 Ibid.

63 Ibid.

64 Ibid.

Second, while critiquing Ambedkar's defence for making individuals as the basic political units, Guha insisted that

> the villages should be the real basis of the machinery [because] individual is the soul of the whole constitution; given the [fact] that the villages remain the basic units of human settlement in India [they] should be made the basis of the machinery of [India's] administration.[65]

Critical here is the point that the Gandhians made in contrast with what Ambedkar proposed, by forcefully arguing to make the village panchayats as the basic units of the independent India's administration because (a) it was a Gandhian ideal and (b) they always remained integral of local governance. In tune with Prakasam, N. G. Ranga from Madras began his critique by criticizing B. R. Ambedkar in strong terms; he mentioned that he was

> most unhappy that Dr. Ambedkar should have said what he has said about the village panchayats. All the democratic tradition of our country has been lost on him. If he had only known the achievements of the village panchayats in Southern India over a period of millennium, he would not have said those things. If he had cared to study Indian history with as much care as he seems to have devoted to the history of other countries, he certainly would not have ventured those remarks.[66]

Critical of the centralization of authority which would lead to 'Sovietization and totalitarianism and not democracy', Ranga was in favour of panchayat-based governance because it would enable 'the villagers to gain as much experience in democratic institutions as possible in order to be able to discharge their responsibilities through adult suffrage in the new democracy that we are going to establish'.[67] As a hard-core Gandhian who was committed to decentralization, he found the panchayats as nurseries of democratic governance. Hence he recommended that

[65] Ibid.

[66] *CA Debates*, Vol. VII, 4/11/1948–8/1/1949, p. 350, the statement of N. G. Ranga, 9 November 1948.

[67] Ibid.

> it is the duty of the State to establish village panchayats in every village or for every group of villages in order to help our villages to gain training in self-government and also to attain village autonomy in social economic and political matters, so that they will become the foundation stone for the top structure of our Constitution.[68]

Being a Gandhian, R. K. Sidhwa, from Central Provinces and Berar, also stressed the importance of strengthening the local bodies, especially the village panchayats, in making India a strong and stable democracy. He, however, believed that 'unless economic conditions are considered equitably, the measure like the Gram Uddhar (village uplift) is not going to prove any use or be successful'.[69] It was appalling that 'local bodies suffer from insufficiency of money and when they approach the Provincial Government, the Provincial Governments express their inability to help them on the ground that the Central Government does not contribute them the money that is due to them'.[70] What was thus required was to give them enough financial support to make them effective instruments of localizing governance. In his words, he thus exhorted that 'local bodies are the root, the basis of our economic conditions in India and unless the better financing of the villages is properly considered and enough money is given to them, [he strongly felt that], average citizen cannot be happy and prosperous'.[71] The draft Constitution lacked serious initiatives to revamp these local authorities which

> are in a very peculiarly miserable conditions [because] the Centre has been made too strong and … provinces have themselves, in the intoxication of power taken away the powers of the local bodies and in the name of mal-administration today more than 50 per cent of the local bodies have been superseded by Provincial Governments.[72]

[68] Ibid, 351.

[69] *CA Debates*, Vol. I, 9/12/1946–23/12/1946, p. 335, the statement of R. K. Sidhwa, 30 August 1946.

[70] Ibid.

[71] Ibid.

[72] *CA Debates*, Vol. VII, 4/11/1948–8/1/1949, p. 265, the statement of R. K. Sidhwa, 6 November 1948.

Due to their financial constraints, these local bodes failed to discharge their responsibilities. The Provincial Governments

> 'would not like to give them the electricity taxes, the entertainment taxes etc., which are the only sources of revenue for these local bodies in Western countries [while] here in India, all these taxes are grabbed by the provinces'. This has left the local bodies mere skeletons today. If this is the tendency, how can you expect the local bodies and villages to prosper?[73]

Once the local bodies lost their vitality, it would lead to collapse of the entire edifice of the constitution, as Sidhwa felt. Unless a direction was given in the Constitution to the Provincial Governments to make these bodies very useful organizations for the uplift of the villagers, he warned, 'this document is not worth presentation in the name of democracy'.[74] In his thinking, he also felt that without villages being financially self-dependent, the democratic aim of making every villagers regardless of gender integral part of administration would remain elusive. By referring to Vallabhbhai Patel's intervention in the Assembly where he exhorted that 'every villager must be made to understand that he is a responsible man or a responsible woman made to realize that he or she has got a share in the administration of the country', Sidhwa concluded that it was clearly unrealistic because 'if you ignore the villagers, the largest portion of the population, the fundamental ethos of democracy will remain unrealized'.[75]

While Sidhwa and Guha stuck to the Gandhian model since it would contribute to India's socio-economic well-being, K. Santhanam from Madras defended his argument while critiquing Ambedkar by reference to the historical role that the village panchayats had played in the sustaining India's civilizational bond. By saying that he did agree with Ambedkar's condemnation of the village panchayats and his statement that 'they were responsible for all the national disasters',[76]

[73] Ibid.

[74] Ibid.

[75] Ibid.

[76] *CA Debates*, Vol. VII, 4/11/1948–8/1/1949, p. 264, the statement of K. Santhanam, 6 November 1948.

Shanthanam justified his point by drawing on their role in preserving Indian life in different phases of her life despite political chaos. As he mentioned, 'in spite of revolutions and changes, [the village panchayats] have sustained Indian life and but for them India will be in a chaos'. Hence, he strongly recommended that

> some statutory provision had to be inserted regarding village autonomy within proper limits' [and] … all the provinces have to set up panchayats, their existence [need] to be recognized in the Constitution, for in the long run, local autonomy for each village must constitute the basic framework for the future freedom of this country.[77]

The voice was uniform: persuaded by the Gandhian idea of village republic, Guha, Prakasam, Sidhwa and Santhanam put a counter to what Ambedkar proposed to build his model of individual-centric liberal democracy. Aware of the fact that the size of the panchayats varied from one place to another, Santhanam thus suggested that it was not desirable to provide a uniform direction in the Constitution. As he stated, 'there may be very small hamlets which are so isolated and even for fifty families, we may require a village panchayat; in other places, we need to group them together so that they may form small townships and run efficient, almost municipal administrations'.[78] Since the variation was so stark, they 'must be left to the provincial legislatures' to decide what was most appropriate under the circumstances.[79] Nonetheless, he stuck to the point that village panchayats could not be done away with simply because they remained an important aspect of participatory democracy which the new constitution strove to inculcate. While concluding his defence, he thus argued that 'what is attempted to do here is to give a definite and unequivocal direction that the state shall take steps to organize panchayats and shall endow them with necessary powers and authority to enable them to function as units of self-government.'[80] Santhanam was led to believe

[77] Ibid.

[78] *CA Debates*, Vol. VII, 4/11/1948–8/1/1949, p. 520, the statement of K. Santhanam, 22 November 1948.

[79] Ibid.

[80] Ibid.

that localizing governance through panchayats was perhaps the best administrative option that could be dispensed with only to the detriment of fundamental Gandhian values which informed India's battle for freedom.

The battle line was therefore drawn because Ambedkar, Nehru, Patel and their colleagues did not seem to have been persuaded while the Gandhi followers remained adamant. An attempt was made to evolve a middle path when K. T. Shah (from Bihar) proposed an amendment to implement Panchayati Raj in a staggered fashion. It was therefore suggested that

> with a period not exceeding ten years of the date when this constitution comes into operation, the distinction or difference embodied in the several Schedules to this Constitution and in the various article that follow shall be abolished, and the number of States of the Union of India shall be organized on a uniform basis of groups of village Panchayats organized inter se, and functioning as democratic units within the Union.[81]

Shah was confident that in 10 years, the differences would be smothered away and a true democratic system was to emerge. As he elaborated,

> the ten-year period would be sufficient to readjust all differences in communications, transport and other common factors which at the present time do cause a great deal of variation, and, in my opinion, a great deal of hardship, impediments and heart-burning as between the various units.[82]

Shah's forceful argument in favour of the amendment failed to generate confidence among the majority of the Assembly members; it was defeated. Despite being critical of Ambedkar for being 'too pessimistic' since he believed that 'we can never reform villages and develop them for self-government',[83] M. Ananthasayanam Ayyangar from Madras opposed the amendment that Shah had proposed because, according

[81] *CA Debates*, Vol. VII, 4/11/1948–8/1/1949, p. 426, K. T. Shah's amendment no. 129 of 17 November 1948.

[82] Ibid, p. 427.

[83] *CA Debates*, Vol. VII, 4/11/1948–8/1/1949, p. 428, the statement of M. Ananthasayanam Ayyangar, 17 November 1948.

to him, 'we do derive all authority from the people who must be trained in the art of government and the responsibility must flow from them'.[84] In a similar vein, Shibban Lal Saksena of the United Provinces opposed the amendment by endorsing what Ayyangar had suggested. According to Saksena, village panchayats, despite being very useful forms of governance, might not be adequately equipped to address the difficulties that India as a new nation was likely to confront. Notwithstanding its conceptual salience, panchayat governance did not seem to be structurally fit to shoulder the huge responsibility in the wake of India's rise as an independent polity.[85]

As the Assembly debates reveal, the Gandhians did not seem to have created a strong opinion in favour of what held so dear to their heart. However, they did voice their discomfort, though it did not carry much weight except to articulate an alternative thought process that had its roots in Gandhian notion of village republics. Since the majority did not seem to have been convinced, the Assembly could have simply ignored these suggestions which would have severe political repercussion since it would have meant rejection of a powerful Gandhian ideal. Hence a compromise formula was worked out by incorporating the concern of the Gandhians into the chapter on the Directive Principles of State Policy which constituted an integral part of the non-enforceable part of the proposed Constitution. The two prominent members, Ayyangar and Ranga, thus proposed an amendment to the Directive Principles of State Policy to the effect that 'the State shall take care to see that village panchayats are reorganized and re-established everywhere, so that, as far as possible, in the interests of democracy, the villages may be trained in the art of self-government, even autonomy'.[86] Besides being forms of self-government, the village republics were also hailed as instruments capable of creating self-sufficient villages. In response to the sceptics who felt otherwise, V. Subramaniam of Madras mentioned that being

[84] Ibid, p. 429.

[85] *CA Debates*, Vol. VII, 4/11/1948–8/1/1949, p. 429, the statement of Shibban Lal Saksena, 17 November 1948.

[86] *CA Debates*, Vol. VII, 4/11/1948–8/1/1949, p. 428, the statement of M. Ananthasayanam Ayyangar, 17 November 1948.

self-sufficient never meant exclusion from the circle of villages which would exchange among themselves those items which they lacked. As he stated, a village

> may produce, say ground-nut in large quantities, and it may export it, even though it may be forced to import Dalda [saturated butter] and other substances for the needs of the people in the village. By saying that it is self-sufficient, we only mean that it may grow all the articles that it can and also import what is necessary from the neighbouring villages.[87]

Based on the concern for one another, the village republic would instil the idea of mutual cooperation as perhaps the most effective means of combatting crisis. In another respect, villages in the circle were to gain enormously out of exchange of experts in various fields of work. As Subramaniam explained,

> we do not know, for instance, how many carpenters are there in the country; if the names of the carpenters are listed in the panchayat office, we will have immediate access to that record and the we can supply carpenters to those villagers where there is none and less than what is required.[88]

Subramaniam drew on Gandhi's conceptualization of village republic while defending the idea of self-sufficient villages. Gandhi suggested a scheme whereby the villages, being a complete republic, were independent of its neighbours for its vital needs and yet interdependent for many others in which dependence was necessary. It was a different kind of socio-economic formation that Gandhi aspired to build in India to take care of India's obvious economic ills. Given the dominating presence of an all-pervasive state in the wake of colonialism that thrived on industrialization, the Gandhian argument was usually brushed aside as being archaic and an impediment towards progress. Insistence on village republic meant putting the cycle of history backwards. In response to a criticism that village republics were nothing but endeavours of bringing back the bullock-cart days, Prakasam rebutted by saying that

[87] *CA Debates*, Vol. VII, 4/11/1948–8/1/1949, p. 525, the statement of V. Subramaniam, 22 November 1948.

[88] Ibid.

> the village republic which is proposed to be established in the country and worked not a bullock cart village republic. The republic that would be established … would be a village republic which would use the bullock carts not for simply taking the fire-wood that is cut in the jungles to the towns and cities and getting some money for hire; these village republic would convert the work of the bullock cart to the work of carrying paddy and other produce which they produce in the village for their own benefit and for the benefit of the public.[89]

Apart from its contributing to self-sufficiency in Indian villages, these village republics also played a critical role in creating and also consolidating an idea of united India since they nurtured a sense of belongingness. In other words, they helped create an identity which ran through all the village republics, despite being physically separate for obvious reasons, by virtue of being ideologically inspired by Mahatma's idealism. This was reverberated when Surendra Mohan Ghose (from West Bengal) conveyed that 'every village like the organic cells of our body was given full freedom to express itself but at the same time with that freedom they were to work only to maintain and preserve the unity of India'.[90] In a different way, V. I. Muniswamy Pillai of Madras expressed the same sentiment. According to him, the suggestion of making villages integral partners to India's growth as a strong nation state remained futile unless they were given substantial authority. Unlike the Gandhians who held a romantic view about Indian villages, Pillai was far more realistic in his assessment when he mentioned that 'villages are in rack and ruin'.[91] Nonetheless, he was willing to make them stand on their own which was explicit in his statement that 'if there is to be any amenities or self-government, it is to the villages that the Sovereign Body must give them'.[92] 'More powers to be given to them [and] they serve a very useful purpose in

[89] *CA Debates*, Vol. VII, 4/11/1948–8/1/1949, p. 522, the statement of T. Prakasam, 22 November 1948.

[90] *CA Debates*, Vol. VII, 4/11/1948–8/1/1949, p. 523, the statement of Surendra Mohan Ghose, 22 November 1948.

[91] *CA Debates*, Vol. VII, 4/11/1948–8/1/1949, p. 524, the statement of V. I. Muniswamy Pillai, 22 November 1948.

[92] Ibid.

developing the country as a whole,'[93] Pillai concluded. Two important ideas seem to have bothered the Assembly members: on the one hand, given the centralized bias of the proposed constitution, they were not persuaded to accept that mere constitutional reference was not enough; only substantial authority could make the village panchayats effective instruments of rural empowerment. They also felt, on the other hand, that without adequate financial support, the idea of village republic merely remained cosmetic!

Concluding Observations

Despite being appreciative of liberalism, Ambedkar and Gandhi articulated their respective ideological predispositions in two contrasting perspectives. For Gandhi, village republics were the vehicle for salvation regardless of one's socio-economic location while, according to Ambedkar, they epitomized instruments of atrocities and degradation. What ran through the debates in the Constituent Assembly over whether village republics were appropriate for newly emerged democratic India was governed by these different ideological proclivities. Two important ideas of participatory democracy and localizing governance seem to have shaped the tenor of the arguments that the Assembly members offered. At one level, there were hardly disagreements because the Assembly members were unanimous in their support for participatory democracy. Adult suffrage was thus readily accepted. At another level, dissension surfaced when a group of Assembly members, especially the Gandhians, insisted on making the villages as the basic units of governance. While seeking to substantiate their points of view, they drew on what Mahatma has said. They were persuaded to believe that with villages being the basic units of administration, the state could not only be well-equipped to discharge its responsibility efficiently, but could also enable the people to get connected with others by virtue of being integral to the oceanic circle. Organically linked, such an administrative set-up would create an environment of mutual give-and-take which would ensure and also strengthen, on the one hand, the communal bond among the villagers

[93] Ibid, 525.

and make the state accountable, on the other, given the powerful voice that the villagers would generate by virtue of being united. This was also a model of social engineering since through intensive social interaction most of the forces alienating one community from another were likely to lose steam in course of time. It was therefore not odd when L. Krishnaswami Bharati of Madras expressed his sentimental attachment with Gandhi's belief by exhorting that

> in my opinion, it is very necessary that this sovereign body [Constituent Assembly] should enunciate and give its views on the fundamental tenet of Mahatma Gandhi, his idea being that there must be decentralization and the village must function as an economic unit [because] ... India dies if villages die, India can live only if the villages live.[94]

As argued, Ambedkar, the chairman of the Drafting Committee did not seem persuaded by this argument because of the prevalence of caste brutality in villages which he suffered himself all through his life. He thus felt that the arguments in favour of making villages as basic units of governance were supportive of the continuity of rigid caste system, which was simply not acceptable in democratic India. Condemning the villages 'as dens of ignorance, brutality and oppression', Ambedkar took up the cudgels against the Gandhians that majority of his colleagues in the Assembly endorsed. Besides his unhappy past when he witnessed the brutal manifestation of caste bias, the influence of John Dewey, his teacher at Columbia University, cannot be ignored. It was Dewey who persuaded him to believe that individual-centric liberalism was an effective instrument to combat social prejudices.[95] Being appreciative of Dewey's insistence on individual as the basic unit of governance, 'a rebel-liberal' thus charted a different path for India's constitutional history to adopt in the Gandhian universe.

There is an issue here: did Gandhi support caste atrocity? One may get the impression that with his strong argument in favour of village republics, the Mahatma seem to have underplayed the aspect of village

[94] *CA Debates*, Vol. VII, 4/11/1948–8/1/1949, p. 527, the statement of L. Krishnaswami Bharathi, 22 November 1948.

[95] B. R. Ambedkar, 'B. R. Ambedkar and the History of Constitutionalizing India,' *Contemporary South Asia* (Oxford: Taylor & Francis, forthcoming).

life that Ambedkar had highlighted. A careful reading of the ideas that Gandhi put forward while elaborating his idea of village Swaraj, however, reveal otherwise. In an unambiguous way, he delved into this issue in his text in *Harijan* where he strongly argued that 'there will be no castes such as we have today with their graded untouchability [and] nonviolence with its techniques of Satyagraha will be the sanction of the village community'.[96] This was a categorical statement. He, in fact, suggested non-violence challenge to those holding caste prejudices which would not, however, disappear overnight; hence he was in favour of a sustained struggle to combat and finally kill the mindset supportive of artificial social distance due to the accident of birth. As part of his social engineering, he also insisted that villagers needed to take up those works which were traditionally given to the untouchables. In his words, 'any lover of true democracy and village life can take up a village [and] treat it as his sole world [where] … he begins by being the village scavenger, spinner, watchman, medicine man and school master all at once'.[97] Reverberating the sentiment that John D. Ruskin articulated while arguing for dignity of labour, Gandhi too found the idea most appropriate to frontally attack caste prejudices. Once the dignity of labour was appreciated, the Mahatma felt, the villagers would come to terms to the fact that they were the same insofar as work for the village improvements was concerned. This would unleash a process whereby there would emerge a sense of unity and fraternity among the villagers who would condemn and denigrate those having caste prejudices. This was easier said than done, as Mahatma was aware given the well-entrenched, age-old social predispositions. Nonetheless, he was confident that constant social communications among the villagers as participants in activities pertinent to common well-being were likely to contribute to the processes of change which were inconceivable when he articulated these ideas in the context of the nationalist movement perhaps due to the prevalent circumstances.

[96] M. K. Gandhi, 'Village Swaraj,' *Harijan*, 26 July 1942, reproduced in M. K. Gandhi, *Village Swaraj* (Ahmedabad: Navajivan Publishing House, 1962), 31.

[97] Ibid, 32.

It is true that the Gandhians lost and individuals became the basic units of governance, as Ambedkar preferred. Nevertheless, the founding fathers left a space for these Gandhian ideas to strike roots by incorporating Article 40 in the final document. Here the Assembly members seem to have been unanimous in their perception because they were aware that the constitution, in order to remain relevant in the days to come, needed to be accommodative of newer demands to sustain being democratic and inclusive in its character. Jawaharlal Nehru expressed this sentiment most explicitly when he exhorted his colleagues to remain united for protecting 'the basic democratic nature' of the constitution. As he unambiguously stated that,

> so far as the basic nature of the Constitution is concerned, it must deal with the fundamental aspects of the political, the social, the economic and other spheres, and not with the details which are matters for legislation. You will find if you go into too great detail and mix up the really basic and fundamental things with the important but nevertheless secondary things, you bring the basic things to the level of secondary things too. You lose them in forest of detail. The great trees that you should like to plant and wait for them to grow and to be seen are hidden in a forest of detail and smaller trees.[98]

This was a clearly stated position that Nehru held while endorsing the fundamental values that the Constitution of India sought to achieve. He left the space open for future generations to work on the details to accomplish the constitutional goals that the founding fathers had preferred. As a living organism, the constitution needed to be responsive, which he articulated by saying that

> a Constitution is something which should last a long time, which is built on a strong foundation, and which may, of course, be varied from time to time—it should not be rigid—nevertheless, one should think of it as something which is going to last, which is not a transitory Constitution, a provisional Constitution, a something which you are going to change from day to day, a something which provisions for the next year or the year after next and so on and so forth.[99]

[98] *CA Debates*, Vol. VII, 4/11/1948–8/1/1949, p. 589, the statement of Jawaharlal Nehru, 25 November 1948.

[99] Ibid.

The idea is very clear. Nehru tackled the dissension at two levels: at one level, he, by referring to the basic nature of the Constitution, upheld the importance of fundamental constitutional ideals which remained sacrosanct even in the years to come. The nationalist movement was directed to achieve democratic form of governance to articulate popular aspirations. Seeking to involve people in governance, the Constitution makers remained committed to this ideal which was never compromised. At another level, he allowed the future generations to accommodate the newer popular aspirations to sustain participatory democracy that the founding fathers so assiduously sought to build at the dawn of India's rise as an independent polity. Futuristic in his vision, Nehru can thus be said to have laid the foundation of a system of governance that was rooted in his urge for participatory democracy. In other words, he might have endorsed what Ambedkar stood for in the Assembly debates by supporting the liberal faith in individualism, though he prepared the ground for decentralization of authority by insisting on the basic nature of the Constitution. Implicit in his argument was the idea that democracy needed to be reinvented to retain its vitality; otherwise, it would become a mere structure of governance without much substance.

Notwithstanding his political thinking, the idea that became synonym to Ambedkar's thought could undoubtedly be said to be that of social justice. Unsurprisingly, Ambedkar was a protagonist of the idea of social justice as an inalienable part of the constitutional democratic framework in India. Conceptually, social justice apparently refers to a distinct aspect of the socio-economic and political system of the country through which concerted and coordinated measures are initiated aimed at ameliorating the disadvantaged position of the depressed classes in society. Ambedkar was of the firm opinion that the provisions for securing only political justice would not suffice to bring about the desired level of socio-upliftment of the untouchables so as to enable them to enjoy a life of social equality in the country. Hence, he vehemently argued for the idea of social justice as the complex and comprehensive set of socio-economic and political preferential and supportive policy measures to uplift the status of depressed classes in society. A unique point of the notion of social justice as propagated by

Ambedkar was his insistence on providing statutory basis to such measures so that they become the policy compulsion of the government and do not remain in the nature of altruistic favours being extended to the depressed classes. Ambedkar's basic concern in arguing for the notion of social justice seems to be his perceptible understanding of the nature of social inequality in India under which the dominant social relations tried to perpetuate it as some sort of natural and logical inequality requiring no corrective measures on the part of the larger society for its eradication. There is a wider concern that is visible in Ambedkar's sociopolitical design for governance. His ultimate goal was to achieve human emancipation which was not possible in view of the well-entrenched prejudices nurtured by the caste Hindus in the then India. While devising his constitutional design he made a significant conceptual contribution to our understanding of social justice. To firmly establish his point, he made a distinction between 'the freedom of the country' and 'the freedom of the people'. Conflating the two was, according to him, misleading. As he elaborated,

> for words such as society, nation and country are just amorphous if not ambiguous terms. There is no gainsaying that "nation" though one word means many classes. Philosophically, it may be possible to consider a nation as a unit but sociologically it cannot but be regarded as consisting of many classes and the freedom of the nation, if it is to be a reality, must vouchsafe the freedom of the different classes comprised in it, particularly of those who are treated as the servile classes.[100]

Social justice cannot thus be secured by the freedom of the country since it may continue with the same kind of sociopolitical and economic interrelationships among the citizens. Hence, for Ambedkar, it was an eyewash for freedom in its genuine sense. This is one powerful exposition of the idea of social justice. The other aspect was articulated when he categorically suggested that genuine freedom of the people remained elusive so long as economic democracy was not established. In his speech before the Constituent assembly on 25 November 1949, he was little uncertain regarding the future of constitutional democracy

[100] Moon, *Dr. Babasaheb Ambedkar Writings and Speeches*; Ambedkar, *Mr. Gandhi and the Emancipation of the Untouchables*, Vol. 9, p. 444.

in India as political democracy (one-man one-vote) was not accompanied by economic democracy. He clearly brought out this concern when he wrote that

> what vitiated parliamentary democracy is the failure to realize that political democracy cannot succeed where there is no social and economic democracy … [which] … are the tissues and fibre of a political democracy. The tougher the tissue and the fibre, the greater the strength of the body.[101]

Even the Western democracies had failed to creatively blend political democracy with economic democracy. The result was disastrous, Ambedkar exhorted which he articulated by saying that

> parliamentary democracy developed a passion for liberty. It never made even a nodding acquaintance with equality. It failed to realize the significance of equality and did not even endeavour to strike a balance between liberty and equality with the result that liberty swallowed equality and has made democracy a name and a farce.[102]

Implicit in this caustic remark was his concern to realize democracy in its true spirit and texture. Based on his existential experience as a Dalit in India and also how Western democracies functioned when he visited the USA and later UK, he was convinced that a mere structure of parliamentary democracy was not adequate to realize human emancipation. Despite being emphatic in his appreciation for the 1950 Constitution of India, he also apprehended whether this was enough to bring about the required socio-economic and political changes appropriate for building a society free from caste prejudices. Nonetheless, he defended a codified set of rules, supported by the court of law being authorized to intervene in case of contravention of these rules. The idea is very clear: an institutionalized system of rules and regulations needed to be put in place to generate constitutional morality which Babasaheb always valued. For him, 'constitutional morality is essential for the maintenance of a constitutional form of government'.[103]

[101] Ibid, 447.

[102] Ibid.

[103] Ibid, 444.

He further argued that by consolidating constitutional morality, which means the habit of being respectful to the codified rules and regulations or strict adherence to them, the edifice of constitutional democracy grew stronger. So, the purpose was to build a strong constitutional government, the continuity of which was dependent on, as per Babasaheb, the creation of a socio-ideological environment in which constitutional rules and regulations reigned supreme.

To Ambedkar, the operationalization of the idea of social justice could be carried on by putting in place a set of constitutional provisions in the nature of both protective and promotional measures. His long-standing demand for an autonomous political representation of the disadvantaged groups in the political institutions of decision-making in the country was to be the major move towards securing social justice. For this, he attempted to provide for an elaborate scheme of definitive political safeguards for depressed classes[104] in the Constitution of India. He was sure that such provisions would enable the depressed classes to conceptualize their common problems and issues in the larger perspective of their all-round development and seek appropriate solutions for them in a formidable manner. Along with distinct and autonomous political representation of the depressed classes in the institutions of Indian polity, Ambedkar also argued for reservation for the depressed sections of society in public employment provided their eligibility for a particular job is complete. In advocating the reservation in public employment, Ambedkar presumably envisioned that such a move would serve two utmost purposes instrumental in securing a comprehensive amelioration in the conditions of the disadvantaged groups of people. First, with the increase in their share in public services, a wider majority of people belonging to the depressed classes would gain social recognition and some degree of preponderance in social relations given the overwhelming status, prestige and power the public services in the feudal mindset of the majority section of Indians. Second, such an assured employment would probably also contribute to the economic upliftment of the depressed groups as regular and fairly sufficient source of income

[104] See, Rodrigues, *The Essential Writings*, 369–81.

in a family might add to the amelioration in the hitherto miserable economic conditions of the family. Thus, combined together, the idea of reservation in public services was considered to be a crucial component in the scheme of social justice envisioned by Ambedkar for the depressed sections of Indian society.

Reiterating the infallible claim of the depressed classes for preferential treatment in various spheres of socio-economic and political life in the country, Ambedkar showed an enormous degree of valiance by conceptualizing preferential measures within the framework of inclusive conception of rights. Such a conceptualization became quite significant ostensibly due to the fact that the preferential treatment to the disadvantaged sections need not be construed as reflection of the benevolence of majority, a viewpoint quite probable given the reticence of such people in accepting the rational imperative of the policy. Moreover, he argued that such a conceptual understanding of the notion of preferential treatment would inspire the depressed classes to fight for these measures if the government showed any leniency in affording them to the people. Thus, it may be said to be a tribute to the conceptualization of social justice as the key element of emancipation of the depressed classes that the protective and promotional constitutional measures have come to be basic framework through which the disadvantaged groups of people are getting empowered and emancipated in the post-independent India.

Mohammad Ali Jinnah (1876–1948)

4

Reconfiguration and Reconceptualization of the Idea of India*

Introduction

Being a socioculturally diverse society, India is a natural habitat of multiple trends of thought. It does not therefore seem odd for the syncretic traditions to flourish along with the tendencies justifying the exclusive existence of a religiously segregated multitude. There are also ideas, widely accepted, which draw on thoughts seeking to creatively blend disparate sets of thinking. Fundamental here is the point that in India sociocultural ideas informing major ideological frameworks are uniquely multidimensional, which are articulated accordingly in the form of specific ideological responses. What is reinforced here is the idea that the contextual variations are certain to contribute to contrasting conceptual frameworks of thinking, shaping one's ideological inclinations. Implicit here is an argument defending the oft-quoted statement of Plato, who declared that every philosopher is a child of his time, which means that the context leaves an imprint in the ideas that gain momentum in particular circumstances. Based on this assumption of transcendental character, the chapter is directed to understand the counterarguments that Mohammad Ali Jinnah (1876–1948) offered while challenging Gandhi in the process of championing his belief of Hindus and Muslims being two distinctly separate nations in view of

* Written by Dr Bhuwan Kumar Jha, Assistant Professor in History at Satyawati College, University of Delhi with inputs from the author Bidyut Chakrabarty who acknowledges his help with deepest gratitude.

their varied religious affiliations. In this academic exercise, the chapter would also engage in unravelling the moments of encounters between the two giants of Indian politics. It is true that Jinnah, also popularly known as Quaid-i-Azam in his later years, was the main architect of Pakistan, which was claimed to have formally appeared on the scene with the adoption of the 1940 Lahore Resolution. Nonetheless, it will also be a little simplistic to argue that Pakistan came into being just because Jinnah alone wanted and worked for it, or because the prevalent socio-economic milieu created an ambience in which separatist ideas gained an easy acceptance. It may be argued that advocating political and economic safeguards or even carving out exclusive communal constituencies represented the first or initial stage of demands that appeared to be working well for the Muslim leaders till at least 1937. However, demanding a separate homeland on the presumption of complete incompatibility of Hindus and Muslims was quite a different approach or ambition not witnessed anywhere else in the world. Articulated for the first time by the Muslim League in March 1940, the demand for a separate Muslim homeland seems to be little baffling since the proposed Muslim state was to be constituted only by the Muslims, with Bengal and Punjab leaving behind the vast population of Muslims not residing in these regions. As the available literature shows, the rise and consolidation of Muslim separatism and the campaign for Pakistan are largely attributed to the Hindu–Muslim socio-economic alienation due mainly to carefully nurtured processes segregating these two communities despite having been together for ages in the same social space. This is also to suggest that the partition was not merely engineered but was an offshoot of peculiar socio-economic circumstances in which the demand for sovereign Muslim state seemingly became the only choice. Two points merit attention here: on the one hand, it is now well established that the idea of Hindu–Muslim separate existence was primarily a context-driven phenomenon, since consciously nurtured prejudices created schisms that remained unbridgeable; the Hindu–Muslim socio-economic chasm, derivative of the contemporary socio-economic imbalances, led, on the other, to alternative, if not starkly contrasting, politico-ideological voices at the level of institutionalized politics which loomed large as the nationalist campaign progressed. So, the argument that the claim for Pakistan had clear socio-economic roots also leads to the argument that the partition of which Quaid-i-Azam was the most powerful votary was to some extent an offshoot of complex interplay of socio-economic forces. However, what is significant here is the point that it was easier for Jinnah to instantaneously build a powerful constituency for partition primarily because the circumstances, aided by the political turmoil of the time, were propitious for such a demand to strike roots. This is, however, not to undermine the contribution of the Quaid-i-Azam and his colleagues in evolving a conducive mindset among a large section of the Muslim population and leadership who became supportive of political mobilization for the cause.

There is another important point that deserves careful consideration. Jinnah and Gandhi were polar opposites in terms of the goals that they sought to achieve while pursuing their respective nationalistic zeal. Both of them devoted their energy to create independent nations: for Gandhi, it was united India, and for Jinnah, it was Pakistan which also meant the bifurcation of India, an endeavour which the former had never endorsed. Their conceptual commitment to nation formation took them to very different and opposite destinations: while Jinnah fought for the creation of Pakistan, Gandhi dedicated himself to the attainment of a united India. They were, in other words, radically different as far as their goals were concerned, and stretched their nationalistic argument in defence of their respective points of view. The chapter therefore makes two major arguments: first, Gandhi developed a template in which multiple nationalistic voices, leading to the evolution of a unified nation with different religious groups coexisting harmoniously, were articulated; being an erstwhile Congress loyalist (till at least 1920), Jinnah can be shown to have been at least partially persuaded (at least initially, and especially during the anti-Rowlatt protests) by what the Mahatma set out for anti-colonial sentiments to seep in among the participants challenging the British rule. Second, despite Gandhi being a dominant (and also mainstream) ideological force, the politico-ideological design that had emerged under his care was heavily influenced by the ideas that his nationalist colleagues evolved while seeking to carve out a space for themselves. So, the so-called Gandhian model of nationalism is a creative blending of multiple ideas striving to realize India's political salvation.

Conceptualizing Mohammad Ali Jinnah

Mohammad Ali Jinnah (M. A. Jinnah or simply Jinnah hereafter) is among the most discussed and debated characters in the history of modern South Asia. To the larger Indian audience, Jinnah remains an enigma, but to the state of Pakistan, he is not only seen as the founding father but also as its most legitimate and acceptable leader. While a portrait of Gandhi is seen donning the most sacred space in the government and official buildings in India, the same is true about Jinnah in Pakistan. Gandhi shaped country's destiny, based on his profound principles of Satya and Ahimsa, operating through the strategy of Satyagraha and *Sarvodya*. Ironically, Jinnah represented Gandhi's biggest failure whose uncompromising demand for a separate homeland, based on the pernicious principle of 'two-nation', denoted everything that he opposed. While Gandhi remained optimistic of placating Jinnah till the very end, even to the surprise of many close associates like Patel and Nehru, Jinnah hardly nursed any such misgivings, remaining terse and categorical in his demands and continuing to be bereft of emotions when he defined politics or circumstances:

> A "United India" means a Hindu-dominated India. It means that and nothing else. Any other meaning you attempt to impose on it is mythical. "India" is a British creation, it is merely a single administrative unit governed by a bureaucracy under the sanction of the sword. That is all. It is a paper creation, it has no basis in flesh and blood.[1]

The only apparent similarities between the two—a Kathiawari–Gujarati lineage, legal education in England and reverence for Gokhale—were simply too small to fathom the gulf that existed in terms of principles, temperament, attitude and commitment. In every department of life and worldview, they were diametrically opposite. Gandhi's constant coaxing of Jinnah to use Gujarati or Hindustani in his speeches, or to take to khadi or spinning, held no meanings for him. While for Gandhi the change to Western style or to the image of 'the English gentleman' was only temporary, for Jinnah 'anglicism was uninhibited

[1] Jinnah's interview to Beverly Nichols, 18 December 1943; Mehrunnisa Ali, ed., *Jinnah on World Affairs (Select Documents: 1908–1948)* (Karachi: Pakistan Study Centre, University of Karachi, 2007), 233.

and permanent'.[2] Hector Bolitho, among the earliest biographers of Jinnah, offered his assessment:

> the two men could not have been less alike: they clashed in mind, temperament and method. Gandhi, with what Jinnah described as his "vague philosophical absurdities", was a humanist.... His heart and his "soul-force" usually governed his actions and his reason. Jinnah shunned emotion, and sentimentality....[3]

Gandhi's politics banked on a profound belief in the innate virtues of every individual, including the perceived opponent(s). In his scheme of things, self-suffering, penance and soul-force constituted active ingredients to be deployed in modern politics. For him Ahimsa or non-violence was the creed of the brave and not of the weak. Jinnah was hardly excited by Gandhi's profound expositions. His politics was rooted firmly around constitution and parliamentary democracy—he was a 'quintessential constitutionalist'—a firm believer in getting his demands met through legal arguments. As time progressed and especially during 1940, while Gandhi continued to display strong faith in his deeply felt principles of Satya and Ahimsa Jinnah became cold and distant, approaching his task through one-track arguments.

What began merely as a difference in how the anti-imperialist struggle was to be led with Jinnah staunchly opposed to the idea of mass mobilization through the Non-cooperation movement, turned later into irreconcilable differences over the geopolitical map of the country. If Jinnah's fear during 1919–1920, of Gandhi challenging his leadership of the country's Muslims by leading them on the Khilafat issue and befriending the Ali brothers, was real, the fear of the Congress (and thereby the Hindus according to him) dominating the Muslims after the British left, was largely imaginary and constructed. If during the first stage of his clash with Gandhi (1919–1920), Jinnah was tentative and also somewhat confused, then during the last stage in the 1940s, he was assured and confident of what he was doing.

[2] B. R. Nanda, *Road to Pakistan: The Life and Times of Mohammad Ali Jinnah* (New Delhi: Routledge, 2010), 4.

[3] Hector Bolitho, *Jinnah: Creator of Pakistan* (Karachi: OUP, 2006), 63. [First published by John Murray (Publishers) Limited, 1954].

To the larger Indian audience, Gandhi was the harbinger of an inclusive society, the one, who till his last breathed at the altar of the Hindu–Muslim unity, but to Jinnah, he remained a great 'Hindu leader' bent upon bringing the massive Muslim populace under a 'Hindu Raj'. Jinnah reserved his choicest words for the Mahatma, for he (Gandhi) and his ideas constituted, under the circumstances then, his greatest stumbling block. He also claimed to see through Gandhi's words and tactics. In a conversation with Lord Ismay, few months after the partition, Jinnah dilated upon the 'wicked guile of Gandhi' who he felt was bent upon destroying Pakistan: 'In every one of his speeches there is a drop of poison. You, of course, can't detect this poison, but the Hindus for whose edification it is instilled, have no difficulty in grasping his meaning, and nor do I, who know him inside out.'[4] Even in his obituary on Gandhi's death, Jinnah retained his contempt towards the universalization of the Mahatma's character, and saw in his death, a loss for Hindus, and not for the nation:

> Whatever our political differences, he was one of the greatest men produced by the Hindu community, and a leader who commanded their universal confidence and respect. I wish to express my deep sorrow, and sincerely sympathise with the great Hindu community and his family in their bereavement at this momentous, historical and critical juncture so soon after the birth of freedom and freedom for Hindustan and Pakistan.[5]

In an interview with B. R. Nanda in 1967, Mountbatten recalled his interaction with Jinnah after he (Mountbatten) had arrived in India as the last viceroy in March 1947. He felt sure that no Muslim leader other than Jinnah could have achieved partition because 'it required an absolutely "disembodied" person who just could not be moved.... You can't argue with a man like that. That was his strength, and I don't think that anybody who did not know him would believe it.'[6] In its

[4] 'Ismay's record of his conversation with Jinnah', 3 October 1947; Ali, *Jinnah on World Affairs*, 561–66.

[5] Ali, *Jinnah on World Affairs*, 630–31.

[6] *Oral Transcript of Lord Mountbatten* (New Delhi: Nehru Memorial Museum & Library), 17.

obituary on the death of Jinnah, *The Times* assessed his attitude and strategy that stood in sharp contrast to that of Gandhi:

> Jinnah provided a striking contrast to Mahatma Gandhi. He lived in stately mansions, was tall and elegantly groomed, with a distinguished presence and fastidious tastes... There was nothing in him of the subtle flexibility of intellect which seems to the Englishman characteristic of the Hindu; all his ideas were diamond-hard, clear-cut, almost tangible. His arguments had none of the sinuosity of Hindu reasoning; they were directed, dagger-like, to the single points he was attacking. He was a formidable antagonist. The clear, cold courage which was the counterpart of his arrogance impelled him along his chosen course without a thought for the feelings of his opponents. His remarkable command of invective enabled him to be outrageously insulting in debate; but he was not thin-skinned, and was ready to take hard knocks as well as to give them.[7]

In the concluding lines of her 'poetical' assessment of Jinnah in September 1917, Sarojini Naidu predicted that 'he whose fair ambition it is to become the Muslim Gokhale may in some glorious and terrible crisis of our national struggle pass into immortality as the Mazzini of the Indian Liberation'. But far from being a Mazzini of the Indian liberation, Jinnah ended up becoming the chief instrument of its vivisection.[8] But for the millions of Muslims, Jinnah was the leader to be followed without asking any question. His suggestion was the command: 'To them, as an Englishman said, he was the King of England, the Prime Minister and the Archbishop of Canterbury rolled into one. For Muslims, he was like the Saladin of the age, the victor of Jerusalem, the defender of the oppressed.'[9] Even his peers in the Muslim League dare not dispute him or speak out of turn:

> Before any of his followers spoke, they would look to him, and if he nodded his head, they would speak... I tried the tactic of breaching the

[7] 13 September 1948, Saleem Qureshi, ed., *Jinnah: The Founder of Pakistan in the Eyes of His Contemporaries and His Documentary Records at Lincoln's Inn* (Karachi: OUP, 1998), 33–38.

[8] Mahomed Ali Jinnah, *An Ambassador of Unity: His Speeches & Writings 1912–1917* (Madras: Ganesh & Co, 1918), 20. (Pen Portrait of Jinnah by Sarojini Naidu).

[9] Akbar S. Ahmed, *Jinnah, Pakistan and Islamic Identity: The Search for Saladin* (London: Routledge, 1997), xi.

> Muslim League defences through them (like Liaquat Ali or Nishtar), but they wouldn't be drawn in the presence of Jinnah. It was quite clear that if I pushed them and they looked across to Jinnah, he would say "No", and call an end to my initiative.[10]

Whether Gandhi's failure in containing the Muslim separatism is up for a debate or whether the failure of the Congress in arriving at a 'settlement of the Hindu–Muslim question' is concerned, Jinnah and his incessant demand for a separate homeland emerges as the typical illustration to be cited. Very recently the issue of Jinnah's portrait donning one of the halls in the Aligarh Muslim University, or BJP leader L. K. Advani's visit to Jinnah's mausoleum in Karachi in 2005 and his subsequent statement about him, became huge controversies.

Jinnah's argument was primarily with Gandhi and the Congress Party and not Savarkar or the Hindu Mahasabha. The argument for nationhood for Muslims was conducted on the basis of regional majorities for Muslims in the north-west of India and in Bengal. Jinnah and Gandhi were lined up on opposite sides of the question of India's Partition. At the Wagah border which separates the Punjab in two halves, the portraits of Jinnah adore the entry to Pakistan and Gandhi is on the Indian side. This is unfair to Gandhi. He fought for the independence of the entire territory of pre-British India (and the princely states). He is the 'Father' of both nations rather than just one. No one on the Indian side, in Congress or outside, claims the fatherhood of the partitioned India. Partition is seen as having been imposed by the British incited by Jinnah or deliberately as part of the imperial strategy of 'Divide and Rule'. (Gandhi once famously said, 'We divide and they rule'.)

The Initial Years: Beginning of Anglicization

Just before Jinnah's birth, his family had settled in Karachi. Jinnah was the eldest of the seven siblings. This was a Khoja family of Shi'ite Muslims, claiming to be disciples of the Ismaili Aga Khan. But similar to many Muslim families of India, Jinnah's immediate ancestors,

[10] *Oral Transcript of Mountbatten*, 16.

informs Hector Bolitho, came of 'old Hindu stock'.[11] Sarojini Naidu called him 'Hindu by race and Muslim by religion'.[12] Early on in his life, Jinnah moved towards the Sunni sect of Islam.[13] His early education in Karachi was initially in the traditional Islamic system, and later through the modern Christian missionary English school. In between, to spend some time with the family of his affluent aunt Manbai (his father's sister) he travelled to Bombay, the city which eventually became the seat of his professional and political life.

The business of his father Jinnahbhai Poonja was taking off in the right earnest. It was around this time in 1892 that Frederick Leigh Croft of the Douglas Graham and Company, a leading British managing agency in Karachi, with which Jinnah's father had a close business association, visited his house. He recommended a young Jinnah for an apprenticeship in the company's home office in London, the proposal changing his life forever. With Jinnah determined to grab this opportunity, his mother insisted on him getting married before he left for England. Therefore, just before his departure in January 1893, at a tender age of 16 years, Jinnah was married off to Emibai, a distant relative and two years younger to him. But both his wife and mother passed away while Jinnah was in London. His wife he had hardly known, but his mother's death had a devastating impact on him.

Apprenticeship in accounts keeping and balance sheets was not something which could engage Jinnah for long. Therefore, few months after his arrival in London, he sought admission to Lincoln's Inn to pursue a career in law, the most cherished profession in those days. It was now that Jinnah's fate turned towards something big. While learning law, he acculturated English habits and also picked up a modern Western vocabulary. Lincoln's Inn was a hub of budding British politicians, a thriving centre of debate and discussions. His fascination for politics only grew further. The urge to fit in with the new place and

[11] Bolitho, *Jinnah: Creator of Pakistan*, 2.

[12] Jinnah, *His Speeches & Writings 1912–1917*, 3.

[13] Akbar Ahmed also informs that Jinnah's family traced its descent from Iran and reflected Shia, Sunni and Ismaili influences. Ahmed, *Jinnah, Pakistan and Islamic Identity*, 3–4.

an anglicized lifestyle made Jinnah drop 'bhai' from his name through a deed poll in 1894. So, the long spelling Mohammad Ali Jinnahbhai now became more British and more simple, M. A. Jinnah, a name that struck greater confidence in him.

It was in 1892 that Dadabhai Naoroji, the Grand Old Man of Indian politics, entered the British House of Commons on the Liberal party ticket through a keenly contested election. His victory meant an added interest for Indians in the contemporary British politics. Indian leaders back home, most of whom fancied themselves as Liberals, impressed as they were by the Liberal shift in politics, looked up to Gladstone, Ripon and John Morley for introducing greater reforms. John Morley's ideas influenced Jinnah too, and Morley soon came to occupy a place of hero in his mind.[14] On 9 August 1892, Jinnah listened raptly to Naoroji's maiden speech from the gallery of the House of Commons where he said:

> For the first time, during more than a century of settled British rule, an Indian is admitted into this House as a Member for an English constituency … it is the spirit of British institutions and the love of justice and freedom in British instincts which has produced this extraordinary result….[15]

Jinnah got a chance to assist Dadabhai for a brief period.

In June 1895, Jinnah applied for admission to the Bar, and a year later a largely transformed young man returned home. But Karachi hardly fascinated him now. So, stopping only briefly at his old home, he landed in Bombay, the city that eventually made him a politician—first a Moderate nationalist-cum-constitutionalist, then a leader seeking safeguard of Muslim rights, and finally an unflinching advocate of a separate homeland. His father Jinnahbhai Poonja had in the meantime suffered huge losses in his business. So, along with his children, the family moved to Bombay and rented an apartment in the Khoja neighbourhood. In Bombay, Jinnah never lived with his father or siblings and nor invited them to live at his house. His father did not live long. Of all his siblings, Jinnah grew fondest of his

[14] Stanley Wolpert, *Jinnah of Pakistan* (New York: OUP, 1984), 12.

[15] Bolitho, *Jinnah: Creator of Pakistan*, 9.

youngest sister Fatima—a relationship that lasted Jinnah's death and even beyond. Jinnah called her 'a bright ray of light and hope': 'She alone kept a place in his cautious affections, from the childhood days in Newnham Road, to the years of his triumph.'[16]

Politics Beckons Jinnah

Struggling to find his foot in the busy life of Bombay, Jinnah was determined to carve out his own space. The young barrister's initial years at the High Court are not chronicled clearly, but it is evident that he struggled to find legal briefs. It was in the year 1900 that his fortunes made upswings when he was invited by John Molesworth MacPherson, the acting Advocate General of Bombay, to work in his chambers. The concession, first of its kind ever extended to an Indian, brought to Jinnah 'a beacon of hope in the dark distress of his early struggles.'[17] His legal credentials received proper recognition when on the recommendation of McPherson he got hired to serve as a third presidency magistrate in a temporary capacity. However, after few months into the job, he concluded that the Bench was 'a much less attractive professional prospect than the Bar'. So even when he was offered a permanent tenure, and that too at a very attractive salary of 1,500 rupees a month, a seemingly confident Jinnah not only declined but also claimed that he would soon earn that much in a single day.[18]

At the dawn of the 20th century, Jinnah either did not voice his opinion prominently or refused to side with those Muslim politicians who saw the Indian National Congress as neglecting the interests of the Muslim community. He kept clear of the bid of some prominent Muslim leaders to meet Minto at Simla in October 1906 to seek concession and special arrangement for the community in return for its loyalty. He was also not part of the subsequent attempt of these leaders to form the Muslim League in Dacca two months later

16 Ibid, 14.

17 Sarojini Naidu in *Jinnah: His Speeches & Writings 1912–1917*, 4.

18 Wolpert, *Jinnah of Pakistan*, 17.

in December 1906. During these years, he was more influenced by the likes of Naoroji, Pherozeshah Mehta and Gokhale. During his early years at Bar in Bombay, he had also worked in Mehta's chamber. The Congress session in Bombay in 1904 was the first big major political conference in which Jinnah took part with Mehta as chairman of the reception committee. This session proved crucial in two ways. First, Jinnah came in contact with Gokhale who immediately cast a spell on him, so much so that he started nursing an ambition to become, in politics, a 'Muslim Gokhale'.[19] Second, Mehta proposed a lobbying mission to England the following year when the Liberals were likely to return to power. And along with Gokhale, already a prominent Moderate, he proposed Jinnah to be its member. Although this lobbying mission did not happen, it brought Jinnah to the limelight of the Congress and consequently the nationalist politics. In 1904 itself he also sought election to the Bombay Corporation.

Jinnah acted as secretary to Dadabhai Naoroji, president of the Congress in December 1906. Dadabhai had grown very weak. So, Jinnah assisted him in drafting his presidential speech. This speech called Bengal's partition a bad blunder and sought greater Hindu–Muslim unity which had been shaken by this decision. Jinnah, while opposing a resolution moved by a Muslim delegate seeking reservation for the educationally backward classes, advocated that there should be no reservation for any class or community. While still in Calcutta, he also criticized the formation of the All-India Muslim League as a separate political body and around the same time was elected vice-president of a newly formed rival organization—the Indian Mussalman Association. Jinnah left Calcutta, in the words of Stanley Wolpert, 'inspired with his mission of advancing the cause of Hindu-Muslim unity'. But, as Wolpert points out, he was 'politician enough' to understand that his only hope of succeeding his liberal mentors was 'by virtue of his secular constitutional national appeal' and 'not through his double minority status'.[20] He had, however, not annoyed the 'new

[19] Ibid, 20–21.

[20] Ibid, 27.

nationalist' or the 'Extremist' faction of the Congress led by Tilak. In 1908, when Tilak was arrested, charged with seditious writings, he hired Jinnah to plead for his release pending trial.

By 1909 Jinnah's growing political ambition saw him transform from opposing the principle of separate electorate outrightly to looking at this strategy as a possible solution to Muslim demands. Although not yet a strong votary of separate electorate, giving his opinion on Morley's scheme, he argued for an increase in Muslim representation from 25 to 33 per cent, and if this was not possible, then, he suggested, separate electorates presented a solution. In February 1909, for the first time, he attended a meeting of the council of the Muslim League. The Indian Councils Act of 1909 increased the number of seats in the Viceroy's Council to 60, out of which 27 were to be elected through provincial legislatures. Out of this number, six were reserved for Muslims, including one from Bombay. This was for the first time that few seats had been carved out exclusively on the basis of religious affiliation. As Hector Bolitho points out—'Jinnah's ascent to power began with this reform.'[21] He was elected to the newly constituted Imperial Legislative Council by the non-official Muslim members of the Bombay Legislative Council. It was the principle of communal electorate that had facilitated for him a prestigious seat in the Council. For the first time, he must have realized the political benefit of his Islamic religious identity. His entry to the highest legislative council of the land at Calcutta in January 1910 proved to be the beginning of his long innings in the lawmaking body that honed his skills as a politician and orator, fuelling further ambitions in his mind. In the esteemed company of such leaders like Surendranath Banerjee, Gokhale and Malaviya in the Imperial Council, Jinnah began his long public–political life.

Gandhi–Jinnah: The First Interactions

As a budding politician in the shadow of the likes of Naoroji, Mehta, Tyabji and Gokhale, Jinnah was sensitive to the developments in

[21] Bolitho, *Jinnah: Creator of Pakistan*, 42.

Transvaal. In a lecture on the 'Indians in Transvaal' in Bombay in July 1908 he denounced the draconian bill of the Transvaal government against which Gandhi had already launched Satyagraha. Describing the hardships brought upon the Indians there, he condemned these Acts as degrading, humiliating and insulting to any self-respecting man.[22] Subsequently, in the Imperial Legislative Council on 25 February 1910, the first time that he spoke here, was in a discussion on indentured labour. He even had a minor tiff with Minto, especially on the words that he chose to use. Jinnah looked at the whole issue as 'a most painful question—a question which has roused the feelings of all classes in this country to the highest pitch of indignation and horror at the harsh and cruel treatment that is meted out to Indians in South Africa.'[23]

The first interaction of Gandhi and Jinnah occurred soon after the former's return from South Africa. Presiding over a reception arranged by the Gurjar Sabha to welcome Gandhi on his return from South Africa (13 January 1915), Jinnah underlined that the greatest problem was 'to bring about unanimity and cooperation between the two communities' so that the demands of Indians could be made 'absolutely unanimously'.[24] After Jinnah and K. M. Munshi had taken their turn to speak, both in English, Gandhi in his characteristic style rose to speak in Gujarati. While in South Africa, Gandhi recalled, Gujaratis were always understood to refer to only the Hindu community. He was therefore glad to find that a function organized by the Gurjar Sabha was being chaired by a Muslim. Pointing to the statement of Syed Ahmad Khan where he had compared Hindus and Muslims as

[22] Ali, *Jinnah on World Affairs*, 61–62.

[23] Ibid, 62–63. Minto took exception to the use of word 'cruelty' to which Jinnah said that he had felt inclined to use 'much stronger language', but did not do so since he did not wish to trespass the constitution of the council. He reiterated that 'the treatment that is meted out to Indians is the harshest which can possibly be imagined, and, as I said before, the feelings in this country is unanimous.' See Bolitho, *Jinnah: Creator of Pakistan*, 43.

[24] Jaswant Singh, *Jinnah: India-Partition-Independence* (New Delhi: Rupa Publications, 2009), 100–01.

the two eyes of Mother India, Gandhi impinged upon the significance of communal unity.[25]

An early cause of difference arose over the language to be used in the conferences in speeches. While Gandhi was a strong votary of Gujarati and Hindustani, Jinnah would almost always prefer to speak and write in English. For Gandhi, it was not merely a question of the medium of communication, but of inculcating pride in one's one language for he thought that a long and durable challenge to colonialism could not be made in the language of the colonizer but by instilling pride in one's own mother tongue. But for Jinnah these arguments hardly held any meaning. Speaking in Gujarati at the Bombay Provincial Conference in Ahmedabad on 21 October 1916, Gandhi was only too happy to propose Jinnah's name for presidentship who, he felt held 'a respectable position' among both the Moderate and Extremist leadership: 'Our President, Mr. Jinnah, is an eminent lawyer; he is not only a member of the Legislature but also the President of the biggest Islamic Association in India. He has placed us under a great obligation by accepting the presidentship of this small conference.'[26] Gandhi wanted Jinnah to deliver his address in Gujarati; Jinnah obliged, but only for the first line—'Gentlemen, I am speaking today in Gujarati as ordered by Gandhiji. Having now made this part of my speech in Gujarati, gentlemen, I shall complete my speech in English.' Thereafter, Jinnah delivered his entire speech in English.[27] At the Muslim League conference at Lucknow in December 1916, Gandhi asked the organizers to conduct their proceedings in Urdu if they wished to carry out their resolution to maintain Urdu as the lingua franca of India. Simultaneously, he also urged them to take some interest in Hindi literature which, he felt, would enable them to arrive at a permanent rapprochement with the Hindus.[28]

[25] *Collected Works of Mahatma Gandhi* (*CWMG*), Vol. XIII (Delhi: Publications Division, January 1915–October 1917), 9–10.

[26] Ibid, 303–04.

[27] Sheela Reddy, *Mr and Mrs Jinnah: The Marriage that Shook India* (Gurgaon: Penguin Viking, 2017), 225.

[28] *Collected Works of Mahatma Gandhi*, Vol. XIII, 326.

In his speech at the Gujarat Political Conference in Godhra on 4 November 1917, Gandhi thanked Jinnah for moving the resolution on the Congress-League Scheme for Reforms in Gujarati and felt that he should learn the language fluently as it would help him in politics as well: 'He is at present a member of the Imperial Legislative Council. But, at no distant date, he will have to approach Hindus and Muslims, Ghanchis, Golas and others not knowing English, for votes. He should, therefore, learn Gujarati if he does not know it.'[29] However, this proved to be the only time that Jinnah obliged Gandhi on the language issue. But in spite of being rebuffed by Jinnah on several occasions, Gandhi in his characteristic style did not lose patience. In 1919, when Jinnah had travelled to England along with Ruttie who was expecting, Gandhi asked Jinnah to take up Gujarati and Hindi: 'May I then suggest that like Macaulay you learn at least one of these languages on your return voyage? You will not have Macaulay's time during the voyage, i.e. six months, but then you have not the same difficulty that Macaulay had.' As if this was not enough, he requested Jinnah to convey his wish to Ruttie that he expected her to join spinning class on her return to India.[30] A year later when Jinnah and his wife were holidaying in Ooty, Gandhi, who had by this time known Ruttie through Sarojini Naidu, a great friend of the Jinnahs, wrote to her directly—

> Please remember me to Mr. Jinnah and coax him to learn Hindustani or Gujarati. If I were you, I should begin to talk to him in Gujarati or Hindustani. There is not much danger of you forgetting your English or your misunderstanding each other. Is there? Will you do it? Yes, I would ask this even for the love you bear me.[31]

Ruttie also contributed to Gandhi's call for fund for setting up the Jallianwala memorial. Gandhi in turn appreciated her concern:

> I would have the future generations remember that we who witnessed the innocent dying did not ungratefully refuse to cherish their memory. As Mrs.

[29] *Collected Works of Mahatma Gandhi*, Vol. XIV (October 1917–July 1918), 68.

[30] Gandhi to Jinnah, 28 June 1919; Reddy, *Mr and Mrs Jinnah*, 226.

[31] Gandhi to Mrs. Jinnah, 30 April 1920; *Collected Works of Mahatma Gandhi*, Vol. XVII (February–June 1920), 361.

> Jinnah truly remarked when she gave her mite to the fund, the memorial would at least give us an excuse for living. After all it will be the spirit in which the memorial is erected that will decide its character.[32]

'Ambassador of Unity' or Advocate of Communal Electorate?

William Metz thinks that Jinnah first demonstrated his leadership skill in the cause of Hindu–Muslim unity through his interventions in the conference of Hindu and Muslim leaders held at Allahabad in 1910.[33] The moving spirit behind the show was the Congress president William Wedderburn. Although the conference did not make much headway in diffusing tensions arising from issues such as cow sacrifice, music before mosque, Hindi–Urdu, national education etc., Jinnah, acting as a 'cross-bencher', tried his bid.[34] Around the same time, at the Congress session in Allahabad, Jinnah moved a resolution disapproving extension of communal electorates to municipalities, district boards and such other local bodies.

Apart from issues involving Muslims specifically, Jinnah also took his turn to speak on or support important legislative measures. An important bill was moved by Gokhale in 1912 related to making elementary education compulsory. While supporting the bill on the floor of the Council in April 1912, Jinnah not only congratulated Gokhale for the services that he had rendered to the country but also prayed that country 'may have many more sons like him'. He underlined that elementary education had not become universal in any country without compulsion.[35] After 1909, be it the Congress sessions, unity conferences or debates in the legislative council, Jinnah made regular appearance at all such platforms.

[32] *Collected Works of Mahatma Gandhi*, Vol. XVII (February–June 1920), 408.

[33] William S. Metz, *The Political Career of Mohammad Ali Jinnah*, ed. Roger D. Long (Karachi: OUP, 2010), 13–14.

[34] Sarojini Naidu in *Jinnah: His Speeches & Writings 1912–1917*, 5–6.

[35] Jinnah, *His Speeches & Writings 1912–1917*, 197, 200.

Jinnah's maiden speech in the Congress was related to the Wakf-i-aulad.[36] It was this issue which he brought before the Imperial Legislative Council subsequently. On 17 March 1911, he introduced the Mussalman Wakf Validating Bill and steered it though two years later. It was primarily the successful passage of this private member's bill, which made 1913 'a distinct landmark' in Jinnah's life.[37] In April 1913, he moved the report of the Select Committee on this bill seeking 'to declare the rights of Mussalmans to make settlements of property by way of wakf in favour of their families, children and descendants'.[38] In the course of his argument, his emphasis that it is the Muhammadan law which should be administered to the Mussalmans must have been music to the ears of the Islamic orthodoxy. Going further, he announced loudly that 'there is no such thing as public policy of any kind, so far as Muhammadan jurisprudence is concerned…', [39] and in any case personal law of the Mussalmans was to be treated as the supreme law applicable to the community: 'I for one am not prepared to accept any provision which is in any way likely to overrule or affect the personal law of the Mussalmans.'[40] His taking up an exclusively Muslim cause with skills of a qualified barrister changed perception about him among co-religionists 'who while still regarding him a little outside the orthodox pale of Islam were so soon to seek his advice and guidance in their political affairs.'[41]

Affirmation of this subtle shift and Jinnah's wider acceptance among Muslims came when he formally joined the All-India Muslim League in 1913, an organization from which he had so far kept aloof. During mid-1912, the chief protagonists of the League met at Calcutta, where Jinnah was also present as a special invitee. This meeting decided to tweak the constitution of the League to bring in a streak of nationalism to it. The new draft was discussed in a meeting of the council of

[36] Sarojini Naidu in *Jinnah: His Speeches & Writings 1912–1917*, 5.

[37] Ibid, 10.

[38] Jinnah, *His Speeches & Writings 1912–1917*, 213.

[39] Ibid, 214.

[40] Ibid, 216.

[41] Sarojini Naidu in *Jinnah: His Speeches & Writings 1912–1917*, 6–7.

the League in December 1912 in Bankipur where Jinnah was again invited. He supported the following clause in the draft constitution:

> Attainment under the aegis of the British Crown of a system of Self-Government suitable to India through constitutional means, by bringing about, amongst others, a steady reform of the existing system of administration by promoting national unity, by fostering public spirit among the people of India, and by co-operating with other communities for the said purpose.[42]

In the League meeting at Lucknow on 22 March 1913, where Jinnah and Sarojini Naidu joined as honoured guests, the draft constitution was adopted. Shafi who presided over this meeting showed his agreement with Jinnah that adoption of a course other than that proposed by the council of the League would be unwise. Thereafter, the very first resolution of this largest political body of the Muslims congratulated Jinnah for his 'skillful piloting' of the Wakf Validating Act.[43] Cajoled by this newly found recognition and limelight, Jinnah yielded to persuasion by Mohammad Ali and Syed Wazir Hasan, while in England few months later, to formally enrol as a member of the Muslim League, but not before asserting his condition '…that loyalty to the Muslim League and the Muslim interest would in no way and at no time imply even the shadow of disloyalty to the larger national cause to which his life was dedicated.'[44] This, he may have felt, would enable him to continue to enjoy the leadership inside the Congress.

After his return from England, Jinnah attended the Karachi Congress in December 1913 wherein he seconded a resolution congratulating the Muslim League for adopting the ideal of self-government within the British Empire and for its declaration that the political future of the country depended on cooperation among various communities.[45]

[42] Ibid, 8–9.

[43] Wolpert, *Jinnah of Pakistan*, 34.

[44] In mid-April 1913, he had sailed for England along with Gokhale. In England, he founded the London Indian Association to organize young Indians there and at his instance, the India Office appointed a committee to look into the legitimate grievances of Indian students. Sarojini Naidu in *Jinnah: His Speeches & Writings 1912–1917*, 11.

[45] Wolpert, *Jinnah of Pakistan*, 35.

From Karachi, Jinnah went to Agra to attend the Muslim League session on 30–31 December 1913. He suggested postponement of League's reaffirmation of faith in the principle of communal representation by another year underlining that such special arrangement would divide the country into watertight compartment.[46] Majority of the League's members were, however, not on the same page and his appeal was rejected. Jinnah returned to England in May 1914 as the head of a Congress deputation in connection with the proposed Council of India Bill. Incidentally Gandhi was also present in England at this time. Jinnah attended the reception in honour of Gandhi held in a hotel in London.[47]

Early on in his legal–political career, Jinnah was open to the idea of a Hindu administrator governing a land with a Muslim majority. Appearing before the Islington Commission in March 1913, to a question whether he felt concerned under a system of simultaneous examinations where the backward communities would be at a disadvantage or whether a Hindu would be an efficient administrator of a population which was largely Mohammedan, Jinnah replied that getting 'competent men' was the priority and also he did not see any reason as to why a Hindu should not be incharge of a district where the majority happened to be Mohammedan.[48]

The years 1915–1916 stand out prominently in his career when Jinnah emerged as the most significant political voice of the Muslims, and as the one who was seeking rapprochement with the Congress on crucial issues concerning the country. During mid-1915, Jinnah wrote to the *Times of India* suggesting the Congress and the League meet to discuss the country's future and asking the Muslim leaders to move along with their Hindu friends.[49] Due to his efforts the annual session of the League was held alongside that of the Congress at Bombay in December 1915. On 30 December, prominent leaders of the Congress—Gandhi, Annie Besant and Sarojini Naidu visited the

[46] Ibid, 36.

[47] Ibid, 36–37.

[48] Singh, *Jinnah: India-Partition-Independence*, 72–73.

[49] Ahmed, *Jinnah, Pakistan and Islamic Identity*, 7.

League session and were welcomed.[50] With his popularity rising, the year 1916 held special significance for Jinnah. It began with his successful law suits—one involving his great friend, Horniman, the editor of the *Bombay Chronicle*, and another involving the great nationalist leader Bal Gangadhar Tilak. Then in autumn, he was once again elected to the Legislative Council on the Muslim seat from Bombay. However, the year had many more significant events to follow.

After a year of the semi-rapprochement of the Muslim League and the Congress in December 1915, Jinnah who became the president of the League in 1916 played his part in bringing the two parties to a historic pact at Lucknow in December 1916. He became president of the League again in 1920 and continued till 1930. After his sabbatical from politics, he again commanded the rein of the organization from 1937 right till the partition and creation of Pakistan. But before the story arrived at Lucknow in December 1916, the homework had begun at Allahabad in April where the Congress committee headed by Motilal Nehru met to discuss the proposed reforms with League leaders. The senior Nehru introduced Jinnah as 'unlike most Muslims…as keen a nationalist as any of us'.[51] The pact or the Congress-League proposals to be decided here was to be sealed at the joint meeting of the two parties which could then be sent to England.

It was in October 1916 in his long presidential address at the Bombay Provincial Conference in Ahmedabad that Jinnah made a categorical demand for separate electorate from a public platform. This marked a decisive shift from the position adopted earlier, say for example in 1913, where he had seen the idea of communal representation to be a divisive factor in the inter-community relationship. He now asked Hindus not to resist this demand of representation in various boards and council chambers through separate electorates which, he felt, was no more open to discussion:

> This question of separate electorates from top to bottom has been before the country ever since 1909 and rightly or wrongly the Mussalman community

[50] Bolitho, *Jinnah: Creator of Pakistan*, 60.

[51] Wolpert, *Jinnah of Pakistan*, 42.

> is absolutely determined for the present to insist upon separate electorates. To most of us the question is no more open to further discussion or argument as it has become a mandate of the community. As far as I understand, the demand for separate electorates is not a matter of policy but a matter of necessity to the Mahomedans who require to be roused from the coma and torpor into which they had fallen so long. I would therefore appeal to my Hindu Brethren that in the present state of position they should try to win the confidence and trust of the Mahomedans who are, after all, in the minority in the country. If they are determined to have separate electorates, no resistance should be shown to their demand.[52]

After the conference at Ahmedabad, Jinnah headed towards Calcutta where the Imperial Legislative Council was meeting for its winter session. With his draft ready, he met the Congress president A. C. Mazumdar in Calcutta in November. The AICC and the League representatives agreed to assure minimum Muslim percentage in the central and state legislatures, that is, one-third at the centre as well as in Bombay, half seats in the Punjab, 40 per cent in Bengal, 30 per cent in the United Provinces, one-fourth in Bihar and Orissa, and 15 per cent in the Central Provinces and in Madras. As an additional safeguard, the agreement provided that any bill or resolution introduced by a non-official member affecting a community shall not be proceeded with if three-fourths of the members of that community in that House were opposed to it.[53]

All his homework complete, Jinnah delivered his presidential address at the Lucknow session of the League. The speech was a mixture of commitment towards self-rule and political safeguards for Muslims. He saw in the Hindu–Muslim rapprochement effort of the last few years 'the first signs of the birth of united India.'[54] He advocated an attitude of 'good-will and brotherly feelings' towards the Hindus since India's real progress could only be achieved 'by a true understanding and harmonious relations between the two great sister

[52] Jinnah, *His Speeches & Writings 1912–1917*, 99–100.

[53] Wolpert, *Jinnah of Pakistan*, 46–47.

[54] Jinnah, *His Speeches & Writings 1912–1917*, 43.

communities.'[55] However, the underlying condition was the issue of political safeguard through assured representation:

> A minority must, above everything else, have a complete sense of security before its broader political sense can be evoked for co-operation and united endeavour in the national tasks. To the Musalmans of India that security can only come through adequate and effective safeguards as regards their political existence as a community…With the satisfactory solution of the most formidable problem that stood in the path of Indian progress towards political co-operation and unity, our constitutional battle may be said to have been half won already.[56]

The Congress, which also met in Lucknow few days before the League session, saw the homecoming of Tilak and his group. The atmosphere was suited to making pacts and agreements. Tilak announced that they were ready to 'make a common cause with any set of men.' Mazumdar informed that the meeting of the AICC and the League representatives at Calcutta had agreed to make a common demand. The deal almost sealed now was formally approved at the joint meeting of the Congress-League in Lucknow in December 1916. The Congress which was attempting to rejuvenate itself had now accepted the principle of separate electorate after years of opposition.

In a book published in the aftermath of the Lucknow Pact and towards the end of the First World War, *Mohomed Ali Jinnah: An Ambassador of Unity—His Speeches & Writings 1912–1917*, the sobriquet 'ambassador of unity', borrowed from Gokhale's prediction about Jinnah, was frequently used by Sarojini Naidu. The book had a 20-page biographical note or 'Pen Portrait' by her and a foreword by the rajah of Mahmudabad. The rajah was full of praise for Jinnah: 'The speeches reveal a study, in a spirit of abiding and inextinguishable faith, of the problems affecting the political destiny of India, of which no other worker among the Indian Mussalmans has so far given proof in an equal degree.'[57] Jinnah confessed that it was his ambition

[55] Jinnah also said, 'Co-operation in the Cause of Our Motherland Should Be Our Guiding Principle.' *Jinnah: His Speeches & Writings 1912–1917*, 59.

[56] Jinnah, *His Speeches & Writings 1912–1917*, 46–48.

[57] Ibid, xi.

to become the 'Muslim Gokhale'. Gokhale made his own prediction about Jinnah—'He has true stuff in him', and that 'freedom from all sectarian prejudice which will make him the best ambassador of the Hindu-Muslim Unity'.[58] Sarojini Naidu, confident that Gokhale's prediction about Jinnah had been proved right, made very eloquent appreciation of the man and his achievements. In her characteristic poetical style, she saw in Jinnah the 'paradox of a rare and complex temperament, of strange limitations and subtle possibilities':

> Never was there a nature whose outer qualities provided so complete an antithesis of its inner worth. Tall and stately, but thin to the point of emaciation, languid and luxurious of habit, Mohammad Ali Jinnah's attenuated form is the deceptive sheathe of a spirit of exceptional vitality and endurance. Somewhat formal and fastidious, and a little aloof and imperious of manner, the calm hauteur of his accustomed reserve but masks for those who know him, a naïve and eager humanity, an intuition quick and tender as a woman's, a humour gay and wining as a child's—Pre-eminently rational and practical, discreet and dispassionate in this estimate and acceptance of life, the obvious dainty and serenity of his worldly wisdom effectually disguise a shy and splendid idealism which is of the very essence of the man.[59]

Jinnah–Gandhi: Home Rule League or Swarajya Sabha?

Jinnah joined the Annie Besant group of the Bombay Home Rule League in 1917 and became its president. His joining the Home Rule movement was born out of his concern at Besant's interment during June 1917. A year later Gandhi advised Jinnah to make Home Rule League a potential recruitment centre for the British War efforts. This he believed will expedite acceptance of the Congress-League Scheme of reforms. He asked Jinnah to see the reason in such an appeal, advising him to make an emphatic declaration regarding recruitment:

> Can you not see that if every Home Rule Leaguer became a potent recruiting agency whilst, at the same time, fighting for constitutional rights, we would ensure the passing of the Congress-League Scheme, with only such

[58] Sarojini Naidu in *Jinnah: His Speeches & Writings 1912–1917*, 1.

[59] Ibid, 1–2.

> modifications (if any) that we may agree to? We would then speak far more effectively than we do today.[60]

Sheela Reddy thinks that Jinnah 'first became acquainted with Gandhi's peculiar views' when he requested Jinnah 'to turn his Home Rule League into a recruitment centre for soldiers for the War': 'It was difficult for Jinnah to take Gandhi seriously after that.'[61]

After Tilak's death, presidentship of the Home Rule League passed on to Gandhi. Sheela Reddy feels that Gandhi outmanoeuvred Jinnah as far as the Home Rule League was concerned. She points out that Jinnah invited Gandhi to take over the Home Rule League and Gandhi went about changing its constitution and name. In protest, Jinnah and 19 other co-signatories resigned from the Home Rule League. Gandhi wrote a long article with the title 'Swarajya Sabha' in *Navajivan* on 24 October 1920 outlining the reasons for this change. The term 'Home Rule', he clarified was a foreign name which could not represent our highest ideal:

> …The meaning, the force, to be found in "swaraj" are not present in "Home rule"…The aim, so far, was to secure Home Rule within the British Empire, like what the Colonies enjoy. Instead, the aim now will be to strive for swaraj of people's choice.[62]

Gandhi wrote that Jinnah, supported by Jayakar, had argued that (a) no amendment would be valid unless approved by a three-fourths majority, and (b) the clause defining the means to be employed for winning Swaraj lends itself to the interpretations that it permits the Swarajya Sabha to carry on unlawful activities. On the first, Gandhi argued that the rule of three-fourths applied to the council and not to the general body where a decision could be taken by a simple majority.

[60] Gandhi to Jinnah, July 4 1918; *Collected Works of Mahatma Gandhi*, Vol. XIV (October 1917–July 1918), 470. Gandhi again wrote to Jinnah on July 9 1918: '…What a proud thing it would be if we recruited and, at the same time, insisted on amendments in the Reform Scheme!', Gandhi to Jinnah, July 4 1918, *Collected Works of Mahatma Gandhi*, Vol. XIV (October 1917–July 1918), 479.

[61] Reddy, *Mr and Mrs Jinnah*, 223.

[62] *Collected Works of Mahatma Gandhi*, Vol. XVIII (July–December 1920), 365–68.

Regarding the second, he emphatically countered the presumption, and argued that since means under all circumstances were bound to be non-violent so any kind of incivility was ruled out, and therefore there was nothing improper in the constitution of the Swarajya Sabha:

> Why, then have all these leaders left it? The simple answer is that the country is moving so fast now that our leaders cannot keep pace with it. In such circumstances, no matter how much we are pained we must go ahead. India will not have such an opportunity for a century. We cannot afford to miss it. We may only hope that when the leaders realize the value of the strong popular current, they will not hesitate to join it.[63]

Gandhi wrote to Jinnah a day later on 25 October 1920 suggesting that he and his co-signatories reconsider their decision.[64] Jinnah, who was already unhappy with Gandhi on various other counts including the boycott and civil disobedience, now published an open letter in the *Bombay Chronicle* accusing that Gandhi's methods had 'already caused split and division in almost every institution' that he had approached hitherto, and 'in the public life of the country not only amongst Hindus and Mohammedans, but between Hindus and Hindus and Hindus and Mohammedans and Mohammedans and even between fathers and sons.' Not stopping here, Jinnah even denigrated Gandhi's followers as inexperienced and ignorant: 'People generally are desperate all over the country and your extreme programme has for the moment struck the imagination mostly of the inexperienced youth and the ignorant and the illiterate.'[65] 'This was the first time in twenty-three years of his public life', Sheela Reddy informs, 'that Jinnah had lost his temper, and, of course he had to pay for this indulgence': 'Almost overnight his popularity crashed, plunging him from the heights of "Bombay's uncrowned king" to its lowest point, hated by the very Muslims who had admired him and followed his lead for at least two decades.'[66]

[63] Ibid.

[64] Ibid, 370–72.

[65] Reddy, *Mr and Mrs Jinnah*, 234.

[66] Ibid.

Clash on Khilafat and Non-cooperation

By 1917, Jinnah had proved his mettle as a forceful speaker, his speeches acquiring a new pungency inside and outside the Imperial Legislative Council. He forcefully argued in the Council opposing the statement of a European member that Muslims might lose out if examinations to ICS were held in India and England simultaneously. Jinnah pointed out that Muslims were in a better position than the member thought and were quite prepared to compete with their Hindu brethren—'Let it be open competition to anyone—Europeans, Hindus, Mohammedans and Parsis, etc.—and the fittest get in; the survival of the fittest should be the rule for recruiting to the highest service.'[67] Appearing on behalf of the Muslim League before the Joint Select Committee of the Parliament on the Reforms Bill in London in August 1919, Jinnah told that Indian Mohammedans had 'very few things' which one could call matters of special interest for them and said that he would be most pleased when a day comes in the political life when there would be no distinction between Mohammedans and Hindus.[68]

By 1918–1919, he had started being counted among the front rank of India's leaders, holding high position in both the Congress as well as the Muslim League. As a young man, he had dreamt of becoming a 'Muslim Gokhale', at 42 years of age, except for his conviction that separate electorates constituted a panacea for the problems faced by Muslims, he was not far behind. It was at the height of his popularity that in April 1918 Jinnah got married again, with Ruttie Petit, 24 years younger his age, after she had converted to Islam. Sheela Reddy has very beautifully brought out the life of Jinnah's young wife, the daughter of Dinshaw Petit, a high class Parsi public figure of Bombay. Jinnah and Dinshaw Petit were great friends, and the latter a supporter of inter-community marriages. But when Jinnah brought this marriage proposal to him, it shattered 'their friendship and Dinshaw's peace of mind forever'.[69]

[67] Nanda, *Road to Pakistan*, 39–40.

[68] Ibid, 43–45.

[69] Reddy, *Mr and Mrs Jinnah*, 11.

In the Gandhi–Jinnah relationship, the years 1919–1920 proved to be the most crucial—the one that defined the irreconcilable dissimilarities. The passage of the Rowlatt bill just after the end of the First World War in which India had participated on the side of the Empire had enraged the nationalist leaders. Indian soldiers had fought in the most difficult terrain in order to safeguard the Empire. And here they were with a most draconian bill which sought to continue the war time restrictions on all kinds of freedom giving endless powers to the state and the police vis-a-vis the common Indian public. In a way it worked to unite the diverse groups of Indian political opinion.

Speaking on the Rowlatt Bill in the Imperial Legislative Council on 6 February 1919, Jinnah called it 'a most inopportune moment' when high hopes had been raised due to impending reforms. He found the bill without any precedent or parallel in any other civilized country and told the government that if the bill was passed it would

> create in this country from one end to the other, a discontent and agitation, the like of which you have not witnessed, and it will have, believe me, a most disastrous effect upon the good relations that have existed between the Government and the people.[70]

Once the Bill became a law, for a while Jinnah was in a dilemma on the question of relinquishing his seat in the Council. On one hand, it could annoy the government and thereby create a lull in his politics, and on the other, it would mean forcing himself to follow Gandhi's strategy 'whom he neither respected nor trusted', but in the end 'reason won over his feelings'.[71] Resigning his seat on 28 March 1919, he accused the government, through his letter to the viceroy, for having 'ruthlessly trampled upon the principles for which Great Britain avowedly fought the war'.[72] A couple of months later, his great friend Horniman, editor of *Bombay Chronicle*, was arrested and sent

[70] *Proceedings of the Imperial Legislative Council*, Part-II (Delhi and Simla, 1919), 15.

[71] Reddy, *Mr and Mrs Jinnah*, 178.

[72] Bolitho, *Jinnah: Creator of Pakistan*, 74.

to England since he had been exposing the government's deed post Jallianwala.[73]

The anti-Rowlatt Satyagraha launched by Gandhi in March 1919 saw the first successful glimpse of his leadership at an all-India level. His method was unique and at great variance with those followed by the Moderates or Constitutionalists like Jinnah. Then the Jallianwala happened. This herculean tragedy shook the very foundations of nationalist consciousness. Leaders after leaders voiced their indignation. AICC in its meeting on 21 April 1919 with Malaviya as president, brought the issue of atrocities by officials and appointed a subcommittee consisting of Jinnah, Jayakar, Kasturi Ranga Iyer, Motilal Nehru and Vithalbhai Patel to prepare a rejoinder to the central government's communique of 14 April which had justified the Rowlatt Act, condemned the agitation and authorized the Punjab government to use all possible force to end the disorder. It also demanded a public enquiry into the happenings in Delhi, Punjab, Bombay and Calcutta. Jinnah delivered a speech in Bombay on the first anniversary of the incident: 'The death-trap in the Jallianwala Bagh, which I witnessed last December, would move even the stones. That horrible butchery was committed in the name of law and order. I have tried to find out one single word…cowardice. No, butchery.'[74]

However, serious differences developed between Gandhi and Jinnah when the former took up the cause of Khilafat as part of the nationalist movement and consequently got closer to the Ali Brothers in the process of mobilizing the Muslim masses. Jinnah, like many others, was sympathetic to the Khilafat cause, but would not like other Muslim leaders to find such prominence at his cost. In his presidential address at the Lucknow session of the Muslim League in 1916, Jinnah had requested the government to pay due regard for the community's 'most dearest and most sacred religious feelings and under no circumstances interfere with the question of the future of the Caliphate.'[75] Then on

[73] Jinnah went to London to make an appeal to the authorities there to free Horniman. Reddy, *Mr and Mrs Jinnah*, 178–79, 182.

[74] V. N. Datta, *Jallianwala Bagh* (Ludhiana: Lyall Book Depot, 1969), 167.

[75] Jinnah, *His Speeches & Writings 1912–1917*, 57.

27 August 1919, a memorandum submitted by Muslim League delegation led by Jinnah to the British premier Lloyd George expressed concern of the Indian Muslims over the British occupation of Turkish territories. The memorandum underlined that the relationship between the Muslims of India and the Turkish Sultan had been always been 'a recognized and established fact'.[76]

In the meantime, Gandhi had greatly grown in both stature and popularity. His taking up the cause of Khilafat on behalf of Indian Muslims had made ordinary Muslims and leaders rally behind him around that time. When he reached Amritsar on 4 November 1919, thousands of people lined up on the streets to have a mere glimpse of the man. This marked the moment of his arrival in Indian politics as a mass leader. The scene was vividly described by Andrews in a newspaper column:

> It revealed, in a light I had not seen before, the psychology of the Indian crowd during a time of intense devotional fervour and excitement. The procession through the city, which occupied altogether nearly five hours, was altogether transformed by the multitude into a religious ceremony. No one had instructed them. From first to last, it was spontaneous, in the fullest sense of the word…In all the varied scenes, throughout the day, the women of Amritsar were, if anything, more prominent than the men. They crowded the balconies and windows and housetops to overflowing in order to perform their act of *Darshan*. They came out of their seclusion to rejoice and worship in a manner which only a great religious festival could evoke. And, on this occasion, the hearts of the Musalman women were beating in unison with those of their Hindu sisters. Of the significance of that fact there could be no doubt whatever. The whole city was one.[77]

Towards the end of 1919, as Gandhi was preoccupied with leading the anti-Rowlatt agitation further and attaching new forms to it, Jinnah was hopeful that the British government would unleash massive reforms to herald some sort of 'renaissance'.[78]

[76] Ali, *Jinnah on World Affairs*, 72–75.

[77] C. F. Andrews, 'Mahatma Gandhi at Amritsar', *The Tribune*, 7 November 1919.

[78] Wolpert, *Jinnah of Pakistan*, 64–65.

When the Congress and the League held their annual sessions at Amritsar, Jinnah could only be in the back seat. The Ali brothers—Mohammad Ali and Shaukat Ali, Gandhi's protégés in the Khilafat movement—had by now hugely gained in popularity among the Muslims. Recently freed from prison, the brothers stole the limelight at the League's meeting, with Shaukat Ali asking the 40 lakh Mussalmans to come forward and die for their religion.[79] At the Khilafat conference, Gandhi spoke in Urdu as Jinnah watched silently. *Bombay Chronicle* highlighted the 'incredible power and lucidity' of Gandhi's speech, which enabled him to win over the 'Muslim heart and mind.'[80]

By mid-1920, it had become evident that Gandhi had made up his mind of leading a protracted movement of non-cooperation including boycott of educational institutions, courts and all other government institutions. This movement was launched on the promise of achieving Swaraj within a year. Gandhian idioms, principles and methods found no sympathy with Jinnah who was only convinced of the impact of agitation through constitutional methods: 'Peace has its victories. We are fighting and can only fight constitutional battles.'[81] The Calcutta and the Nagpur sessions of the Congress during late 1920 sealed the fate of the Indian national movement in favour of Gandhi. As his leadership of the Congress stood affirmed as never before, Jinnah with his incessant opposition to the boycott and non-cooperation and with the Khilafat issue hijacked by the Khilafat committee, found his isolation from Congress and Gandhi complete.

Presiding at the Muslim League session in Calcutta on 7 September 1920, Jinnah squarely blamed the British government for the situation that the Indian Muslims found themselves in: 'First came the Rowlatt Bill—accompanied by the Punjab atrocities—and then came the spoliation of the Ottoman Empire and the Khilafat. The one attacks our liberty, the other our faith.' Then he affirmed, as if confronted with

[79] Reddy, *Mr and Mrs Jinnah*, 228–29.

[80] Ibid, 229.

[81] Jinnah's presidential address at the Lucknow session of the Muslim League, 1916; Jinnah, *His Speeches & Writings 1912–1917*, 41.

stiff competition from the Khilafat conference, that from a purely Mussalman point of view, the question of Khilafat was 'a matter of life and death'.[82] The special session of the Congress in Calcutta held around the same time in September 1920, approved Gandhi's scheme of non-cooperation in spite of stiff opposition from certain quarters including Jinnah. This marked a decisive shift in the history of the Indian national movement, and established for all times to come Gandhi's unchallenged supremacy over the nationalist body. On 8 September, B. C. Pal moved an amendment to Gandhi's resolution on non-cooperation saying that for all their wrongs, they could not possibly paralyze the government through this method. He wanted to be cautious, to take only one step forward. He was supported by most Bengal leaders and others like Baptista, Satyamurthi, Malaviya, C. R. Das and Jinnah. Jinnah said that though the only remedy that there was for all the piles of wrongs heaped upon the country was non-cooperation, he was not convinced of the practicability of Mr Gandhi's scheme. Before putting non-cooperation into practice, he should like to take stock of the materials and forces of the country.[83] He wanted to know why Gandhi did not put into practice the whole programme at once, and neither did he see any hope in the policy of non-cooperation: 'The policy of non-cooperation was excellent and effective, but there was a great "if".' He attempted to restrain the Congress from adopting the programme without giving the country some more time: 'Before you commit the country to your programme, do you believe, are you convinced that Mr. Gandhi's programme is practicable? Will you tell me here the day on which I should give up my practice?'[84] Motilal had changed his position at the last moment. Umar Sobhani and Shankarlal, Jinnah's associates in the Home Rule League also crossed over. Shaukat Ali was so unhappy at Jinnah's opposition that after the meeting he almost beat him up but 'Jinnah walked away seemingly unperturbed.'[85]

[82] Ali, *Jinnah on World Affairs*, 88–91.

[83] *Indian Annual Register*, Vol. II, Part III (1921), 112 (d).

[84] Ali, *Jinnah on World Affairs*, 91–93.

[85] Reddy, *Mr and Mrs Jinnah*, 233.

Opposition to Gandhi at Calcutta in September had considerably mellowed down by the time the scene shifted to Nagpur in December 1920. Interestingly it was C. R. Das (who had supported B. C. Pal's amendment in Calcutta session) who now moved the non-cooperation resolution at the annual session in Nagpur. While supporting the resolution, Gandhi mentioned that Malaviya had written about his inability to attend but had conveyed his disagreement with the resolution. The resolution found support from B. C. Pal, Lajpat Rai, Shyam Sundar Chakravarty, Kitchlew, Hakim Ajmal Khan, K. Iyengar, J. L. Banerjee and others. At this session of the Congress which sought to change the creed of the Congress and attain Swaraj within one year, Jinnah was the lone voice to dissent. On the last day, the moment he rose to speak he faced hooting and shouting with the audience demanding that he address Gandhi as 'Mahatma' and Mohammad Ali as 'Maulana'. Calling the weapon of non-cooperation for attaining Swaraj as both illogical and unsound, he asked Gandhi to use his 'vast influence' to stop the programme that was sure to end in disaster.[86] Highly frustrated, Jinnah left for Bombay without attending even the Muslim League session:

> In less than twelve months, the political career that he had built so assiduously over twenty-three years had unraveled a nonentity... He didn't entirely blame Gandhi for all of it—that would be giving him too much importance. But he did blame the British government, convinced that it was their blunders that were making people desperate enough to fall into Gandhi's hands. What frustrated him was that between Gandhi and the government, he was stuck in a bind.[87]

While Nagpur confirmed Gandhi's ascendancy in the Congress, it also proved to be the beginning of Jinnah's huge disenchantment with Gandhi and the Congress. Speaking in Bombay six weeks later, on Gokhale's death anniversary, he described Gandhi as a great man but his programmes impractical, and relegated his doctrine of soul force as an 'essentially spiritual movement'.[88] At the next session of the Congress at Ahmedabad (1921), the annual session which he attended

[86] Ibid, 236–37.

[87] Ibid, 242.

[88] Nanda, *Road to Pakistan*, 76.

for the last time, while everyone wore khadi and spun it too, he was seen in foreign clothes refusing to spin khadi. Jinnah's refusal to join the Non-cooperation movement or endorse aspects of constructive swadeshi like spinning khadi, denoted a sharp dislike for the principles espoused by Gandhi:

> He was repelled by the religious overtones of Gandhi's campaign, and even by his asceticism. He did not relish the idea of discarding his Savile Row suites, putting on khadi shirts and *dhotis*, squatting on the floor and haranguing mobs of illiterate peasants and the urban proletariat on the inequities of foreign rule. Nor could he accept Gandhi's programme of non-cooperation with the government, which included the boycott of Councils and courts and renunciation of the two Spheres, law and politics, in which he had won his laurels.[89]

In his *Autobiography*, Jawaharlal Nehru assessed Jinnah in the context of the new Congress which, under the influence of Gandhi, had now vastly changed its creed:

> He (Jinnah) disagreed on political grounds, but it was not politics in the main that kept him away. There were still many people in the Congress who were politically even less advanced than he was. But temperamentally he did not fit in at all with the new Congress. He felt completely out of his element in the *khadi*-clad crowd demanding speeches in Hindustani. The enthusiasm of the people outside struck him as mob hysteria. There was as much difference between him and the Indian masses as between Savile Row and Bond Street and the Indian village with its mud huts.[90]

Towards the end of 1921, many leaders including Jinnah were keen to find a meeting ground between the government and the non-cooperators. Jinnah met the viceroy on 1 November 1921. They discussed various issues including the Khilafat, non-cooperation and Turkish questions. Jinnah found Gandhi's policy as 'destructive and not constructive', and informed the viceroy that he had met both Gandhi and Malaviya seeking a way out.[91] Led by Malaviya a conference of

[89] Ibid, 74.

[90] Jawaharlal Nehru, *Autobiography* (New York: John Day Company, 1941), 68.

[91] Viceroy to the Secretary of State, 1 November 1921; Ali, *Jinnah on World Affairs*, 96–99.

some 300 eminent representatives from different parts of the country representing all shades of political opinion was held in the Cowasji Jehangir Hall, Bombay. The letter convening this conference had been signed by Malaviya, Jinnah, Jayakar, A. Sarabhai, K. Natarajan and G. M. Bhurgi. Gandhi also attended. Malaviya criticized the repressive policy of the government during the period of non-cooperation.[92] Explaining the objectives of the conference, Jinnah said that the idea was to put a stop to certain activities on both the sides, that is, government as well as the non-cooperators. However, there could be no Round Table Conference (RTC) with the viceroy unless he gave an assurance that he had the sanction of the British government to implement the decision arrived at such a conference. Gandhi proposed certain conditions like release of all political prisoners before holding such a conference with the government. He wished to know whether the heart of the government had changed and that it showed true repentance. However, the idea of truce did not make any substantial impact.

Inside the New Council: The Politics Jinnah Excelled at

While Jinnah remained on the sidelines of the nationalist politics during 1920–1922, his chance to redeem himself came after the suspension of the Non-cooperation movement in February 1922. Muslim League had fallen in line with the Khilafat demand. Jinnah was now keen to bring the League back to the mould of constitutional politics by abandoning non-cooperation. Although he was able to get his friend G. M. Bhurgri elected as the president of the Muslim League in March, Ansari leading the Khilafatists inside the League opposed his move to abandon non-cooperation. Therefore, he was left with the space and opportunity provided by the Central Legislative Assembly, whose elections were due in 1923, to display his innate talent and pursue his political ambitions. He had not contested the 1920 elections to the Assembly lest he would have been seen as defying the boycott call given by the Congress and supported by the League. The Assembly, based on the Government of India Act of 1919 was a much better

[92] *Indian Annual Register*, Vol. I (1921–22), 353–56.

forum (with an elected majority) than the Legislative Council of the earlier years for espousing the nationalist cause. His resolve was also helped by the emergence of Swarajists who favoured entry to the legislatures. He successfully contested the 1923 election from the Muslim reserved constituency of Bombay city neither as a Swarajist and nor as a Khilafatist. The opportunity of working in the legislature opened a new vista for him, as B. R. Nanda rightly opines:

> Little did he know that the focus of politics was about to shift to the legislatures, a political forum in which he was at home, and his victory would not only break his political isolation, but enable him to occupy a pivotal position on the national stage.[93]

Once inside the legislature, he brought together those nationalists who were not keen to join the Swarajist rank. Thus was born an umbrella group or party called the Independent Party consisting of 16 members from different provinces consisting of some eminent names like Madan Mohan Malaviya, Purushottam Das, Thakurdas, Kasturbhai Lalbhai, B. C. Pal and K. C. Neogy. Besides Jinnah, there was only one other Muslim member—G. M. Bhurgri—who died soon after. C. R. Das and Motilal Nehru, leaders of the Swarajist group persuaded Jinnah to agree to form a joint front of the two groups inside the legislature called as the Nationalist Party. Together, the new group (with addition of some Moderate members) reached a figure of 75, sufficient to outwit the government on important issues. With his oratorical skills and a deft understanding of constitutional and other legal issue, Jinnah commanded respect inside the legislature. With his group—the Independent Party—maintaining the delicate balance between the government and the Swarajists, his importance rose all the more. Recalling his impression as he saw Jinnah in 1924, Percival Spear writes:

> He was then important because his group held the balance between the Swarajists and the government. Thin to leanness and icily handsome, he affected at that time an overpowering sartorial elegance in the western manner. His voice was quiet, his gestures, his manner Olympian and aloof, as if he was surveying a world of insects or distastefully prodding with as needle some lifeless exhibits. Perhaps his manner suited the occasion by

[93] Nanda, *Road to Pakistan*, 82.

repaying to the government benches the disdain with which they had until recently regarded the nationalists.[94]

The coalition which almost worked fine during 1924 (except for few differences) developed serious ruptures by early 1925 when Jinnah's support for pursuing an anti-government line, could not no longer be taken for granted. Sharp and bitter exchanges followed between Motilal Nehru and Jinnah. He told Motilal point blank that he would no longer agree to a policy of 'wrecking and recklessness' by merely resorting to these tactics.[95]

Reading, the viceroy, thought that Jinnah made a tremendous mistake by aligning with the Swarajists. Had he (Jinnah) remained absolutely independent, then he would have held the 'key to the situation'.[96] Inside the central legislature, the viceroy noted, the Nationalist Party had 'turned its back upon the original Swarajist programme'. Referring to the alliance which the Independents under Jinnah concluded with the Swarajists at the beginning of the assembly session, the viceroy very wittingly painted its implications:

> Jinnah evidently thought that by the terms of the alliance he would be sitting in the driving seat of the motor car holding the steering wheel with Motilal Nehru beside him powerless to control except by means of advice. The exact opposite resulted. Motilal Nehru was in the driving seat and Jinnah was even scarcely beside him; but his Party were inside the car being driven along without realizing whither they were going or what would happen.[97]

The serious Hindu–Muslim riots in many parts of the country during 1922–1924 had also worked to change the communal climate and the unity of the non-cooperation days had been seriously compromised. But in the midst of his strife with the Swarajists, when confronted with an allegation by Jamnadas Mehta (Swaraj party member in the

[94] Percival Spear and Margaret Spear, *India Remembered* (Delhi: Orient Longman, 1981), 14.

[95] Nanda, *Road to Pakistan*, 91.

[96] Reading to Leslie Wilson, 12 March 1924, *Reading Papers*, Nehru Memorial Museum & Library, Microfilm, Roll No. 11.

[97] Reading to Ramsden (secretary of state), 13 March 1924, *Reading Papers*, Roll No. 2.

legislature) that he had become 'a leader of communal strife', Jinnah shot back sharply that he was 'a nationalist first, a nationalist second and a nationalist last'. Speaking at the League's 15th session at Lahore on 24 May 1924, Jinnah pointed out that the triple boycott of courts, schools/colleges and council had failed and that lawyers barring few exceptions had not paid much heed to Gandhi's call and students 'after a first rush of an impulsive character, realised that it was a mistake'. He nonetheless concluded that that though blunders had been committed, 'the result of the struggle of the last three years has this to our credit that there is an open movement for the achievement of Swaraj for India', and one essential component for achievement of Swaraj is the political unity between Hindus and the Muhammadans.[98] However, Jinnah appears to have shifted his position from the agreed solution of the Lucknow Pact of 1916. At the All-Parties Conference in January 1925 (chaired by Gandhi), though Jinnah vindicated his own dislike of separate electorate but underlined that Mussalmans did not agree to the population basis for representation. During 1926 as the Swaraj Party headed for a split because of the conflict between Motilal Nehru on one hand and the Marathi group led by Jayakar, Moonje, Kelkar and Aney on the other, Jinnah refused to accept the offer of Jayakar to form part of the newly formed Responsive Cooperation Party.[99] Jayakar expressed his disappointment at Jinnah's attitude of not showing much enthusiasm about the new outfit.[100]

Failure of the Nehru Report

From 1927 onwards, the situation had changed significantly. With the Congress and the government putting forward their respective proposals and strategies for a future constitution, Jinnah hogged the limelight as the representative voice of the Muslims. While the Congress under Gandhi, Nehru and Patel resented the idea of some party or group

[98] Ali, *Jinnah on World Affairs*, 102–04.

[99] Jayakar wired Jinnah to join the new party and strengthen it at Delhi. Jayakar to Jinnah, *Telegram*, 20 February 1926, *Jayakar Papers*, National Archives of India, File No. 497.

[100] Jayakar to Sadanand, 26 February 1926, *Jayakar Papers*, File No. 497.

representing the Muslim voice and thereby reducing it (the Congress) as the representative of Hindus alone, the Hindu Mahasabha challenged any arrangement in which its own position was ignored. The Delhi Proposals of the Muslim League on 20 March 1927 encapsulated the political demands of a large body of the Muslim leadership.[101] They agreed in principle to give up separate electorates in return for four demands: (a) representation of Bengali and Punjabi Muslims in the legislatures according to their population, (b) reservation of one-third seats in the central legislature for Muslims, (c) separation of Sind from the Bombay Presidency and (d) extension of reforms to the Frontier Province. This meeting which was convened by Jinnah included 16 members of the Legislative Assembly. The viceroy Irwin noted that these proposals were given to the press by Jinnah without any vote perhaps in a bid to re-establish his old Independent Party, and that the Punjab Muslims were upset about them.[102] For Jinnah, these proposals were the 'outcomes of many heads': 'You cannot expect everyone to commit himself to every word and every clause of this long resolution. But so far as the spirit of the proposals is concerned it is undoubtedly just and fair to both communities'.[103]

The Congress working committee hoped that a satisfactory settlement could be arrived on the basis of the new manifesto.[104] However, a section of the Hindu Mahasabha leadership was not happy about the proposals. Around the same time, many Hindu members of the Central Legislative Assembly met under Malaviya to outline certain principles which ought to act as the basis of discussion, namely (a) joint electorate for all legislatures, (bi) reservation of seats on the basis of population, (c) safeguards for the protection of religious and quasi-judicial rights

101 Mushirul Hasan, 'The Delhi Proposals: A Study in Communal Politics,' *Indian Economic and Social History Review* 17, no. 4 (1980): 381–96.

102 Irwin to Birkenhead, 24 March 1927, *Halifax Papers*, Nehru Memorial Museum & Library, Microfilm, Roll No. 1.

103 Jinnah's speech in the All-India Muslim League session, 31 December 1927; *Indian Quarterly Register*, Vol. II (1927), 449.

104 *Nehru Report*, i.e. *Report of the Committee Appointed by the All Parties Conference to Determine the Principles of the Constitution for India* (1928). Allahabad: All India Congress Committee, 18; *Indian Quarterly Register*, Vol. I (1927), 4, 34.

and (d) question of redistribution of provinces on linguistic and other essential bases to be left open for consideration.[105] *Hindustan Times* pointed out the absence of any viable link between joint electorate and separation of Sind and introduction of reforms in Baluchistan and the Frontier Province. It asked if, on similar grounds, Hindus could also seek readjustment of the Punjab and Bengal to suit a communal purpose.[106] On the question of the boycott of the Simon Commission, barring the Punjab faction under Md. Shafi, the main faction of the League under Jinnah met in Calcutta on 30 December 1927–1 January 1928 and decided to oppose the commission. However, while reiterating the Delhi Proposals, it underlined that separate electorates could be abandoned only after separation of Sind and reforms in Baluchistan and NWFP.[107]

After the Delhi Proposals and the boycott of the Simon Commission, what came as a big challenge to the Congress-led nationalist leadership was to evolve the blueprint of a future constitution with a broad consensus among the Indian political leadership. Accordingly, the All-Parties Conference in its meeting in Bombay on 19 May 1928 presided over by Ansari appointed a subcommittee under the veteran leader and lawyer Motilal Nehru to draft such a constitution. However, Jinnah had sailed for England on 5 May following his wife Ruttie who had gone there along with her mother on 10 April. However, by the time Jinnah reached England, Ruttie had left for Paris and few weeks later he came to know that she was extremely unwell.[108] Motilal was keen to have Jinnah as a member of the subcommittee or appoint someone as his representative, but his telegram to Jinnah failed to elicit any response.[109]

The report of the subcommittee, popularly known as the Nehru Report, was ready by the month of August. The report was by far the most elaborate work meticulously prepared by representatives of

[105] *Indian Quarterly Register*, Vol. I (1927), 34.

[106] Ibid, 34–35.

[107] *Indian Quarterly Register*, Vol. II (1927), 443, 447–48.

[108] Reddy, *Mr and Mrs Jinnah*, 341–43.

[109] Nanda, *Road to Pakistan*, 110.

different shades of the Indian political opinion. However, while rejecting the demand for separate electorates, the report did not agree to the major Muslim demands in entirety that would be applicable to a situation where joint electorate with reservation of seats for minorities was conceded. The report was placed before the All-Parties Conference in Lucknow on 28 August. Jinnah was still in Europe. Motilal wrote to Jayakar that they had to do without Jinnah, but they could not help the situation.[110] Ansari who presided over the conference appreciated the report as a rare example of consensus and the 'last hope' of the millions of Indians.[111] Demand for Sind's separation was accepted subject to the condition that the new province was found to be financially viable and that the Hindu minority in the new province acquired the same weightage as Muslims enjoyed in those provinces where they were in a minority.[112] The Punjab and Bengal delegates accepted provisions related to their provinces prompting Annie Besant to enthusiastically declare that Indian unity and freedom had triumphed over communalism and sectarianism.[113] The All-Parties Conference concluded on a happy note approving major recommendations and making only minor amendments. An excited Ansari heaved a sigh of relief that his life's work, that is, unifying people, had been achieved.[114] M. C. Chagla, a prominent Muslim leader and a close associate of Jinnah, told the *Hindustan Times* that these decisions were more comprehensive as compared to the Lucknow Pact of 1916, since at Lucknow only the Congress and the League were involved, whereas the current scenario involved all prominent groups like Congress, Mahasabha, Sikh League, Muslim League and Khilafat organizations.[115]

[110] Motilal Nehru to Jayakar, 17 August 1928; Ravinder Kumar and Hari Dev Sharma, eds., *Selected Works of Motilal Nehru*, Vol. V (New Delhi: Vikas Publishing, 1996), 348–49.

[111] *Indian Quarterly Register*, Vol. I (1928), 62–63.

[112] R. J. Moore, *The Crisis of Indian Unity, 1917–1940* (New Delhi: Oxford University Press, 1974), 36.

[113] *Indian Quarterly Register*, Vol. I (1928), 66.

[114] Nanda, *Road to Pakistan*, 115.

[115] *Selected Works of Motilal Nehru*, Vol. VI, 232.

But Motilal was sceptical since Jinnah's opinion was not known as yet. He shared his worries with Gandhi:

> There is only one man about whom I am very anxious and that is Jinnah. He has not yet returned from England and has not expressed himself one way or the other. But for one weakness, he (Jinnah) is thoroughly sound. He is always afraid of losing his leadership and avoids taking any risks in the matter. This weakness often drives him to support the most reactionary proposals.[116]

In July, Chagla wrote to Jinnah to return to India so that he could discuss the draft report with Motilal before it was presented to the All-Parties Conference. Motilal mailed a draft of the report to him on 2 August assuring him that the committee was open to any suggestions he might have and asking him to return latest by 29 August to attend the Lucknow conference.[117] From London, Jinnah had gone to Paris where Ruttie's health had deteriorated fast. He looked after her, but on 5 October, she suddenly left for Bombay along with her mother. Sarojini Naidu, who reached Paris on 10 October en route America, discussed the Nehru Report with Jinnah. In her letter to Chagla, she felt that Jinnah's pessimism about the report had to with his personal situation as well: 'I have had long talks with him in Paris.... He has had to endure such incalculable personal troubles lately that I do not wonder that he is shaken and uncertain about vital public problems.'[118]

After a long and crucial gap of six months, Jinnah reached Bombay on 26 October. Motilal quickly wrote to him that he had been invited to a meeting of the Motilal Nehru subcommittee scheduled on 5 November in Delhi in which he had been co-opted.[119] With Jinnah not showing any interest, Motilal's anxiety grew only further as he wrote to Gandhi on 25 November that the Muslim members of the Legislative Assembly belonging to Jinnah's party were bitterly opposed to the Nehru Report and the decision reached at the Lucknow con-

[116] Motilal to Gandhi, 2 October 1928; *Selected Works of Motilal Nehru*, Vol. V, 368–70.

[117] Reddy, *Mr and Mrs Jinnah*, 348.

[118] Ibid, 348–49.

[119] *Selected Works of Motilal Nehru*, Vol. V, 385–86.

ference, and it was 'in his anxiety to keep his hold on these people', that Jinnah was 'playing into their hands': 'The game is to put off the consideration of the Report by the Muslim League at its annual Session which means a protracted controversy during the whole year 1929'.[120] Things started falling apart very soon. On 27 November, the Bombay Presidency branch of the League where both Jinnah and Shaukat Ali were present rejected the report for, what it called, ignoring Muslim interests.[121] The crucial All-Parties Convention began in Calcutta on 22 December 1928. The Muslim League session was also scheduled in Calcutta around the same time. The two bodies appointed respective delegations to negotiate with each other. While the League's delegation was represented by Jinnah, Kitchlew, Chagla, Barkat Ali and the raja of Mahmudabad, that of the Congress consisted of Gandhi, Sapru, Malaviya, Ansari, Azad, Motilal, Jayakar and others. Their meeting failed to reach any consensus. Consequently, Jinnah presented his demands in the All-Parties Convention on 28 December: (a) reserving one-third seats in the central legislature for Muslims; (b) in the event of adult suffrage not being introduced, seat should be reserved for Muslims in Bengal and the Punjab for 10 years; (c) residuary powers to rest with the provinces and (d) separation of Sind should not be made contingent upon the establishment of dominion-hood.

On the question of one-third seats in the central legislature, Sapru who was a part of the Motilal subcommittee, said: 'If he (Jinnah) is a spoilt child, a naughty child I am prepared to say, give him what he wants and be finished with it.' However, he hoped that Jinnah would not insist on reservation of seats for Muslims in the Punjab and Bengal.[122] Jayakar alleged that amendments put forward by Jinnah had their origin in a communal spirit.[123] Jinnah underlined that minorities could support a constitution only when they felt secure in it—'The security of the minority was the test'.[124] Though Jinnah's amendments

120 Ibid, 397–98.

121 Irwin to Peel, 12 December 1928; *Halifax Papers*, Roll No. 2.

122 *Indian Quarterly Register*, Vol. I (1928), 125–27.

123 Ibid, 128–29.

124 Ibid, 130.

were defeated, his persistent demands seeking reservation of seats for Muslims of the Punjab and Bengal won him the support of many Muslim leaders, especially of these two provinces who had earlier supported the Nehru Report. Jamshed Nusserwanjee, a Parsi and a friend of Jinnah, was present when he spoke. Next morning, as Jinnah left Calcutta by train he remarked: 'Jamshed, this is the parting of the ways'.[125]

Back to Bombay, Jinnah continued to work on his demands. In March 1929 he proposed his 'fourteen points' which while incorporating most demands from the Delhi Proposals and those made by him at the All-Parties Convention in Calcutta, also included, among others, (a) separate communal electorates and only the particular community in future could decide to go for joint electorates (b) no such territorial redistribution in future as to affect Muslim majority in a province, (c) no amendment to constitution unless okayed by all state legislatures and (d) no cabinet at the centre or in the states without ensuring a minimum of one-third Muslim ministers. Although his 'fourteen points' found favour with the Jamiat-Ulema-i-Hind, other groups like the Shafi faction of the Muslim League, the Congress Muslims and the Khilafatists were not on board.[126] The Muslim League met in Delhi towards the end of March 1929 and engaged in long-drawn deliberations. Jinnah now made clear his strong dislike of the Nehru Report. Citing the opposition of the Hindu Mahasabha delegates to amendments in the Nehru Report at the All-Parties Convention, Jinnah concluded that the proposals of the report could therefore be treated only as 'counter Hindu proposals to Moslem proposals'.[127] Azad, who had been present at the League's session, told the *Free Press* that both Jinnah and Mohammad Ali disagreed with any resolution which did not reject the Nehru Report.[128]

[125] Bolitho, *Jinnah: Creator of Pakistan*, 38.

[126] Moore, *The Crisis of Indian Unity*, 38–39.

[127] Jinnah's statement and draft resolution at the meeting of the council of the Muslim League, Delhi, 28 March 1929. There were strong differences among various factions within the League over Jinnah's draft resolutions. *Indian Quarterly Register*, Vol. I (1929), 363–65, 367.

[128] *Indian Quarterly Register*, Vol. I (1929), 370–72.

Early in 1929, Jinnah was also confronted with unprecedented problems on the personal front. Ruttie who was living separately was in and out of hospital. With Kanji Dwarkadas, a close friend of the Jinnahs around, Jinnah would drop in regularly to see an ailing Ruttie. Finally on the evening of 20 February 1929, the day she was born 29 years ago, she breathed her last. Later in 1968, in an interview Kanji Dwarkadas revealed that Ruttie had died of an overdose of sleeping pills.[129] Jinnah who was in Delhi rushed back. When Ruttie's body was kept in the grave, Jinnah got emotional, the only time, Chagla wrote later, when he found 'Jinnah betraying some shadow of human weakness.'[130] Kanji felt Ruttie's death left Jinnah with a deep wound turning him from a 'cheerful, pleasant and social friend with a dry sense of humour' to someone 'egocentric and sensitive to criticism'.[131]

Jinnah's Sabbatical from Active Politics: 1930–1934

In the midst of the Civil Disobedience Movement during 1930, Jinnah felt himself out of gear. The Muslim leadership was hardly talking in one voice and Jinnah's leadership within the League itself was no longer commanding, a situation which was not to his liking. Therefore, with his characteristic vanity, he announced his intention to stay in England and carry on his struggle through the British Parliament there:

> Indeed, vanity could soar no higher when he declared: "There I shall meet British statesmen on a footing of equality. They shall be accessible to me not in the sense that I shall seek them and beg for interviews. They will want me…" The bubble, however, burst. The British electorate gave short shrift to his vaunting ambitions. Right from 1930 to 1934, when the new Reforms Scheme was published, he kept away in England in comparative obscurity, from which he was rescued by the Government. They summoned him to the first two RTCs. At these, however, he played no conspicuous part, and showed but little interest in the solution of the communal problem.[132]

129 Reddy, *Mr and Mrs Jinnah*, 358.

130 Ibid, 360.

131 Ibid, 371.

132 '"Architect of Pakistan": Life Sketch of Jinnah', *Hindustan Times*, New Delhi, 12 September 1948.

Later, talking to the students at Aligarh in 1938, Jinnah said that it was due to pessimism and disappointment about the country that he had decided to stay in London during the early 1930s. It was 'the Hindu sentiment, the Hindu mind, the Hindu attitude', Jinnah clarified, which had made him lose hope of any unity. And the Muslims were dwelling in no man's land since 'they were led by either the flunkeys of the British government or the camp followers of the Congress' and attempts to organize the community were frustrated by 'toadies and flunkeys on the one hand, and traitors in the Congress camp on the other.'[133]

Jinnah attended the first and the second RTCs in 1930 and 1931. In the second conference, among the Muslim leaders, Aga Khan received more prominence. Jinnah was not even invited to the third RTC, but he stayed on in England 'haunted by the memory of his unfortunate marriage, and discouraged as a politician.'[134] However, in the eyes of the British Empire, the Congress party even at the height of its popularity had to make stupendous efforts to drive home its all-community inclusive character. In the second conference, Gandhi asserted the claim of the Congress to represent the whole of India, while all other parties at the meeting, he pointed out, represented only 'sectional interests'. Far from being a communal organization, the Congress, he clarified, was 'a determined enemy of communalism in any shape or form'. He expressed unhappiness at the treatment of the Congress as 'one of the Parties':

> The Congress is the only all-India-wide national organisation, bereft of any communal basis; that it does represent all the minorities which have lodged their claim here and which, or the signatories on their behalf, claim—I hold unjustifiably—to represent 46 percent of the population of India. The Congress, I say, claims to represent all these minorities.[135]

[133] Bolitho, *Jinnah: Creator of Pakistan*, 94.

[134] Ibid, 93

[135] 'Proceedings of the Plenary Session', *Indian Round Table Conference (Second Session)* (Calcutta: Central Publication Branch, 1932), 266.

The failure of the Nehru Report, subsequent RTCs and the Communal Award of 1932 worsened the inter-community relationship. The Communal Award radically altered the balance of power, especially inside Bengal, and the Poona Pact further reduced the number of unreserved seats in the province for Bengali Hindus.[136]

Liaquat Ali Khan and his wife met Jinnah at his house in Hampstead Heath in London in July 1933 pleading with him to return home. Twenty years younger to Jinnah and educated at Oxford, Khan was always ready to play a second fiddle to Jinnah. Hector Bolitho remarks that Khan was the ally Jinnah needed, fostering thereafter a life-long partnership leading to the final designs for creation of Pakistan and even after: 'A great part of the fortunes of Pakistan were decided on the day, in July 1933, when Liaquat Ali Khan crossed Hampstead Heath, to talk to his exiled leader.'[137] Between April 1934 and January 1935, Jinnah visited India twice, first to attend a session of the Muslim League and then to attend the session of the Central Assembly to which he had been elected by the Bombay Muslims. His final return in October 1935 was quickened by the passage of the Government of India Act 1935 and the inauguration of provincial autonomy. This Act incorporated many of his significant communal demands.

Post-1937 Elections and Onset of the Second World War: Shifting the Agenda

Muslim League led by Jinnah fared miserably in the elections of 1937 in the Muslim majority provinces. Out of 30 million voters in British India, 30 per cent were Muslims; League received just 5 per cent of the Muslim votes that were cast. This humiliating defeat appeared to take the wind out of the League's sail. The fight was not only with the Congress now but also with other Muslim parties like the Unionist Party and the Krishak Praja Party. The latter dimension required the League to acquire a more divisive agenda, more intense than it had

[136] See Bidyut Chakrabarty, *The Partition of Bengal and Assam, 1932–1947* (London: Routledge Curzon, 2004), 55–84.

[137] Bolitho, *Jinnah: Creator of Pakistan*, 98.

already injected. And thus began the journey for a separate homeland through a newly invented two-nation theory. These results prompted him to make strategic shifts resulting in the Lahore Resolution of 1940 incorporating this theory. Gandhi described the two-nation theory as untruth. He underlined that the vast majority of Muslims in India were converts to Islam or descendants of converts. They had not become a separate nation the moment they had converted.

Jinnah had earlier not given much importance to Muhammad Iqbal (1876–1938) or his distinct ideas. The defeat in the 1937 elections prompted him to revisit the poet and his solutions for the problems faced by the Indian Muslims. Both had regularly met in London. Iqbal participated in the RTCs. He had shown his disagreement with Jinnah's demand for safeguards to Muslims through communal and increased representation. A constitution based on the 'conception of a homogenous India', said Iqbal in 1930, would unwittingly 'prepare her for a civil war'. Only a partition of the land, he believed, would provide a long-lasting solution. In the north-west, he advocated amalgamation of the Punjab, NWFP, Sind and Baluchistan into a single state.[138] At the third RTC, Iqbal argued that the Muslims were against a central government as it was bound to be dominated by the Hindus.[139]

Results of elections to provincial assemblies held during the winter of 1936–1937 were declared in February 1937. Following soon after these election results, in his letter of 20 March 1937, Iqbal advised Jinnah to counter Nehru's idea of 'aesthetic socialism' with the argument that the Muslim problem was cultural, and not economic.[140] Jinnah went to Lahore to meet Iqbal at his house on 21 May 1937. On 28 May 1937, he wrote to Jinnah that the only solution was a redistribution of the country leading to the birth of one or more states with Muslim majority, and that time for such a move had already arrived.[141]

[138] Ibid, 93.

[139] Nanda, *Road to Pakistan*, 319.

[140] V. N. Datta, 'Iqbal, Jinnah and India's Partition: An Intimate Relationship,' *Economic and Political Weekly* 37, no. 50 (2002): 5033–38.

[141] Bolitho, *Jinnah: Creator of Pakistan*, 106.

Iqbal warned that if such a redistribution was impossible, then the only alternative was civil war which, in any case, had been going on in the form of communal riots.[142] Following up on this, he asked in his letter of 21 June 1937, why Muslims of north-west and Bengal should not be considered as a nation 'as any other nation in India and outside', and then he suggested that the Muslims of this region would be better off ignoring the political compulsions of Muslims in rest of the British India where they were in a minority.[143] Iqbal bestowed lot of faith in Jinnah's leadership for the Muslims and felt that it was only he who could guide the community through the storm. Shifting his strategy, Jinnah now changed the tenor and content of his speeches and writings. In a speech in Lucknow in October 1937, he opened his mind that the policy of the Congress would lead to class bitterness and communal war. Gandhi felt it amounted to a declaration of war. Jinnah said it was 'purely in self-defence'. Gandhi doubted if it was the same Jinnah who was once dubbed a nationalist and the hope of both Hindus and Muslims.[144] After the 'Pakistan Resolution' had been passed at the Lahore session of the Muslim League in March 1940, Jinnah acknowledged Iqbal's contribution: 'Iqbal is no more amongst us, but had he been alive he would have been happy to know that we did exactly what he wanted us to do.'[145]

When the Second World War began, Jinnah tried to take advantage of the situation. He asked the government to take the Muslim India into confidence through their accredited organization, the

[142] Datta, 'Iqbal, Jinnah and India's Partition'.

[143] Analysing the impact of Iqbal on Jinnah, V. N. Datta concludes: 'It was Iqbal who blazed a trail that Jinnah followed. Iqbal conceived an idea of Pakistan, Jinnah realised it. As an intellectual godfather, Iqbal gave a concept of the two-nation theory and offered a map of the redistribution of territory…As an ideologue, he rejected Maulana Azad's notion of composite culture and religious pluralism. Iqbal had no truck with Jawaharlal Nehru's secular-socialist nationalism. Committed to the notion of Millat, he repudiated the British constitutional measures, such as separate electorates and weightage for resolving the communal disease.' See Datta, 'Iqbal, Jinnah and India's Partition'.

[144] Bolitho, *Jinnah: Creator of Pakistan*, 106–07.

[145] Ibid, 120.

Muslim League, if the British wanted to be successful in the War.[146] In November 1939, in response to the unilateral decision of the British government to make India a party in the War, the Congress ministries in various provinces resigned. Jinnah smelt his chance. From this vantage point, he fired the first salvo, asking his followers to observe 22 December as a day of deliverance and thanksgiving because the Congress governments had ceased to function.

Jinnah met Linlithgow on 4 November 1939 and wrote to him next day that the British government should meet all reasonable demands of the Arabs in Palestine and ensure that Indian troops were not used outside India against any Muslim power.[147] He reiterated this demand in his presidential speech at Lahore session of the League in March 1940: 'What we wanted the British government to give us assurance of was that the Indian troops should not be sent against any Muslim country or any Muslim power.'[148] Jinnah used this concern about Islamic countries to consolidate his following at home. The viceroy assured him that the British government was on friendly and sympathetic terms with all the Muslim powers, and if a contingency arose Jinnah's suggestion would not be overlooked.[149] On another occasion, addressing a joint meeting of the Muslim Conference and the Muslim Students Federation in Jammu on 9 May 1944, he underlined that 'all Muslims whether they live in China or Palestine are brothers' and therefore it was his duty to interfere whenever Muslims anywhere were terrorized.[150]

The working committee of the League in its session on 3 February 1940 assured its wholehearted support to the British war effort on behalf of the Mussalmans of India.[151] It was in this atmosphere of the early months of 1940 that Jinnah and the League spelt out their most

[146] 'Press Statement of Jinnah', 7 September 1939; Ali, *Jinnah on World Affairs*, 147–48.

[147] Jinnah to Linlithgow, 5 November 1939; Ali, *Jinnah on World Affairs*, 150–51.

[148] Ali, *Jinnah on World Affairs*, 158–59.

[149] Linlithgow to Jinnah, 19 April 1940; Ali, *Jinnah on World Affairs*, 160–61.

[150] Ali, *Jinnah on World Affairs*, 240–41.

[151] Jinnah to Linlithgow conveying the view of the League's working committee, 24 February 1940; Ali, *Jinnah on World Affairs*, 153–56.

significant demand—creating a separate homeland and thereby affecting India's destiny forever. Speaking to an English correspondent early in 1940, Jinnah launched a frontal diatribe on the Congress, calling it the worst variant of a fascist and authoritarian organization whose sole aim was to annihilate every other organization in the country. He had already shifted his tactic from fighting a battle for Muslims within the parliamentary democracy to creating a separate nation. So, he continued 'democracy can only mean Hindu Raj all over India.... This is a position to which Muslims will never submit.'[152]

To convince his Western audience, Jinnah wrote an article in the *Time and Tide* on 9 March 1940 drawing attention to how Hinduism or Islam was different from Christianity or other religions of the world. There are reasons to believe that Jinnah while defending his claim for Muslims being a socioculturally distinct community was influenced by another powerful proponent of the Muslim cause independent of what the Congress stood for. In a letter to Jinnah, he thus argued that

> [a]fter long and careful study of Islamic Law I have come to the conclusion that if this system of Law is properly understood and allied, at least the right to subsistence is secure to everybody. But the enforcement and development of the Shariat of Islam is impossible in this country without a free Muslim state or states. This has been honest conviction for many years and I still believe this to be the only way to solve the problem of bread for Muslims as well as to secure a peaceful India. If such a thing is impossible in India, the only alternative is a civil war which, as a matter of fact, has been going on in the shape of Hindu Muslim riots.[153]

Following this line of argument that Iqbal made, Jinnah pursued the contention further which he defended by highlighting the sociocultural differences that Muslims had naturally had with their Hindu counterparts. While insisting that Hindus and Muslims were different, he, in his *Time and Tide* article (referred earlier) thus contended that the uniqueness of Hinduism and Islam, he contended, had made their followers socially and culturally incompatible. British people,

[152] Bolitho, *Jinnah: Creator of Pakistan*, 116.

[153] Cited in Hafeez Malik, ed., *Iqbal: Poet-philosopher of Pakistan* (New York: Columbia University Press, 1971), 385–86.

he wrote, considered religion as a private matter between man and God, but Hinduism and Islam, in contrast, were 'social codes' which governed 'not so much man's relation with his God, as man's relation with his neighbour: They govern not only his law and culture, but every aspect of his social life, and such religions, essentially exclusive, completely preclude that merging of identity and unity of thought on which Western democracy is based.' And then, he ended his write-up with his most famous demand—a constitution that recognized 'two nations' in India 'who must both share the governance of their common motherland'.[154] A liberal democrat in his faith, Jinnah felt that the partition between the Hindus and Muslims were instinctively structured because civilizationally they were poles apart, which he persuasively argued in his 1940 address to the Muslim League when he exhorted that Hinduism and Islam

> are not religious in the strict sense of the word, but are, in fact, different and distinct social orders, and it is a dream that the Hindus and Muslims can ever evolve a common nationality, and this misconception of one Indian nation has gone far beyond the limits and is the cause of most of your troubles and will lead India to destruction if we fail to revise our notions in time. Hindus and Muslims belong to two different religious philosophies, social customs [and] literatures. They neither intermarry nor interdine together and, indeed they belong to two different civilizations which are based on conflicting ideas and conceptions. Their outlook on life and of life are different. It is quite clear that Hindus and Muslims derive their inspirations from different sources of history; they have different epics, different heroes and different episodes. ... To yoke together two such nations under a single state, one as a numerical minority and the other as a majority, must lead in growing discontent and final destruction of any fabric that may be built up for the government of such a state.[155]

In a way, the demand for Pakistan that was unambiguously spelt out from the platform of the Muslim League in March 1940 had already been delineated and spoken about. Iqbal's ideas had now found the exceptional mind of Jinnah who, having discovered the potential

[154] Bolitho, *Jinnah: Creator of Pakistan*, 117–18.

[155] India Office Records, L/I/1/R, Jinnah's Press Statement of 8 February 1940.

contained in the demand for Pakistan, stood like a rock against all arguments and persuasions to the contrary.

Just prior to the League session, Gandhi in his speech at the Subjects Committee of the Congress at Ramgarh on 18 March 1940 pleaded for better sense to prevail. He addressed Jinnah as his brother and lamented that he (Gandhi) had lost the confidence of the Muslims:

> We are all brothers—even the Quaid-i-Azam is my brother. I have meant all that I have said about him, never has a frivolous word escaped my lips, and I say that I want to win him over…There was a time when there was not a Muslim whose confidence I did not enjoy. Today I have forfeited that confidence and most of the Urdu Press pours abuse on me…I am also a reader of the Koran like them, and I will tell them that the Koran makes no distinction between the Hindus and the Mussalmans. But if they feel that they should have the Heaven without the Hindus, I will not grudge it to them.[156]

It is evident that the Mahatma was determined to avoid partition by seeking to persuade Jinnah that Hindus and Muslims could never be segmented since they were culturally interlinked since times immemorial. It perhaps had dawned on him by then that his arguments were not persuasive enough to deter Jinnah from pursuing his politico-ideological mission of creating a separate Muslim state. Nonetheless, his effort towards mitigating the fear that Quaid-i-Azam had falsely nurtured was also illustrative of how he felt when the latter was reluctant to even listen to the views that the Mahatma so assiduously held to scuttle the campaign for India's partition.

The Lahore session of the League was held after 15 months of its previous session in Patna in December 1938. In his presidential address on 22 March 1940, Jinnah narrated the 'difficulties' faced by the League ever since January 1939 when the Muslims and the League were subjected to the 'Vidya Mandir in Nagpur', 'Wardha Scheme all over India' and 'ill-treatment and oppression to Muslims in the Congress-governed provinces'. He dwelt on how an organized strength of the League had tilted the scale in its favour after the declaration of

[156] *CWMG*, Vol. LXXI (1 December 1939–15 April 1940), 352–53.

the War. Up to that time (declaration of the War), Jinnah lamented, the government thought only of Gandhi, and though he (Jinnah) had been the leader of 'an important political party in the Legislature for a considerable time, larger than the one' that he was leading then, he was never thought of by the viceroy. Now, his sudden promotion in the eyes of the viceroy had put the Congress in a state of 'worst shock' since the step had challenged the party's 'sole authority to speak on behalf of India'. In this speech, he also attempted to create serious doubt in the mind of Muslims about the likely situation if the British left without creating a separate homeland. Making light of Gandhi's speech that he had lost confidence of the Muslims, Jinnah clarified that Gandhi and the Congress were actually hell bent on having a Constituent Assembly where the Muslims will be pitted against the Hindus in a ratio of one to three. And in such a situation there could never be a 'real agreement from the hearts' so necessary to work as friends. He was able to drive home the point that the Muslims would then be left in perpetual bondage of a Hindu majority led by the Congress:

> Mr. Gandhi says that if the minorities are not satisfied then he is willing that some tribunal of the highest character and most impartial should decide the dispute… In the event of there being a disagreement between the majority of the Constituent Assembly and the Mussalmans, in the first instance, who will appoint the tribunal? And suppose an agreed tribunal is possible and the award is made and the decision given, who will, may I know, be there to see that this award is implemented or carried out in accordance with the terms of that award?... We come back to the same answer, the Hindu majority would do it; and will it be with the help of the British bayonet or the Gandhi's "Ahimsa"? Can we trust them anymore? Besides, ladies and gentlemen, can you imagine that a question of this character, of social contract upon which the future constitution of India would be based, affecting 90 million of Mussalmans, can be decided by means of a judicial tribunal? Still, that is the proposal of the Congress.[157]

He wanted Gandhi to acknowledge that the Congress was a Hindu body and that he represented nobody except the solid body of Hindu people: 'Why should not Mr. Gandhi be proud to say. "I am a Hindu.

[157] Presidential address of Jinnah, Muslim League, Lahore, March 1940, http://www.columbia.edu/itc/mealac/pritchett/00islamlinks/txt_jinnah_lahore_1940.html (accessed on 10 October 2019).

Congress has solid Hindu backing"? I am not ashamed of saying that I am a Mussalman.' Concluding his address, Jinnah hit through his recently found idea of Muslims constituting a nation, and how they needed to come forward as servants of Islam:

> Mussalmans are a nation according to any definition of a nation, and they must have their homelands, their territory, and their state. We wish to live in peace and harmony with our neighbours as a free and independent people… I therefore want you to make up your mind definitely, and then think of devices and organise your people, strengthen your organisation, and consolidate the Mussalmans all over India. I think that the masses are wide awake. They only want your guidance and your lead. Come forward as servants of Islam, organise the people economically, socially, educationally, and politically, and I am sure that you will be a power that will be accepted by everybody.[158]

Next day, that is, 23 March 1940, Fazlul Haq, premier of Bengal, moved the 'Pakistan Resolution' which said that no constitutional plan would be acceptable unless it is designed on the basic principle of demarcating geographically contiguous units into regions which should be so constituted, with such territorial readjustments as may be necessary 'that the areas in which the Muslims are numerically in a majority, as in the North-Western and Eastern Zones of India, should be grouped to constitute "Independent States" in which the constituent units shall be autonomous and sovereign.'[159]

The Mahatma's rejoinder to Jinnah's speech at Lahore followed soon. Writing on 26 March 1940, Gandhi accepted that he was 'proud of being a Hindu', but retorted that he had 'never gone to anybody as a Hindu to secure Hindu-Muslim unity', since his Hinduism demanded 'no pacts'. On the charge of the Congress being a Hindu party, he asked if a Hindu organization could have a Muslim as president, and could its working committee have four Muslims out of 15? He stuck

158 Presidential address of Jinnah, Muslim League, Lahore, March 1940, http://www.columbia.edu/itc/mealac/pritchett/00islamlinks/txt_jinnah_lahore_1940.html (accessed on 10 October 2019).

159 Bolitho, *Jinnah: Creator of Pakistan*, 119; Newspapers next day reported it as 'Pakistan resolution'. Jinnah went along with it. In a speech later that year he said—'No power on earth can prevent Pakistan.'

to his dictum of 'no swaraj without Hindu-Muslim unity'. On the constituent assembly front, he clarified that its only sanction would be an agreed solution of communal questions, and in case it failed to reach an agreement, it would be dissolved automatically:

> I cannot understand the Muslim opposition to the proposed Constituent Assembly. Are the opponents afraid that the Muslim League will not be elected by Muslim voters? ... If the vast majority of Indian Muslims feel that they are not one nation with their Hindu and other brethren, who will be able to resist them? But surely it is permissible to dispute the authority of the 50,000 Muslims who listened to Quaid-e-Azam to represent the feelings of eight crores of Indian Muslims.[160]

In March 1942, a British mission led by Stafford Cripps arrived in India. Its draft declaration allowed the right of any province which was not ready to accept the new constitution, to retain its current constitutional position. Both the Congress and the League rejected the proposals based on their logic and their own interpretations. Then in August 1942, the Congress launched the Quit India Movement. All top leaders of the party were imprisoned to be released only after the war was over. Gandhi was released in 1944 on health grounds.

To the charge that he had deliberately left many details of Pakistan vague, Jinnah in an interview to Beverly Nichols in December 1943 argued that neither was there a blueprint when Burma or Sind were separated. When the interviewer asked him to describe the 'vital principles' of Pakistan, Jinnah's reply could not have been more brief and candid: 'In five words. The Muslims are a Nation.'[161] Then another significant question followed—whether he thought in terms of religion when he talked of Pakistan. 'Partly', confirmed Jinnah, but 'by no means exclusively', and then he went on to delineate 'radically antagonistic' differences between Hindus and Muslims:

> You must remember that Islam is not merely a religious doctrine but a realistic and practical code of conduct. I am thinking in terms of life, of everything important in life. I am thinking in terms of our history, our

[160] *Collected Works of Mahatma Gandhi*, Vol. LXXI, 371–72.

[161] 18 December 1943, Ali, *Jinnah on World Affairs*, 229–30.

> heroes, our art, our architecture, our music, our laws, our jurisprudence. In all these things our outlook is not only fundamentally different but often radically antagonistic to the Hindus. We are different beings. There is nothing in life which links us together. Our names, our clothes, our foods, they are all different; our economic life, our educational ideas, our treatment of women, our attitude to animals. We challenge each other at every point of the compass. Take one example, the eternal question of the cow. We eat the cow, the Hindus worship it.[162]

In his presidential address at the Muslim League session in Karachi in December 1943, Jinnah said that their (Muslims') problem was not one of non-cooperation with the Congress, but rather of defence against its attitude, pursued since 1937, of dominating the Muslim community and 'to establish, by hook or crook, Hindu Raj and Hindu Government. We are defending ourselves against that monstrosity, those machinations and those designs.'[163] In contrast with Gandhi's insistence that Hindus and Muslims were not, at all, separate, but were culturally mingled communities, Jinnah, in his very strongly worded letter to the Mahatma, firmly reiterated that

> [w]e maintain and hold that Muslims and Hindus are two major nations by any definition or test of a nation. We are a nation of hundred million, and what is more, we are a nation with our own culture and civilization, language and literature, art and architecture, names and nomenclature, sense of value and proportion, legal laws and moral codes, customs and calendar, history and traditions, aptitudes and ambitions; in short, we have our own distinctive outlook on life and of life.[164]

Key to Jinnah's contention are two complementary points: on the one hand, he was pushing the view that given the inherent sociocultural differences between the Hindus and Muslims despite being part of the same geographical space, the arguments opposing partition were not persuasive; by strongly defending his claim for India's dismemberment, the Quaid-i-Azam, on the basis of the distinct character of

[162] Ibid, 230.

[163] Ali, *Jinnah on World Affairs*, 234–236.

[164] Jinnah to Gandhi, 17 September 1944; *The Collected Works of Mahatma Gandhi*, Vol. 78, 407.

Islamic civilizational traditions, provided, on the other, a challenging argument in favour of a sovereign Muslim state following the transfer of power in India.

On the British policy towards India, Jinnah made an interesting observation in an interview in May 1944. He said that the idea of one nation had been deliberately fostered among Indians by the British imperialists with a sinister motive: 'They know Hindus and Muslim cannot unite. If put together they will always keep on quarrelling. So the British encourage this idea of unity in order to continue their domination.'[165] When asked by a newspaper about his views on Gandhi's threat of civil disobedience in the event of non-acceptance of his proposal for a united India, Jinnah quickly replied that he (Jinnah) could not be accused of being pro-British, but if they (Muslims) joined the threat and the British government surrendered then the 'Muslim India would be faced not only by Hindu majority rule but a Hindu majority triumphant with British co-operation.'[166]

'Gandhi–Jinnah Talks'— Last Elusive Attempt at Reconciliation

Released from imprisonment in May 1944, Gandhi was keen to find a solution to the communal deadlock. In a letter on 17 July, Gandhi addressed Jinnah as 'Bhai Jinnah', reminded him that there was a time when he was able to persuade him (Jinnah) to speak in 'our mother tongue', and pleaded not to be regarded 'as an enemy of Islam and the Muslims here'.[167] Jinnah told Gandhi that they could meet in Bombay in August. However, the meeting was delayed by a month due to Jinnah's indisposition.[168] Beginning 9 September and ending 27 September 1944, 14 interviews were held between Gandhi and

[165] Jinnah's interview to Prem Nath Bazaz in Sri Nagar, 28–29 May 1944; Ali, *Jinnah on World Affairs*, 241–42.

[166] Jinnah's interview to the *News Chronicle*, 4 October 1944; Ali, *Jinnah on World Affairs*, 243–44.

[167] *Collected Works of Mahatma Gandhi*, Vol. LXXVII (17 December 1942–31 July 1944), 393.

[168] Bolitho, *Jinnah: Creator of Pakistan.*

Jinnah in Bombay. In between these talks several letters were also exchanged between the two leaders. Gandhi, in his individual capacity, had carried the Rajaji's formula to Jinnah to reach to a settlement. This was the last serious attempt to bring the warring leaders on a common platform.

Rajaji explained:

> I have tried to understand the case of the Muslims and the case of the Congress and to be just to both parties. This claim may not be accepted either by the Muslim League leader or by the leaders of Hindu communalists. But I believe that impartial judges will see the justice in the claim.[169]

The C. R. or the Rajaji formula set such conditions as (a) subject to the terms of constitution for a free India, the League would endorse the demand for independence and shall cooperate with the Congress on the formation of the interim government in the transitional period, (b) after termination of the War, a commission shall demarcate contiguous areas with Muslim majority in the north-west and in the east; within such areas, plebiscite shall decide the issue of separation from Hindustan, (c) all parties can advocate their points of view before holding the plebiscite, (d) in the event of separation, mutual agreements shall be entered into for safeguarding defence, commerce, communications and for other essential purposes, (e) transfer of population only on voluntary basis and (f) these terms to become binding only in case of transfer by Britain of full power and responsibility for the governance of India.[170]

The first round of talk on 9 September lasted for three and a half hours. Gandhi said: 'It was a test of my patience.... I am amazed at my own patience. However, it was a friendly talk.' He noticed in Jinnah a staggering contempt for Rajaji and his formula.[171] Jinnah asked Gandhi whether he had come to meet him as a Hindu or as

[169] C. Rajagopalachari, 'Gandhi-Jinnah Talks: Text of Correspondence and Other Relevant Matter', Preface, *The Hindustan Times*, New Delhi, 1944, iii.

[170] *Gandhi-Jinnah Talks*, 36.

[171] *Collected Works of Mahatma Gandhi*, Vol. LXXVIII (1 August 1944–31 December 1944), 87–88.

a representative of the 'Hindu Congress'. Gandhi said he had come as an individual and Jinnah could talk to him as an individual or as president of the League.[172] Jinnah was, however, not to be moved. He asked for Pakistan before, and not after, independence from the British rule. Gandhi said all Muslims did not want Pakistan, and more so, the willingness to separate should be put to the vote of all inhabitants of the area. Jinnah asked: 'Why should you ask non-Muslims?' Gandhi replied: 'You cannot possibly deprive a section of the population of its vote. You must carry them with you, and if you are in the majority why should you be afraid?'[173]

Jinnah wrote to Gandhi on 10 September and referred to Gandhi's refusal to accept the basis of the Lahore Resolution and his remark that there was 'an ocean' between him and Jinnah.[174] Gandhi told Jinnah that his life mission had been Hindu–Muslim unity which could not be achieved without the foreign power being ousted. He accepted having made the statement—'an ocean separated you and me in outlook'—but that was not in reference to the Lahore Resolution: 'Lahore resolution is indefinite. Rajaji has taken from it the substance and given it a shape.'[175] Jinnah refuted any connection between the Lahore Resolution and the Rajaji formula. 'On the contrary', he observed, 'he (Rajaji) has not only put it (the Lahore Resolution) out of shape but mutilated it' and therefore, the only solution, Jinnah told Gandhi, was to accept the division of India as Pakistan and Hindustan, as briefly laid down in the Lahore Resolution of March 1940, and then proceed to settle the details forthwith.[176]

Following another round of talks on 13 September, Gandhi told Jinnah that there was no parallel in the whole of world of converts or their descendants seeking a nation on that basis alone:

[172] *Collected Works of Mahatma Gandhi*, Vol. LXXVIII, 88.

[173] *Collected Works of Mahatma Gandhi*, Vol. LXXVIII, 88–89.

[174] *Gandhi-Jinnah Talks*, 3.

[175] Gandhi to Jinnah, 11 September 1944, *Gandhi-Jinnah Talks*, 5–6.

[176] Jinnah to Gandhi, 11 September 1944, *Gandhi-Jinnah Talks*, 6–7.

> The more our argument progresses, the more alarming your picture appears to me. It would be alluring if it were true. But my fear is growing that it is wholly unreal. I find no parallel in history for a body of converts and their descendants claiming to be a nation apart from the parent stock. If India was one nation before the advent of Islam, it must remain one in spite of the change of faith of a very large body of her children. You do not claim to be a separate nation by right of conquest but by reason of acceptance of Islam. Will the two nations become one if the whole of India accepted Islam? Will Bengalis, Andhras, Tamilians, Maharashtrians, Gujaratis, etc., cease to have their special characteristics if all of them became converts to Islam? ... You seem to have introduced a new test of nationhood. If I accept it, I would have to subscribe to many more claims and face an insoluble problem.[177]

Responding to Gandhi on 17 September, Jinnah agreed that the word 'Pakistan' was not mentioned in the Lahore Resolution, but the word had by then, he clarified, 'become synonymous with the Lahore resolution'. He refused to accept Gandhi's contention that he represented the whole of India: 'It is quite clear that you represent nobody else but the Hindus, and as long as you do not realize your true position and the realities, it is very difficult for me to argue with you....'[178] Gandhi told Jinnah that he hoped not to be expected to accept the Lahore Resolution without understanding its implications, and if his last letter was the final word, then there was little hope:

> Can we not agree to differ on the question of "two nations" and yet solve the problem on the basis of self-determination? It is this basis that has brought me to you. If the regions holding Muslim majorities have to be separated according to the Lahore resolution, the grave step of separation should be specifically placed before and approved by the people in that area.[179]

Jinnah pointed to the 'inconsistencies and contradictions' in various positions adopted by Gandhi in the course of their correspondence. He wanted Gandhi to appreciate Muslims' claim of the 'right of self-determination as a nation and not as a territorial unit', a claim, which

[177] *Gandhi-Jinnah Talks*, 12–13.

[178] Ibid, 16–18.

[179] Gandhi to Jinnah, 19 September 1944, *Gandhi-Jinnah Talks*, 18–19.

he emphasized, was their 'birthright'.[180] Gandhi was 'disturbed' by Jinnah's letter since the consequences of accepting his proposition of Muslims constituting a separate nation would be extremely dangerous. Once this principle was admitted, he lamented, 'there would be no limit to claims for cutting India into numerous divisions which would spell India's ruins':

> I have therefore suggested a way out. Let it be a partition as between two brothers, if a division there must be...You summarily reject the idea of common interest between the two arms. I can be no willing party to a division which does not provide for the simultaneous safeguarding of common interests such as defence, foreign affairs and the like. There will be no feeling of security by the people of India without a recognition of the natural and mutual obligations arising out of physical contiguity.[181]

Gandhi–Jinnah talks meandered. Gandhi complained that the talk on 22 September had left 'a bad taste' and the process had almost reached a breaking point. Their talks and their correspondence, Gandhi felt, were following a parallel course.[182] Finally on 24 September, Gandhi summed up his suggestions which, he felt, would reasonably satisfy the claim embodied in the Lahore Resolution. The foundational assumption in Gandhi's proposal was that India was not to be regarded as two or more nations but as one family whose Muslim members in the north-west zones and in the east desired to live in separation. These areas were to be demarcated by a commission approved by the Congress and the League. Thereafter, the wishes of the people of these areas should be ascertained through adult voting or through some equivalent method. If the vote was for separation, then they would be separated and constituted into two sovereign independent States as soon as India became free. The treaty of separation should provide for efficient administration of foreign affairs, defence, internal communications, customs, commerce and the like which must continue to be

[180] Jinnah to Gandhi, 21 September 1944, *Gandhi-Jinnah Talks*, 19–21.

[181] Gandhi to Jinnah, 22 September 1944, *Gandhi-Jinnah Talks*, 22.

[182] Gandhi to Jinnah, 23 September 1944, *Gandhi-Jinnah Talks*, 25.

matters of common interest between the contracting parties. The treaty shall contain safeguards for rights of minorities in the two States.[183]

Jinnah complained that Gandhi had, through these suggestions, changed the fundamental basis of the Lahore Resolution as there was no acceptance of the assumption that (a) Muslims in India were a separate nation, (b) they had an inherent right of self-determination and (c) they alone were entitled to exercise the right of theirs for self-determination.[184] Gandhi advised Jinnah to 'think fifty times' before throwing away an offer which had been made 'entirely in the spirit of service in the cause of communal harmony'. He requested Jinnah to place this offer before the council of the League, and if the council was not inclined to accept it, then he (Jinnah) could advise the council to place the proposal before the open session of the League. In that situation, Gandhi was willing to attend and address the open session of the League.[185] Jinnah's response was stern—only a member or a delegate was entitled to participate in the deliberations of the meetings of the council or the open session, and therefore Gandhi was not entitled to address the open session of the League.

Except for generating lot of interest in the press and some hope among the Congress supporters, the Gandhi–Jinnah talks did not yield any fruitful result. The differences between the principles and attitude of the two leaders were too fundamental to be diluted through such methods. Jinnah would accept nothing less than the acceptance of the idea of a separate nationhood for Muslims, and then every other measure was presumed to naturally emanate from such an acceptance. Gandhi had made an honest attempt and put up for consideration the maximum that he could yield, even at the cost of annoying many of his own party men. But Jinnah was not the one to be moved through such tactics. Yet, the month of talks and close correspondence was the only time they had met at close quarters ever since the early years of their association. At the close of the talks, the 'ocean' between Gandhi

[183] *Gandhi-Jinnah Talks*, 26–27.

[184] Jinnah to Gandhi, 25 September 1944, *Gandhi-Jinnah Talks*, 27.

[185] Gandhi to Jinnah, 25 September 1944, *Gandhi-Jinnah Talks*, 32.

and Jinnah remained as wide as ever, and the Mahatma's 'life mission' of achieving Hindu–Muslim unity appeared more elusive than before.

Soon after the end of these talks, Gandhi told the *News Chronicle* on 29 November 1944 that though Jinnah was sincere and a good man, he was 'suffering from hallucination when he imagines that an unnatural division of India could bring either happiness or prosperity to the people concerned'. Gandhi, however, added that they had parted as friends and hoped to meet again.[186] Jinnah furiously replied:

> Here is an apostle and a devotee of non-violence threatening us with a fight to the knife, and according to him the talks have only adjourned *sine die*. But apart from that, what kind of separate State does he concede to the obvious Muslim majority in their national homelands?[187]

Few months later in February 1945, in his interview to the *News Chronicle*, Jinnah stated that 10 crores of Muslims would never agree to be transferred from British raj and British imperialism to 'Hindu raj and Hindu imperialism of the Brahmin–Bania combination' as that would be 'sure as death' for them.[188]

The Final Leg of the Journey: 1945–1948

When the War ended in May 1945, the Congress leaders languishing in jails were freed immediately. The political events moved at a fast pace from here onwards. Wavell showed his inclination to meet Indian leaders in Simla on 25 June to decide further course of action on providing self-government and to remove the deadlock on the communal question. A day before the summit, Wavell met Azad, Gandhi and Jinnah and reported that Gandhi and Jinnah were behaving like 'very temperamental prima donnas'.[189] During the summit on 25 June Azad, as president of the Congress, pointed to the non-communal

[186] 29 September 1944, *Gandhi-Jinnah Talks*, 47–48.

[187] Press Conference, Bombay, 4 October 1944, *Gandhi-Jinnah Talks*, 52–53.

[188] Ali, *Jinnah on World Affairs*, 247–48.

[189] Wolpert, Jinnah of Pakistan, 243.

nature of his party, but Jinnah would not settle for anything less than painting the Congress as a Hindu body. Jinnah made it clear that he would not agree to any constitution except on 'the fundamental principle of Pakistan.'[190] When the meeting was reconvened on 29 June, the viceroy asked for panels of names for his new council, Azad agreed immediately, but Jinnah sought time for consulting his working committee. He wanted a guarantee from the viceroy that all Muslim members of his council would be nominated by the League only. Wavell refused to extend such a guarantee. They met again on 8 and 11 July, but Jinnah refused to budge. Wavell's grand plan ended there. Although Jinnah's bid to secure parity for his party on the basis of religion had failed for the time being, it nonetheless showed his power to wreck the process if his agenda was not on the list. After the abortive talks in Simla in 1945, Jinnah in his address to the Muslim League in Bombay reiterated his utter contempt for Gandhi:

> When it suits Mr. Gandhi, he represents nobody, he can talk only in his individual capacity…Yet when it suits him again, he is the supreme dictator of the Congress. He thinks he represents the whole of India. Gandhi is an enigma. How can we come to a settlement with him…Unless Mr. Gandhi and the Congress give up their demands of establishing Hindu Raj and by hook or crook bringing the Muslims into it, for which they have been determinedly working, they cannot expect us to transfer ourselves from the British Government to a Hindu Raj.[191]

K. M. Munshi felt that Jinnah held Gandhi, Patel and Nehru in supreme contempt, and recalled that when on one occasion Wavell asked him (Jinnah) to see Gandhi, he met Gandhi and then told the viceroy that 'he (Gandhiji) is the worst Hindu in the country; he wants to dominate all of us.'[192] When asked if his demand for Pakistan inferred loyalty to the community before loyalty to the country, Jinnah bluntly refused to concede nationhood to India: 'There is no country in that sense. I don't regard myself as an Indian. India is a state of

[190] Ibid, 243.

[191] 6 August 1945, *Indian Annual Register*, July–December 1945, 158–59.

[192] *Oral Transcript of K. M. Munshi*, NMML, 17.

nationalities including two major nations, and all we claim is a distinct sovereign state for our nation—Pakistan.'[193]

Fortunes of Jinnah and his Muslim League shot up sharply after the general elections of 1945–1946. In sharp contrast to the results of the 1937-elections, he had now bagged the majority of the Muslim seats. It was an election the League had fought in the name of Islam and Pakistan, the two, made almost inseparable. A vote for Pakistan was seen as a vote for Islam. Religious preachers and Sufi *pirs* were also pressed into League's electoral campaign. The imaginary fear of the 'tyranny' of a 'Hindu Raj' was made to appear real, paying huge dividends in the end. The party won all the thirty Muslims seats in the Central Assembly, and as many as 439 out of 490 seats in the state assemblies. This landslide victory enabled Jinnah to emerge fully capable in the negotiations with the Congress and the government. Fresh from this victory, and in an attempt to put additional pressure on the stakeholders, the League leaders after March 1946 started talking in terms of a civil war if their demands were not met. Abdur Rab Nishtar, an important leader of the League announced that the Mussalmans belonged to a 'martial race' and were not believers in 'non-violent principles of Mr Gandhi.' Similarly, Abdul Qaiyum Khan, leader of the League from the NWFP declared that the 'well-armed' people in the tribal areas were for Pakistan.[194] This threat was effectively realized through the 'Direct Action Day' of 16 August 1946 when Jinnah in his own words 'bid goodbye to constitutional methods' and told the council of the League: 'today we have also forged a pistol and are ready to use it.'[195]

Mountbatten arrived towards the end of March 1947 to lead the most momentous change in the modern history of the country. However, by that time the die had been cast. Mountbatten later admitted that he had met nobody except Gandhi 'who seriously thought we could go back':

[193] Jinnah's interview to Norman Cliff of *News Chronicle* (London), 12 April 1946; Ali, *Jinnah on World Affairs*, 295–97.

[194] Nanda, *Road to Pakistan*, 320–21.

[195] Ibid, 321.

> Gandhiji never agreed. Up to the very last day when I saw him, when I came back to London before the June 3rd meeting, I thought I was going to have awful trouble with him, but he said it was his day of silence. I think it was his way of accepting gracefully that nothing could be done.[196]

Mountbatten recalled that Gandhi put up a 'hare-brained scheme' one day: 'You should invite Jinnah Sahib to form the government and then he will remain without partition.' Mountbatten replied: 'If you could get the Congress party to accept that, I would go along with it.'[197] In the final stages of negotiations, in order to save partition, Gandhi again suggested to Mountbatten to dismiss the interim government and invite Jinnah to form the government. But Mountbatten argued with him, and said that his 'suggestion was impractical' and unless the Congress party, Nehru, Patel and Kripalani also endorsed his suggestion, he would not speak to Jinnah about it: 'I said those three, if those three will come back with you and say, "Yes, go ahead", I will speak to Jinnah. I won't see him unless they do because it would absolutely fail.'[198]

Mountbatten felt Jinnah was very serious about partition, even threatening civil war if his demand was not met:

> You have got to remember Jinnah's political history. He was old man already then. Though we didn't know it, I suppose he was dying. He had now reached the stage where he had brought the Muslim League up the road to fight. Look at the Direct Action Day Calcutta in 1946. He had shown his power. He told me over and over again that he would fight, that there would be a civil war throughout India. He rather boasted this would not be confined to the Punjab and Bengal, because he said, there were forty million Muslims in the rest of India who would fight. I said, "They all will be killed." Nevertheless he said, "They should die gloriously" and so forth. I think he intended to fight. He showed me no signs of not wishing to do so.[199]

From the beginning to till very late, Jinnah had deliberately avoided giving the demand for Pakistan a precise definition or a well-defined

[196] *Oral Transcript of Mountbatten*, 13–14.

[197] Ibid, 10–11.

[198] Ibid, 20–21.

[199] Ibid, 11–12.

map. As Ayesha Jalal points out: 'A host of conflicting shapes and forms, most of them vague, were given to what remained little more than a catch-all, an undefined slogan.'[200] But when it started becoming clear that the Hindu majority districts of the Punjab and Bengal would be partitioned, Jinnah put in all his might to prevent it, even going to the extent of forwarding logic in contradiction of his two-nation theory. With the two major provinces to be partitioned along religious lines, consequently reducing the area that would ultimately constitute Pakistan, Jinnah went crazy. He sought the maximum possible area under the new State and a corridor connection the north-west and the east regions:

> He wanted the maximum. He really wanted to have the whole of north India. This is the way he would have liked to start with. If he could not have that, he wanted the whole of undivided Punjab, the whole of undivided Bengal and of course Sind and Assam, the North Wes Frontier Province and any other area he could get. At one stage when he thought he had really managed to achieve a certain amount, he demanded a corridor, a land corridor between West and East Pakistan, which shows how extravagant and unrealistic his demands were.[201]

Jinnah was highly upset with what he started calling a 'moth-eaten Pakistan'. He argued that a man was a Bengali first or a Punjabi first rather than a Muslim or a Hindu. Mountbatten quickly retorted that that logic applied to all of India and to partition itself.[202] Jinnah felt that the idea of partitioning the two provinces was a 'bluff on the part of the Congress to frighten him off Pakistan.' He appealed to Mountbatten not to destroy the unity of Bengal and Punjab 'which had national characteristics in common; common history, common way of life; and where the Hindus have stronger feelings as Bengalis or Punjabis than they have as members of the Congress.' Mountbatten countered his arguments: 'I am afraid I drove the old gentleman mad, because whichever way his argument went I always pursued it to a

[200] Ayesha Jalal, *The Sole Spokesman: Jinnah, the Muslim League and the Demand for Pakistan* (Cambridge: Cambridge University Press, 1985), 4.

[201] *Oral Transcript of Mountbatten*, 17.

[202] Ibid, 13–14.

stage beyond which he did not wish it to go.'[203] Ironically, as Ayesha Jalal argues, it was Jinnah's two-nation theory which was now acting as 'the sword' to cut 'his Pakistan down to size.'[204] Jinnah demanded a corridor through Hindustan connecting the two halves of Pakistan, and then in order to lure the Hindus of the Punjab and Bengal, he assured them full protection with regard to their religion, faith, life, property and culture: 'They will be in all respects treated as citizens of Pakistan without any distinction of caste, colour, religion or creed.'[205]

Post Partition: The Concluding Journey of a Heavily Punctured Relationship

In his press conference in Delhi on 13 July 1947, now since the new State of Pakistan had been decided upon, Jinnah asked minorities to be loyal to the State: 'You cannot have a minority which is disloyal and plays the role of sabotaging the state. That minority of course, becomes intolerable in any state. I advise the Hindus and Muslims, I advise every citizen to be loyal to his state.'[206] And on his departure from India, he sent a message appealing people to bury the past and start 'afresh as two independent sovereign States of Hindustan and Pakistan.'[207] After Pakistan was created, a tactful politician that he was, Jinnah no longer talked about the two-nation theory. The theory having achieved its objective lay redundant now. Inaugurating the first session of the Pakistan Constituent Assembly on 11 August 1947, after being elected its President, he told his countrymen—

> Any idea of a United India could never have worked and in my judgment it would have led us to a terrific disaster. May be that view is correct; may be it is not; that remains to be seen... If you will work in co-operation,

[203] 'Record of Interview between Mountbatten and Jinnah regarding Jinnah's position on the Cabinet Mission', 8 April 1947; Ali, *Jinnah on World Affairs*, 354–56.

[204] Jalal, *Jinnah: The Sole Spokesman*, 255.

[205] Jinnah's Press Conference in Delhi, 13 July 1947; Ali, *Jinnah on World Affairs*, 446–52.

[206] Ibid.

[207] 'Farewell Message of Jinnah, GG Designate, on the Eve of His Departure from Delhi', 7 August 1947; Ali, *Jinnah on World Affairs*, 490.

> forgetting the past, burying the hatchet you are bound to succeed. If you change your past and work together in a spirit that every one of you, no matter to what community he belongs, no matter what relations he had with you in the past, no matter what is his colour, caste or creed, is first, second and last a citizen of this State with equal rights, privileges and obligations, there will be no end to the progress you will make. ...You may belong to any religion or caste or creed—that has nothing to do with the business of the State... We are starting with this fundamental principle that we are all citizens and equal citizens of one State...in course of time Hindus will cease to be Hindus and Muslims would cease to be Muslims, not in the religious sense, because that is the personal faith of each individual, but in the political sense as citizens of the State.[208]

However, Jinnah's emphasis on treating religion only in a personal sense and looking at all citizens as equal, ended here. 'With the assumption of power of the new State', *Hindustan Times* wrote,

> the master plan of Jinnah to make of it an Islamic State was forthwith put into execution. This involved many operations of a rather drastic nature. But the indomitable and ambitious Quaid-e-Azam would not relent.... With his will prevailing as command in Pakistan, he has weeded out all non-conforming persons and parties....[209]

Jinnah was essentially looking at the new State as a Muslim or Islamic nation which should borrow its laws strictly from the tenets of Islam, and commit itself additionally to the cause of Muslims all over the world. On the inauguration of the Pakistan Broadcasting Service few days following his statement in the Constituent Assembly, he told his countrymen that the birth of Pakistan marked the 'fulfillment of the destiny of the Muslim nation' and that the Muslims of India had shown to the world that they were 'a united nation'.[210] When the process of constitution-making actually began, he favoured *Sharia* or Islamic law to form the foundational basis of a future Pakistan.

In a nascent state, founded on the basis of the idea that adherents of Islam were fundamentally different and poles apart from their Hindu

[208] Ali, *Jinnah on World Affairs*, 499–501.

[209] 'Architect of Pakistan'.

[210] Ali, *Jinnah on World Affairs*, 509–11.

counterparts, theocracy was the logical outcome. One could argue on the actual shape of an ideal theocratic state, but there could be little argument that the new country had to be an Islamic state. Jinnah repeatedly propounded the theory of a close proximity between the Islamic principles and a democratic set-up. Addressing the Karachi Bar Association on 25 January 1948, he emphatically declared that those rejecting the idea of an Islamic State were actually creating a 'mischief' and some were led by propaganda. Insisting that Pakistan's constitution should be based on Sharia, he emphasized that Islamic principles were as applicable to life than as they were 1300 years ago: 'Let us lay the foundations of our democracy on the basis of truly Islamic ideals and principles.'[211] He had echoed these sentiments on the eve of partition too: 'When you talk of democracy, I am afraid you have not studied Islam. We learnt democracy thirteen centuries ago.'[212] In his broadcast to the people of the United Sates on 26 February 1948, Jinnah felt sure that the shape of Pakistan's constitution would be of a democratic type, 'embodying the essential principles of Islam'. These principles, he contended, were applicable in 'actual life as they were 1300 years ago': 'Islam and its idealism have taught us democracy.'[213]

He even moved a significant step ahead in this discourse when he asked the State Bank of Pakistan on the occasion of its inauguration on 1 July 1948 to evolve 'banking practices compatible with Islamic ideas of social and economic life'. To strengthen his argument, he claimed that the economic system of the West had failed to do justice between man and man and therefore Pakistanis must work their destiny in their own way and present to the world an economic system 'based on true Islamic concept of equality of manhood and social justice' and thereby fulfil 'our mission as Muslims'.[214] In his last 'Eid message on 6 August 1948, around a month before he passed away, Jinnah exhorted the Muslim States, including the Muslim majority areas, to unite as they

[211] Nanda, *Road to Pakistan*, 326.

[212] Jinnah's Press Conference in Delhi, 13 July 1947; Ali, *Jinnah on World Affairs*, 446–52.

[213] Ali, *Jinnah on World Affairs*, 638–39.

[214] Ibid, 681.

were all passing through perilous times': 'The drama of power politics that is being staged in Palestine, Indonesia and Kashmir should serve as an eye-opener to us. It is only by putting up a united front that we can make our voice felt in the counsels of the world.'[215]

Jinnah's diatribe against Gandhi continued unabated even after the creation of Pakistan. In a conversation with Ismay on 3 October 1947, he complained that the Indian government and Gandhi were 'determined on the destruction of Pakistan' and interestingly made a change from his earlier claims of seeing through the operation of the 'Hindu mind': 'That I, and indeed most of my countrymen, are totally incapable of understanding the working of the Hindu mind, and that we are very gullible.' When Ismay asked him if he doubted Nehru's sincerity and statesmanship, Jinnah directed his anger at Gandhi and said that Nehru was merely 'a figurehead, vain, loquacious, unbalanced, unpractical, and that the real and almost absolute power lay with Patel, who was actively aided and abetted by Gandhi'.[216] Gandhi, in sharp contrast, was positively disposed towards the new State of Pakistan. He even pressurized Patel when, during mid-January 1948, he insisted and got through the pending payment of 55 crore rupees to Pakistan. A week before that, Patel had told his cabinet colleagues that this payment would 'be converted into sinews of war against India'. In this, he had been supported by Mookerjee, Gadgil and Ambedkar. Nehru had also agreed initially. Patel had even informed a press conference that the settlement of financial issues could not be isolated from that of other vital issues and had to be implemented simultaneously.[217]

Drawing the 'Life-sketch' of the Quaid-i-Azam, a day after his death, the *Hindustan Times* very appropriately captured the leader's mind and his action:

> With all his strength and tenacity, he is a strangely negative person, whose appropriate symbol may well be a "No". Indeed, vanity is his most characteristic trait…Mr. Jinnah dictates, he does not parley. Jinnah talks, he does

[215] Ibid, 684–85.

[216] Ibid, 561–66.

[217] Rajmohan Gandhi, *Patel: A Life* (Ahmedabad: Navajivan Publishing House, 1991), 462.

> not listen. Jinnah is perfect. He is mysterious. He is magnificent. Jinnah's greatest admirer is Mr Jinnah himself. And he cannot be bought perhaps because he sets too high a price upon himself. The religion of *la Patrie* in Mr Jinnah's career is a glorified *moi*, writ large. For his is the *culte du moi*. Mr Jinnah was himself the League formerly. He is Pakistan today.[218]

Despite the fact that the religion-driven two-nation-theory failed to sustain Pakistan as one nation following the rise of Bangladesh in 1971, M. A. Jinnah created a new genre of political mobilization in which separatism was justified as legitimate. He was perhaps one of those nationalists who rose to prominence without a solid political base even in Muslim-majority provinces of Bengal and Punjab. A political activist with the capability of evolving appropriate strategies, the Quaid-i-Azam charted a course of action which finally led to the fulfilment of his dream, namely, the creation of Pakistan. History was, however, unkind to him because he hardly had a chance to contribute to a liberal Pakistan as he passed away just little more than a year after independent Pakistan was created. Nonetheless, history will remember him as a successful nationalist politician who intelligently utilized the well-entrenched Hindu–Muslim socio-economic differences as his defence for an independent Muslim state following the British withdrawal. It was, to his credit, that the regional leaders, Fazlul Haq from Bengal and Sikander Hayat Khan of Punjab, stood by him when he put forward his demand for Pakistan in the face of Gandhi's stiff opposition. So, Jinnah can be said to have generated mass enthusiasm for Pakistan which he successfully projected as a panacea for the socio-economically deprived majority of the Muslims. And, this is how he will be remembered in history.

Concluding Observations

For those keen on dismemberment of India concurrent with the process of the British withdrawal, M. A. Jinnah was a messiah; Gandhi was, in contrast, a tragic hero who, despite being vehemently opposed to partition, restrained himself from openly campaigning or leading a mass movement against it. Gandhi was confronted with this vital

218 'Architect of Pakistan'.

question in the months preceding the actual division of the country. With the memories of riots in Noakhali and Bihar fresh in his mind, he lamented that neither the Hindus and nor the Muslims were heeding to his advice. In his prayer meeting on 4 June 1947, Gandhi told the gathering that they should not feel sorry that India was to be partitioned because they had asked for it: 'The Congress never asked for it. I was not even present here. But the Congress can feel the pulse of the people. It realized that the Khalsa as also the Hindus desired it.'[219] In another meeting, he clarified that he could take the lead, but only if all non-Muslims were ready to follow what he had to say: 'And today I can say with confidence that if all the non-Muslims were with me, I would not let India be divided. But I must admit that today the general opinion is not with me, and so I must step aside and stay back.'[220] In a discussion with visitors, just a month before partition, Gandhi asserted that he could show the miracle if Hindus maintained peace and showed courage, but with what face could he tell the League not to indulge in atrocities? And if at all he was expected to give a lead, then against whom and to whom could he give the lead—

> The British have not partitioned the country. It has been done with the consent of the Muslim League and the Congress. Isn't that so? The leaders had no other alternative. They thought it was better to partition the country so that both the parts could live happily and peacefully rather than let the whole country go to pieces.[221]

There are two interrelated aspects of the Gandhi–Jinnah contention which deserve reiteration: first, some believe that Jinnah's insistence

[219] *Collected Works of Mahatma Gandhi*, Vol. LXVIII (25 May 1947–31 July 1947), 75. In his prayer meeting on 1 April 1947, Gandhi appeared peeved by what he felt about erosion of his authority within the Congress: 'Whatever the Congress decides will be done; nothing will be according to what I say. My writ runs no more. If it did the tragedies in the Punjab, Bihar and Noakhali would not have happened. No one listens to me anymore. I am a small man. True, there was a time when mine was a big voice. Then everyone obeyed what I said; now neither the Congress nor the Hindus not the Muslims listen to me. Where is the Congress today? It is disintegrating, I am crying in the wilderness.' *Collected Works of Mahatma Gandhi*, Vol. LXVII, 187.

[220] Prayer Meeting, 9 June 1947; *Collected Works of Mahatma Gandhi*, Vol. LXVIII, 118.

[221] 17 July 1947, *Collected Works of Mahatma Gandhi*, Vol. LXVIII, 356.

on partition was an afterthought since he, as some historical evidences point out, was persuaded to accept the Cabinet Mission's 1946 scheme of confederal India which would have not only marginalized the role of some leading Congressmen, including Jawaharlal Nehru and Vallabhbhai Patel but also considerably weakened the centre thereby creating eventually a weak State in the final negotiations for power. This was nothing new, as India's constitutional development since the adoption of the 1935 Government of India Act demonstrates. Some believe that Jinnah would have been happier had his Congress colleagues conceded some of his demands which would have substantiated his claim of being a pan-Indian (and not merely a Muslim) leader in India. The idea was floated by the viceroy John Linlithgow (1936–1943) when he mentioned that for Jinnah, Pakistan was primarily 'a bargain counter' to ascertain his indispensability in constitutional negotiations for power-sharing with his Indian counterparts. He appeared to have, as the argument goes, given enough indications to the viceroy who held this opinion despite the Muslim League being supportive of the creation of separate Muslim land following the acceptance of the Lahore Resolution in 1940. In this view, it was the failure of the Congress leadership to pre-empt the processes that finally culminated in India's division. And, therefore, consequently Gandhi, despite being a dominant voice in the nationalist campaign was unable to gauge the situation, was a testimony of a strategic failure that eventually led to the consolidation of Muslims in Jinnah's favour when he exhorted them to unite for Pakistan.

As an alternative, one may argue that Jinnah's coming up with the idea of two nations in the aftermath of the astounding defeat of the Muslim League in 1937 elections and resignation of the Congress ministries after the start of the Second World War in 1939 tells its own story. On the one hand, he was seeking to establish himself as the sole spokesman of the Muslim voice in India, and on the other, by attempting to undermine the mainstream nationalist opinion led by Gandhi he created a binary of leadership and parties strictly along communal lines—'Hindu Congress' led by Gandhi and the Muslim League led by Jinnah as representative voices of the Hindus and the Muslims, respectively. This hypothesis deprived Gandhi and the

Congress from speaking on behalf of all the communities or the whole of British India. In this sense, the deadlock in the Simla conference in 1945 on Jinnah insisting to nominate all Muslim members to the proposed council, thereby denying any representative authority to the Congress to speak on behalf of Muslims, was a well-thought-out strategy. K. M. Munshi, a prominent Congress leader, recalled that the 'greatest blunder' committed by the Congress was its decision to resign from the ministries in 1939.[222] And, therefore, by the time the Cabinet Mission came, its proposals could not have promoted unity, as by that time a stage had been reached 'where mere phrases could not bring about a harmonious spirit.'—

> Every time, you see, Jinnah raised his demands. There was first the Lucknow Pact which was accepted on the assurance that it would bring harmony. Later he said: "Give me my Fourteen Points and separate electorates and I will bring the Muslims to you." We submitted to it. Later still he said: "Accept the Communal Award, and everything will be all right." Every time he talked, his price became much higher. He did not expect that Pakistan would be ever consented by the Congress. He wanted to dominate the whole situation till he could have the whole of India at his feet.[223]

In the annals of Indian nationalism, Jinnah can be said to have represented an alter ego of Gandhi in the sense that both of them participated in the freedom struggle for fulfilling binary opposite nationalist aims. The model of nationalism that Gandhi nurtured, which was meant to be inclusive of all the communities, did not allow Jinnah to articulate his own exclusivist nationalist vision for Muslims. In the Gandhian framework, Muslims were sought to be accommodated in the pan-Indian politico-ideological framework. In Jinnah's perception, since Gandhi's scheme was a ploy to establish a 'Hindu Raj' at the cost of other communities, it was not only despised but also rejected instantaneously. Core here is the point that Jinnah and Gandhi interaction was interdependent in the sense that they reacted to each other as soon

[222] That was the only time in all those years, Munshi felt, when the British government was keen to make friends with the Congress: 'My view was that, if we had to fight a war of independence, helping England to fight the War would have been our own war of independence.' *Oral Transcript of K. M. Munshi*, 10–11, 26.

[223] *Oral Transcript of K. M. Munshi*, 11–12.

as an issue was brought up in the public domain. Here one needs to be sensitive to the colonial policy of divide et impera critically shaping the responses that both the Mahatma and the Quaid-i-Azam had articulated. So, India's colonial context remained an important variable in so far as the ideas which were conceptualized and flourished in the wake of the British rule.

Jinnah's concern for an independent Muslim state was a counter to the Congress insistence on undivided India that gained credibility presumably because of the colonizers' determination to take advantage of communal chasm that manifested itself in multiple ways, and which to some extent also reflected the socio-economic disparities dividing Muslims from their Hindu counterparts. In the context of carefully nurtured socio-economic imbalances between Hindus and Muslims, Gandhi's design of communal harmony did not appear to have been as effective during 1930s and 1940s, as it was expected to be, or as it had worked during the preceding years say for example during the non-cooperation days. Despite being a rebuttal of the Congress ideal of a united India, Jinnah's two-nation theory that created partition gained acceptance among large number of Muslims. This acceptance primarily evolved from their connecting the Muslims' socio-economic conditions with non-Muslim regimes, and invoking the fear of an impending danger to the Islamic culture and ideals. They believed that if the British left without partitioning the country, then the Congress, through its Hindu Raj, would further worsen these conditions. In this thinking, the image of common Muslims being the victims was readily endorsed. Fundamental here is the point that for conceptualizing Gandhi and Jinnah as alternative voices one need not ignore the prevalent socio-economic milieu and also the inspirational intellectual inputs that contributed to the contrasting viewpoints that they represented.

In such circumstances, the divide and rule strategy gave maximum dividends to the alien authority which further consolidated the Hindu–Muslim division beyond rapprochement. Speaking on 9 August 1945, after the Simla conference had hit the roadblock, Patel accused the British policy of divide and rule for actually creating the communal animosity:

> The British talk of Hindu-Muslim quarrels but who has thrust this burden on their shoulders? If they are sincere let them hand over to Congress or the League or accept international arbitration. Give me just a week's rule over Britain. I will create such disagreements that England, Wales and Scotland will fight one another for ever.[224]

The aforementioned discussion on Gandhi–Jinnah debate is, conceptually speaking, most instructive for it highlights the critical importance of specific sociocultural traits of a community in the creation of a multitude with specific goals. A sentiment of attachment and loyalty, nationalism is a sociocultural construct drawing on what is considered to be primary to the existence of the community in question. Hence, it does not seem odd if one's religio-cultural identity is highlighted to cement a bond with those having identical religious faith. Because it is purposefully invented, one should not also ignore the prevalent sociocultural milieu in which some of the claims receive general approbation. Here lies the source of strength of some nationalist interventions that succeed in contrast with those that fail presumably because they are not strong enough to establish the claim. Despite being derivative of the context, nationalism, as the story of Indian freedom struggle demonstrates, is primarily an ideological endeavour in the sense that it requires to be consciously nurtured and engendered with focus on predetermined goals. Not only is the Gandhi–Jinnah dialogue illustrative of a uniquely textured nationalist voice, it also testifies the contention that there can also be a nationalist critique within the widely accepted nationalist discourse that unfolded in India at the behest of Gandhi and his colleagues in the Congress. By being sensitive to the distinct sociocultural characteristics that the Indian Muslims evinced, and by constantly invoking the fear of an impending Hindu Raj, Jinnah succeeded in creating a persuasive language that almost immediately created a context in which separatism was hailed as desirable and empowering. Whether the processes could have been halted does not seem to be a relevant query because history has shown that it was inevitable given the existent socio-economic context in which the attempts at bridging the Hindu–Muslim schism did not seem to have been made as seriously as was needed. So, Jinnah was not an accident

[224] Gandhi, *Patel: A Life*, 345–46.

of history, but rather more an outcome of the circumstances that finally culminated in the rise of Pakistan, an independent Muslim state that Jinnah aspired in the face of stiff opposition from his Congress colleagues and other secular-minded nationalist Muslims. Being revered as the Quaid-i-Azam (great leader) and Baba-i-Quam (father of the nation), it was to Jinnah's credit that he successfully raised a voice which, dismissed as transitional at the outset, helped build a nationalist discourse for those who were part of the Muslim majority areas and were also simultaneously socio-economically peripheral and ideologically marginalized. The critique that he put forth of the Mahatma was no less important because it allowed him to conceptualize Indian Muslims differently by reference to the prevalent socio-economic milieu that hardly gave them an opportunity to be treated at par with their caste-Hindu counterparts.

Gandhi–Jinnah encounters heavily influenced the trajectory of how India moved towards independence and partition. This division continues to shape the destiny of both the countries and their interrelationship. While the theory of two nations, turning into three in 1971 with the creation of Bangladesh, stands somewhat disapproved in the way these countries have progressed, and have become modern powers in South Asia in their own right, what is significant is that the image and memories of Gandhi and Jinnah continue to provide legitimacy to politics, actions and policies on the two sides of the border. While Pakistan has been faced with a highly unstable democratic experience interspersed with military coups, India has grown to be the biggest democracy in the world. The conflict between the ideas of Gandhi and Jinnah need to be tested against these results.

CONCLUSION

I

Politics, Ideology and Nationalism: Jinnah, Savarkar and Ambedkar versus Gandhi is a new argument based on familiar historical evidences. Implicit here is a two-fold idea: on the one hand, the book makes the point that the historico-political processes cannot be grasped, if not conceptualized, without comprehending the dialectical interconnections among the conflicting and also compatible ideas that surfaced in the nationalist context immediately before the 1947 transfer of power in India. The context was, of course, relevant and thus pertinent to understand the ideas that seem to have critically shaped India's rise as an independent polity in the comity of nations. What is striking is the fact that despite having been nurtured in the same colonial milieu, the nationalists held views which were also divergent on many occasions. While the book delves into the ideas of individual thinkers, it also deals, on the other hand, with the processes in which ideas contrary to their mainstream counterparts were also articulated with the objectives of attaining political freedom and human salvation. This does not seem to be odd since the contextual inputs behind the formation of ideas were not of similar types. Once these ideas were formed and had gained acceptance in the public domain, they led to an ideational battle which makes the study of Indian nationalism so interesting and conceptually innovative.

The first part of the title of the book, *politics, ideology and nationalism*, is explicit in its connotation because it highlights the importance of processes leading to the privileging of an idea or a set of ideas over others. This is a follow-up of the argument, made above, suggesting that the nature of the inputs that one receives from the context is also contingent on how these are internalized by those being engaged in the battle of ideas. Here, the second part of the title makes the argument far more explicit and intelligible by drawing on the empirical inputs that the specific individual thinkers garnered while defending their specific points of view. This is the crux of the argument that, notwithstanding being raised and nurtured in the same colonial socio-economic and political environment, M. A. Jinnah, V. D. Savarkar and B. R. Ambedkar differed with Gandhi in fundamental ways, though their goal did not seem to be exactly dissimilar. In other words, being nationalists, the Gandhi opponents espoused political liberation as perhaps the first step towards realizing their politico-ideological priorities. So, despite being nationalists par excellence, neither Jinnah nor Savarkar nor Ambedkar was hardly persuaded by what the Mahatma put forward as his nationalist vision. As a consequence, freedom was won, but punctured by the traumatic partition. Jinnah's two-nation theory gained credibility notwithstanding Gandhi's vehement opposition; in a similar vein, Savarkar's fascination for a majoritarian-driven Weltanschauung gradually caught people's imagination and Ambedkar's opposition to caste-based discrimination created a definite politico-ideological space for voices challenging the well-entrenched prejudicial mindsets that the mainstream nationalists were alleged to have epitomized. There is one fundamental point here, which is, Gandhi was the point of both confluence and departure: confluence because by being opposed to Gandhi, Jinnah, Ambedkar and Savarkar can be said to have consolidated a bond that appears to have flourished in a context when Gandhian ideas appear to have lost their appeal presumably because of the rise and consolidation of those ideas which helped articulate the nationalist zeal far more effectively than what Gandhi represented. The nationalist scene thus became a platform where multiple ideas jostled for space in a milieu in which the Mahatma reigned supreme as a nationalist leader. It was easier for him to remain so presumably because he was backed by the Congress which had its organization spread out in colonial India. In other words, that the Congress endorsed what Gandhi stood for explains, rather persuasively, why the Mahatma became a powerful voice across the length and breadth of the country in comparison with those who also had a powerful message, but their voice was hardly as effective as that of the former. Jinnah's Muslim League had its support base only in two British Indian provinces, Bengal and Punjab, while Savarkar and Ambedkar sought to create their constituencies by couching their appeal in emotions and sentiments: for Savarkar, the clamour for freedom was futile so long as the interests of the Hindus were sacrificed for protecting those of the minorities, especially the Muslims. By implication, it meant that Gandhi, by being soft, particularly to the Muslims, pursued a partisan agenda which alienated those supportive of the claim that Hindus were betrayed by the Gandhi-led Congress. Being ideologically baptized by the philosophy of Enlightenment, Ambedkar, while evolving his model of social justice, had also an appeal which was, however, confined to a specific segment of India's demography. In other words, despite being revolutionary in his ideas and approach, Babasaheb did not seem to have succeeded in creating a nationalist persona that was visible and ideologically appealing to the masses irrespective of class, clan and region. There are two important ideas that merit attention here: first, Gandhi had a pan-Indian appeal primarily because the nationalist discourse that he evolved had created a space in contrast with the competing ideological modes of conceptualizations. The second important idea stems from the claim that Gandhi seems to have put in place a format of the nationalist campaign setting the tone and tenor of anti-British counteroffensive which also created a space for competitive, if not contrary, politico-ideological priorities. This is therefore not an exaggerated claim that Gandhi being the pivot of the nationalist agitation had helped others build their counter narratives by drawing on those sociopolitical concerns which the Mahatma appears to have paid less attention to while being engaged in political mobilization for freedom. There is also the point that the Gandhian ideas had also drawn on those which his bete noire, Jinnah, Savarkar and Ambedkar, represented during their ideational battle with the Mahatma. In other words, the point, being made here, reinforces the claim that the Gandhian nationalist discourse had elements which had their roots in the ideas of Jinnah, Savarkar and Ambedkar; it was a creative amalgamation of competing politico-ideological inputs which Gandhi appears to have internalized presumably because they were complementary to the nationalist goal that he strove to achieve.

II

According to Plato, every philosopher is a child of his time. This is a profound statement since by highlighting the dialectical interconnection between the text and context, Plato reinforced the point that the ideas that the philosophers evolve are context-driven. In other words, since the context and text are dialectically interlinked, the latter cannot be understood without reference to the former. In terms of their origin, ideas are invariably locational; but, in terms of their nature, they can also be transcendental both locationally and also historically. For instance, the Upanishadic exaltation *Vasudhaiva Kutumbakam* (the world being a family) has its roots in the ancient past, which was articulated by the Enlightenment philosophers in Europe in the form of compassion, care and concern for others. The same ideas were reverberated in North America in the Jeffersonian claim for all men being born equal. Fundamental here is the point that ideas do not emerge in a vacuum; they are organically connected with the prevalent socioeconomic and political milieu. So, whatever a thinker or an activist seeks to do by creating a new template of thinking cannot be absolutely immune for the context in which they are born and nurtured. While defending Marxism as a context-driven doctrine, VI Lenin most explicitly referred to this aspect by suggesting that by disregarding the intimate interaction between the text and context, 'we pursue an argument that is devoid of substance'. By losing sight of this, 'we', he added further,

> turn Marxism into something one-sided, disfigured and lifeless; we deprive it of its living soul; we undermine its basic theoretical foundation – dialectics, the doctrine of historical development, all-embracing and full of contradictions; we undermine its connection with the definite practical tasks of the epoch, which may change with every new turn of history.[1]

[1] V. I. Lenin, *Marx, Engels, Marxism* (Peking: Foreign Language Press, 1978), 300.

Core to Lenin's argument is the idea that context remains most critical in ideological conceptualization; bereft of which it is clearly ahistorical. The argument also entails the point that also emphasizes the claim that context also generates urge for both deifying and acceptance. Even a cursory look at history confirms that socio-economic and political changes do not come so easily because the same context contributes to the arguments which are both supportive and also oppositional to the existent system. Here lies the clue as to why the British colonialism in India survived almost 200 years, despite nationalist challenge, largely with support from its Indian collaborators who justified their being with the alien authority as appropriate, notwithstanding being integral to the same context providing impetus to the campaign for freedom. Rather than being uniform, the nature of the influence that the context exerts varies from one situation to another, from one generation to another. This does not seem to be unusual, as history has shown. Basic here is the contention that context remains an important determinant of the ideas which can both be contextual and transcendental. One should add a caveat here because the ideas which are contextual today may be transcendental tomorrow; or, what is a transcendental idea today was a contextual one in the past since the former stemmed from specific contexts in which they were articulated and put into practice.

The above, rather long, prefacing remark is useful to provide a conceptual perspective for the argument that the book provides. Here, there is one central figure, the Mahatma, and there are not-so-central figures that also played a critical role in shaping India's nationalist response till independence was won in 1947. Broadly speaking, the campaign against the British for freedom was largely non-violent, though the role of other parallel forces of opposition cannot be overruled; they were not mainstream, though their impact in various parts of the country was felt. It is now established that Gandhi set the tone of the nationalist campaign which retained its non-violent character barring the major exception of the Chauri Chaura incident in 1922, which forced him to withdraw the Non-cooperation movement. In other words, it was Gandhi who evolved the macro strategy while challenging the alien power, and his colleagues who fought for independence seem to have been in agreement with him. What is argued here is the point that despite being supportive of Gandhi's non-violent campaign against the British, his critics, M. A. Jinnah, V. D. Savarkar and B. R. Ambedkar, held completely contrary sociopolitical views which put in a completely different steed in the annals of India's nationalist past. An earlier Congress activist Jinnah stuck to his demand for a separate Muslim homeland in opposition to his colleagues in the Congress. Nonetheless, he never sought to mobilize his supporters for a violent attack on the British government which reinforces the contention that he appeared to have endorsed the Gandhian method of non-violent struggle to get rid of political slavery. This is also true of V. D. Savarkar. Although he was baptized in the revolutionary nationalist ideology which led to his long incarceration in the Cellular Jail in Andaman, he did not appear to have been inclined to pursue a violent struggle for freedom once he was released and allowed to carry on his political activities in the constitutional format. In a similar vein, B. R. Ambedkar, being overwhelmed by the Enlightenment values, had hardly had inclination for violent struggle; he too seems to have upheld non-violence as perhaps the best option in the nationalist struggle. To reiterate the point made earlier, Gandhi's critics appear to have been persuaded by the argument that the Mahatma made in favour of non-violence as perhaps the most appropriate macro strategy in the nationalist mobilization for freedom. Similarity ends here. The three critics evolved powerful critiques of Gandhi's sociopolitical views. For instance, Jinnah's insistence on Hindus and Muslims being separate socio-cultural communities despite having lived together for ages contributed to his claim for vivisection of India into two sovereign states. Gandhi, as is well-known, was never persuaded to accept the argument which, to him, was based on his misconception of how India had evolved as a socio-cultural compact in which religion did not appear to be as dominant as was conceived. It was not Gandhi alone who critiqued Jinnah's point of view; nonetheless, India was partitioned and Pakistan was created on the basis of Jinnah's two-nation theory. On the basis of his conceptualization of Hindutva which is largely a cultural construct, Savarkar created a space for a religio-cultural argument to strike roots in the nationalist campaign. However, Gandhi, in his zeal to develop India as one unit regardless of religious schism, did not find Savarkar's argument persuasive since it was directed to create a Hindu

Pakistan. As an ideologue of the Hindu Mahasabha that championed the Hindu interests, Savarkar stood by his faith so long as he was active politically even after India's independence in 1947. Here too, in spite of being not so hard on Gandhi insofar as his macro strategy of non-violence was concerned, Savarkar differed from Gandhi since his endeavour at mobilizing the Hindus as a separate entity did not match with that of the Mahatma. The pattern is evident in case of the views of Ambedkar who, like Gandhi, was a firm believer of constitutional methods for grievance redressal. Being heavily influenced by the Enlightenment ideas, Babasaheb, as Ambedkar was popularly known, readily accepted the politico-ideological method of non-violence that Gandhi had deployed to win freedom. Differences had, however, surfaced as soon as Ambedkar questioned Gandhi's fascination for the foundational principles of Hinduism, based on the Vedic instructions, since they justified the discriminatory caste system which was, to him, a deterrent to India's rise as a nation.

As is evident, at one level, Gandhi's fierce critics such as Jinnah, Savarkar and Ambedkar seem to have found in non-violence an effective device for political mobilization for the nationalist cause. Even Jinnah, who carved out Pakistan, was favourably inclined to attain his political goal by resorting to non-violence. Ambedkar too ascertained that non-violence was perhaps the most effective means that drew on the core values of Enlightenment. The 1927 Mahad Satyagraha which Babasaheb led to claim the rights of Dalits to use water in a public tank catapulted him on to the centre stage of nationalist politics. It was possible for him to launch the struggle since the practice of Dalits being debarred from taking water from the tank was legally banned by the Bombay Legislative Council in 1923. The local municipal council was unable to implement the government decree due to opposition by the caste Hindus. According to Ambedkar, it was clearly illegal given the fact that the decree was adopted by the government after following due processes. That he partook in the non-violent struggle to ascertain Dalit rights over benefits that the public authority guaranteed is a testimony to his faith in the mode of struggle that the Mahatma had spearheaded for freedom. Savarkar's appreciation for non-violence came later in his career since he, being involved in revolutionary nationalist activities at the beginning of his political career, dubbed Gandhian non-violence as nothing but an intelligently crafted design for deceiving the masses especially when the British Raj was ruthless in containing the nationalist upsurges in the country. Once he was released from the Cellular Jail when he was serving a life sentence, he seemed to have undergone a radical metamorphosis in his political belief. In this phase of his political activities, he was clearly in favour of struggles that drew on constitutional methods, like the Congress. So long as he presided over the activities of the Hindu Mahasabha, he non-violently protested against the alien government for its misgovernance which, he felt, needed to be combatted by involving the masses at large. It was articulated in a series of speeches that he delivered during his stint as the supreme commander of the Hindu Mahasabha. A scan of the speeches helps us build the argument that Savarkar was also inclined to follow the democratic means of protests despite being a revolutionary nationalist when he arrived on the nationalist scene in India.

III

There is no denying that the context is critical in shaping the individuals and their socio-economic and political ideas. However, the impact of the context on how an individual evolves varies from one to another, which means that it is not uniform. While making this point, one has to be sensitive to the claim that with the change in the context, the individual also transforms in a way which may not have been conceived earlier. For instance, B. R. Ambedkar never came to terms with caste atrocities which he rightfully condemned as an artificial social design to deprive a section of Hindus of their legitimate rights as human beings. In other words, being born as a Dalit, he was subject to social humiliation which was unacceptable to him as it was an engineered device by the caste Hindus to put the Dalits in permanent subjugation. This was further illustrated when he abjured Hinduism in 1956 and accepted Buddhism as his religious creed. Shifting his faith to Buddhism was, for Ambedkar, a panacea in the sense that it would relieve him of the difficulties that he and his compatriot Dalits had encountered so long as they remained within the fold of Hinduism. It was a relief that he had reasons to cherish his achievements in circumstances when there was hardly an opportunity for the untouchables to be treated at par with the caste Hindus. It can thus be argued that Ambedkar chose Buddhism not out of his appreciation but out of his disenchantment with Hinduism; the reason was thus not positive but negative as he realized that no other religion was adequately equipped to enable the Dalits to fulfil their aspired goal. The conversion was also the culmination of his search for an appropriate conceptual framework to view human beings as equal to one another, which was not possible so long as caste hierarchy remained sacrosanct. This was thus a libertarian endeavour because Buddhism, by being opposed to discrimination of any kind, created a space for the socially disenfranchised communities to legitimately demand their rights as equal partners which they had been denied so far. The conversion, then, was Ambedkar's attempt 'to dissociate himself and his people from the humiliating role assigned to them' largely to historically evolved and socio-economically supportive discriminatory and prejudicial practices.[2] Buddhism was, to him, not merely a religious sect but a design for human emancipation; it was a design which was neither deceitful nor adversarial to human beings simply because of the accident of birth. In a number of ways, Buddhism thus provided Ambedkar with a persuasive alternative within his nationalist concern because of its typical Indian roots; it also helped him to resolve his emotional dilemma that he encountered while exploring the possibilities of being converted to Islam or Christianity since they were 'foreign' in terms of their origin and evolution. Conversion was like the killing of two birds with one stone since: (a) it was a powerful critique of Hinduism that always privileged atrocious social customs to segregate one section of the community from another, and (b) it also helped the untouchables evolve as a self-conscious collectivity with a well-defined goal. Hence, it has been fairly argued that 'with the conversion to Buddhism, Ambedkar achieved what Phule and Periyar for all their resistance to Hinduism had failed to achieve: making a conscious non-Hindu identity a collective material and radicalizing force in India'.[3] Conversion was thus not an isolated event, but one that

[2] Ananya Vajpeyi, *Righteous Republic: The Political Foundation of Modern India* (Cambridge: Harvard University Press, 2012), 225.

[3] G. Omvedt, 'Undoing the Bondage: Dr. Ambedkar's Theory of Dalit Liberation', in *From Periphery to Centre Stage: Ambedkar, Ambedkarite & Dalit Future*, ed. K Yadav

was a significant component of his politico-ideological vision seeking to liberate an equally significant section of India's demography, being stigmatized, if not completely dehumanized, for fulfilling the partisan aims of the caste Hindus.

What provoked Ambedkar to go for conversion to Buddhism was: (a) he was fascinated by its concern for absolute equality among human beings regardless of one's birth, and (b) it was a religion which was neither discriminatory nor prejudicial in character. Denouncing Hinduism for having endorsed graded inequality, he thus opted for Buddhism that clearly stood for equality in its substantial sense. While defending his decision, he further argued that he preferred Buddhism because it was a combination of three principles. In contrast with other religions that were primarily concerned with God, soul and life after death, Buddhism, according to Ambedkar, 'teaches *Prajna* (understanding as against superstition and supernaturalism), ... *Karuna* (love) [and] ... *Samata* (equality)'.[4] The Buddhist Sangha epitomized, as he also emphasized, 'communistic organization because it disallows private property [and came into being] as a result of a change of mind'.[5] The explanation that Babasaheb provided reveals that his decision to convert to Buddhism was not just a strategic device but one that was drawn on his politico-ideological faith in the values of the philosophy of Enlightenment. His final decision to lead his followers to renounce Hinduism and convert to Buddhism showed that he could not be an atheist like Savarkar, but he could not remain a Hindu either. Savarkar formed his theory of nationalism around the question of who belonged to India. Religion for him was an ideology of nationalism but not the credo by which he led his life. Jinnah was similar. He displayed no fondness for Islam and its practices, and yet he leveraged the idea of religion as defining the other 'nation' within India and achieved his dream of creating Pakistan, the first newly created nation in the 20th century. By winning a Muslim nation

(New Delhi: Manohar Publications, 2000), 136.

[4] B. R. Ambedkar, 'Why I Like Buddhism', in *Dr. Babasaheb Ambedkar Writings and Speeches*, ed. Vasant Moon, Vol. 17, Part III (New Delhi: Dr. Ambedkar Foundation, Government of India, 2014) (reprint), 515.

[5] Ibid.

state in what Savarkar had theorized as a solely Hindu nation, Jinnah disproved Savarkar. The existence of Pakistan became for Savarkar and other Hindu nationalists the principal failure of the Congress and Gandhi in winning independence for India. The ideal dream for Hindu nationalists became the recovery of the ceded regions to recreate *Akhand Hindustan*, undivided India.

His conversion was, at one level, a protest, and, at another, a rejuvenation of the individual self presumably because of Buddhism being inherently favourably disposed towards absolute equality. It was evident in his statement that he made immediately after his conversion. According to him,

> by discarding my ancient religion which stood for inequality and oppression today, I am reborn. I have no faith in the philosophy of incarnation; and it is wrong and mischievous to say that Buddha was an incarnation of Vishnu. I am no more a devotee of any Hindu gods or goddesses. I will not perform *Shraddha* (Hindu funeral rite). I will strictly follow the eight-fold path of Buddha. Buddhism is a true religion and I will lead a life guided by the three principles of knowledge, right path and compassion.[6]

Fundamental here is the claim that Ambedkar's existential experience as a Dalit led him to prefer Buddhism to other Indian religions. It is clear that he took this extreme step when he realized that being a Hindu, he would continue to be subject to oppression by the caste Hindus. Guided by the urge for knowledge, concern for others and also search for locating the right path for self-realization, Buddhism was, for Babasaheb, an empowering religion capable of setting things right for him and his fellow companions.

While his existential recounting acted decisively in shaping most of his critiques to Hinduism, it was his stint at Columbia University with John Dewey as his academic mention which helped him build a persuasive mode of reasoning in support of his arguments. It will therefore not be an exaggeration to suggest that the sharp critique of caste that he articulated later was the outcome of his experience

[6] Cited in Dhananjay Keer, *Dr. Babasaheb Ambedkar: Life and Mission* (Bombay: Popular Prakashan, 2012) (reprint), 500.

of being in the USA where he was introduced to the Enlightenment values. There were two sources of influences: on the one hand, the US socio-cultural context in which he was treated at par with the American citizens introduced him to a milieu that was free from the birth-based discrimination as was the case in India. Besides the prevalent context in the USA, the individual influence of his tutor, John Dewey, acted decisively in shaping his sociopolitical thoughts in the form of critiques of social discrimination, based on the accident of birth. What he imbibed from the context was conceptually justified by what Dewey articulated in his *Democracy and Education*, published in 1916. It is true that his being in the USA helped him understand the nature of a liberal society in which birth-driven hierarchy was abhorred. These ideas were further consolidated by Dewey's persuasive arguments in support of equality for all contributing to social equity in particular. Basic here is the point that Ambedkar's arguments questioning the caste system had drawn on his conceptualization of liberalism, which cannot be comprehended independent of his experience in the USA, and also his regular interaction with his academic mentor at Columbia University.

As the contemporary evidence suggests, Jinnah rose to prominence since the First Round Table Conference, held in November 1930. The battle that he had waged against Gandhi was settled in his favour in the 1931 Second Round Table Conference because, it was in this conference, Jinnah stood out with his persuasive arguments to defend the claim that he only represented the Indian Muslims, and not Gandhi, as was asserted so far. Regarding the future constitution, he thus made it clear that no constitution was acceptable without the approval of the Indian Muslims. It was articulated very forcefully when he emphasized that 'no constitution will be acceptable to the Mussalmans of India unless the due safeguards are provided to their rights and interests which will give them a complete sense of security in the future constitution'.[7] For Jinnah, the task was made easier since the Muslim delegates, those who attended the Conference, were unanimous in

[7] *Indian Round Table Conference, 12 November 1930–19 January 1931 (Sub-Committees' Reports, Conference Resolution, and Prime Minister's Statement).* Presented by the Secretary of State for India to Parliament by Command of His Majesty, H. M. S. O., London, *January* 1931, Vol. A, 300.

supporting the argument that he offered in favour of the rights of the religious minorities. A confident Quaid-i-Azam thus declared that 'I am authorized on behalf of the Muslim delegation to state that under the circumstances … we strongly [feel] that unless and until the Muslim demands and safeguards are not incorporated in the future constitution it will not be acceptable to us'.[8] So, a former Congress loyalist, M. A. Jinnah, who had accepted Gandhi as its leader, became a staunch opponent to the Mahatma since he felt that the latter was not equally sensitive to the interests of the minorities, especially the Muslims. He, in other words, carved out a definite space by being fiercely critical of the Mahatma who appeared to have lost out presumably because of the Congress' strategic failure in really establishing its claim of being truly secular. The story, so far narrated, reveals one trend demonstrating how a nondescript Congress follower gradually became an effective leader of the Indian Muslims by meaningfully championing their cause in a context when Gandhi was at his zenith as a mass leader. It is true that the peculiar unfolding of socio-economic and political processes in the presence of a mighty colonial power contributed to the creation of a milieu in which Jinnah's claim of Muslims being victims of circumstances found an easy acceptance, cutting across class and regions. In view of his pan-Indian concerns, the Mahatma did not appear to have paid adequate attention to the socio-economic imbalances at the grassroots affecting the Muslims adversely, which strengthened Jinnah's critique of the Congress and its leadership. A majority of the Muslims got easily swayed presumably because Gandhi, being a pious Hindu, could never be a true defender of Muslims' rights and interests. Hence, Jinnah's critique of Gandhi was easily accepted at large. Core here are two points which need reiteration: on the one hand, there is no doubt that M. A. Jinnah established his claim for being the sole spokesman for the Muslims by being a staunch opponent of Gandhi; that means, Jinnah's political-ideological views evolved out of his critique of the Gandhian mode of nationalist campaign. There is another point that also deserves to be mentioned, that is, being a smart strategist, Jinnah couched his critique of Gandhi in such a way as to highlight the socio-economic grievances of the majority of the

[8] Ibid., Vol. B, 1101.

Indian Muslims which the Mahatma seemed to have set aside given his primary concern for political freedom which would have been weakened had he challenged the well-entrenched anti-Muslim prejudices of the caste Hindus. What was unique about Jinnah was his success in evolving an alternative nationalist model to galvanize the Muslims which gained mileage when it evolved out of his forceful critique of the Mahatma's multicultural mode of nationalist intervention; it was hardly pan-Indian, Jinnah exhorted, because the rights and interests of the Indian Muslims were seldom meaningfully addressed.

Amidst those thinkers who challenged Gandhi's universalist vision of Indian nationalism, Savarkar stands out for his particularly compelling alternative to the same. Despite Gandhi and Savarkar being at opposite ends ideologically, their ideas bloomed in identical contexts: a fact that explains their similar concerns. Like Gandhi, Savarkar was passionate about securing India's political freedom, though his activism and his methods of combatting the colonial authority differed radically from Gandhi's, at the outset of his political career. Because of his involvement in revolutionary nationalist activities, he was exiled in Andaman as a political prisoner. It was during this period in his life that he penned *Eighteen Fifty Seven*, the book that fundamentally changed the mainstream conceptualization of the so-called Sepoy Mutiny from an isolated outburst of a set of aggrieved soldiers of the British Indian Army to a glorious first war of independence.

While Jinnah and Ambedkar regularly and famously confronted Gandhi in the public domain, there are not many instances of Savarkar and Gandhi battling it out face to face. Their oft-quoted exchange in London was the only occasion that saw the two highly original thinkers laying out their ideological approaches to Indian nationalism in opposition to each other. As contemporary evidence shows, they met each other in 1907 in a meeting of the Indians which was addressed by both Gandhi and Savarkar. Both of them argued for selflessness and patriotism as means for national rejuvenation. They also converged on the need for Hindu–Muslim amity, the absence of which, they both felt, was a casualty resulting from the colonialists' divide et impera strategy. By linking Hindu–Muslim animosity with colonial rule, Savarkar drew our attention to the deliberate design that the ruler developed to pursue partisan aims. He was always for Hindu–Muslim togetherness and his sole enemy was the British Raj. His concern for Hindus was also articulated, though in a rudimentary form, in this London speech in the presence of the Mahatma. Supportive of Indian syncretic tradition, he thus exhorted that 'Hindus are the heart of Hindustan. Nevertheless, just as the beauty of the rainbow is not impaired but enhanced by its varied hues, so also Hindustan will appear all that is best in the Muslim, Parsi, Jewish and other civilizations'.[9] Not only did he echo the Gandhian voice in regard to the need for Hindu–Muslim unity, but he also admired Gandhi as a '*desh bhakt*'.[10] The parallel stops there. Savarkar remained unmoved with the assumptions that he offered in the 1909 *Hind Swaraj* in support of non-violence as the only means for India's political liberation. Opposed to Gandhi's non-violence-driven politico-ideological formula, Savarkar countered the argument by unambiguously stating that the non-violent means of resistance was bound to fail 'because it presupposes all me to be selfless and that they will not cooperate with the aggressor; perhaps worse, it blindly presumes that the aggressor has a high sense of morality'.[11] Being fiercely critical of Gandhi's non-violence, he now laid out, in a 1909 speech in London, his own ideological predisposition supporting violence as perhaps the only option to meaningfully combat the ruthless colonial power. According to him,

> we feel no special love for secret organizations or surprise and secret warfare. ... It would be a crime to talk of revolution when there is a constitution that allows the fullest and freest development of a nation. Only because you deny us light, we gather in darkness to compass means to knock out the fetters that hold our Mother down. You rule by bayonets [and hence] ... it is a mockery to talk of constitutional agitation when no constitution exists.[12]

[9] V. D. Savarkar, *Newsletters from London* (Kolhapur: Riya Publications, 2013), 143, quoted in Vaibhav Purandare, *Savarkar: The True Story of the Father of Hindutva* (New Delhi: Juggernaut Books, 2019), 88.

[10] Ibid.

[11] V. D. Savarkar's 1909 London speech was quoted by M. Asaf Ali, in his memoirs entitled *M Asaf Ali Memoirs: The Emergence of Modern India* (New Delhi: Ajanta Publications, 1994), 72.

[12] Ibid, 73.

The above statement is illustrative of the ideational differences that Savarkar had with Gandhi. It was crystal clear that he did not appreciate non-violence as a means to effectively challenge the colonial power that hardly had compassion for the colonized. For him, the preference for violent means was dictated by the ruthlessness of the colonial administration which, under no circumstances, was liberal in its approach and belief; it was a draconian rule violating the basic Enlightenment values which purportedly laid the foundation of British rule in India. Implicit here are two fundamental assumptions: on the one hand, given his faith in constitutional governance, he held views which are compatible with those of Gandhi. He differed from the Mahatma when he emphatically argued for violence as the only available alternative to contain the colonial power. A hard-core pragmatic, he, unlike Gandhi, was not willing to concede space to human morality which was inconceivable in the prevalent circumstances when the main objective of the aggressors was to exploit the ruled for their partisan aims. Hence, he was fiercely critical of Satyagraha that Gandhi espoused to mobilize people for the nationalist cause. According to Savarkar, Satyagraha which

> demands the preaching of absolute nonviolence and condemnation of all armed resistance even to alien aggression ... is highly detrimental to our interests as a nation.... By insisting that the spinning qualities are more spiritual than the fighting the enemies, Gandhi undertook an endeavour to emasculate those involved in the freedom struggle. It pays the British at the cost of the nationalists.[13]

His criticism of the Mahatma was directed towards the means that did galvanize the Indians for the nationalist cause, which is a testimony to the claim that Savarkar's insistence on a violent counter to colonialism did not seem to have attracted supporters to the extent he had expected. It is now well established that with the arrival of Gandhi on the nationalist scene, the nature of anti-British campaign had undergone a sea change; no longer was the attack against the

[13] V. D. Savarkar's address in the 22nd session of the Hindu Mahasabha at Madura in 1940, reproduced in V. D. Savarkar, *Hindu Rashtra Darshan* (a compilation of his presidential addresses) (Bombay: Veer Savarkar Prakashan, 1992) (reprint), 154.

British sporadic and a surprise; it became far more organized and widespread, cutting across regions and classes. The campaigns that the Mahatma had launched were pan-Indian in character, while the earlier nationalist outbursts were confined to the scattered areas of India, particularly in the provinces such as Bengal, Punjab and Maharashtra. One should add a caveat here: in his avatar as a revolutionary nationalist, he always championed violence; but this was not the case once he floated the Hindu Mahasabha and took charge of the organization as its president. For him, resorting to violence was dictated by the circumstances in which the constitutional democracy which the British government had assured was denied; by implication, it meant that had there been an effective and fair constitutional government in India, Savarkar would not have espoused violence at all. This was exactly articulated in his personal interaction with the Governor of Bombay during his incarceration in the Cellular Jail in Andaman. He candidly admitted that

> I was compelled to be a revolutionary and a conspirator when I had discovered that there was no peaceful or constitutional method open to me to attain the goal I had in view. But if the present reforms prove to be useful for the furtherance of our hopes in a peaceful way, we shall very willingly turn to constitutional method and pursue gladly the constructive work on the principle of responsive cooperation. As revolutionaries, as we are described to be, our policy was as much of responsive cooperation as that of those who swore by other methods. We will utilize to the full the present reforms in pursuance of that principle and with a similar object in view. National good was our objective and if peaceful means served that end, we had no reason to cling to our old ways.[14]

Implicit here are three major points which are useful to comprehend the evolution of Savarkar as an ideological crusader. This is also pertinent here since it will help us understand that Savarkar's opposition to Gandhi was not based on diverse approaches to nationalism, but was governed by the concern for carving out a definite ideological space

[14] http://savarkar.org/en/pdfs/my-Transportation-for-Life-Veer-Savarkar.pdf; V. D. Savarkar, *The Story of My Transportation for Life: A Biography of Black Days in Andamans* (Mumbai: Rashtriya Smarak Trust), 371.

for his distinctive mode of conceptualizing nationalism in a language which was derivative of indigenous values and ideas. First, it is clear that he adopted violent means as he found the available means to be inadequate for fulfilling his politico-ideological goal. It was, in other words, a choice that he had to make primarily due to the lack of any other effective means for purposefully pursuing his nationalist ambition. Second, that he was willing to fulfil his political objective by constitutional means was also evident when he categorically expressed his views in their support. His willingness to explore the constitutional methods also shows that being nurtured in the Enlightenment tradition, it was naturally ingrained in him just like his other nationalist colleagues, including Gandhi. Third, he appears to have been favourably disposed towards the reform schemes that the British government had adopted for 'national good'. Being persuaded to believe that common good was possible through peaceful constitutional means, the erstwhile revolutionary nationalist appears to have wavered in his appreciation for militant nationalism which he admired by being appreciative of revolutionary nationalism.

On the basis of a careful assessment of the evolution of V. D. Savarkar as a nationalist, one can safely argue that there are two completely contrasting phases in his political career: on the one hand, as a revolutionary nationalist, he held views which were obviously contrary to those of Gandhi; it was evident in his meetings with the Mahatma in London in 1906 and 1909. Basic here is the point that careful analysis of his statements reveals that despite being vehemently opposed to Gandhi's non-violence, he evolved his views out of a serious engagement with the Mahatma, which suggests that the former was always a referent insofar as his approach to nationalism was concerned. The phase that had begun once Savarkar became the Hindu Mahasabha president in 1937 also reveals that Gandhi continued to remain a source of irritation and also opposition since the latter was mild in his opposition to the British rule. For Savarkar, Satyagraha was simply not adequate to bring about India's political liberation since its success was contingent on a high sense of morality of the rulers. It was therefore anything but realistic. Fundamental here is the point that while devising his own nationalist strategies, it was not possible for him to ignore Gandhi, which further confirms the claim that the politico-ideological views that Savarkar had evolved had emerged out of his critique of the mainstream nationalism of which the former was the chief priest.

IV

Gandhi and his critics were politically baptized in the spirit of nationalism, which means that, for them, the principal objective was to liberate India from British rule, though they held divergent views on how it was to be fulfilled. For Jinnah, the culmination of the British rule was desirable since it also led to the creation of Pakistan following India's partition. Babasaheb was persuaded to accept India's vivisection on the condition that the Congress leadership had agreed to adopt a liberal constitution with the commitment of protecting Dalit's interests. The Hindu Mahasabha that Savarkar led did not appear to be a significant political force in comparison with the Muslim League and the Congress, though it had articulated an alternative voice highlighting the demands of a segment of Hindus couched in Hindutva. According to Savarkar, independence was necessary for India's growth as a strong nation. Since, in his opinion, Hindutva was not an exclusive category, he insisted that those who lived in India were instinctively drawn to the cultural ethos that Hindutva represented. As will be shown later, Hindutva and Hinduism are two different constructs: while the former denotes specific cultural traits and mores, Hinduism refers to a well-defined religion that largely flourished in India for specific historical reasons. Being a believer of syncretic civilizational existence of disparate religio-cultural communities in India over centuries, the Mahatma differed from both Savarkar and Jinnah for obvious reasons. Opposed to partition since it was contrary to his lifelong mission, he was never convinced that partition was the only option left to the nationalists. It is true that despite his endeavour, India was divided, which was a testimony of his political failure at a time when he appeared to have lost his ideological appeal to his disciples and comrade-in-arms. History seems to have been cruel to the Mahatma and the joy for freedom was marred by the pangs of partition. Savarkar did not appear to have posed a serious challenge to the mainstream nationalism and the so-called threat of Hindutva never assumed devastating proportions as the claim for Pakistan had. Similarly, the politico-ideological objectives that Ambedkar held were not radically different from those of Gandhi; his only concern, as the events leading to the 1932 Poona Pact show, was not to further divide the Hindus which, he rightly apprehended, was likely to weaken the nationalist onslaught. Otherwise, there were no serious disagreements between him and Babasaheb. In fact, being appreciative of the Enlightenment values, both of them can be claimed to have held identical ideological beliefs. Differences between them were governed by the contextual compulsions in which both of them fought for defending politico-ideological values which, they strongly felt, were just in the prevalent milieu. That Gandhi held Ambedkar in high esteem as a fair-minded individual was proved when he strongly argued for him to be the chairperson of the Drafting Committee that was formed in 1946 to frame independent India's constitution following the 1946 Cabinet Mission's suggestion. Due to his insistence, it was possible since Jawaharlal Nehru was in favour of assigning the responsibility to a British legal expert, Ivor Jennings. Implicit in the act of the Mahatma is the view that Ambedkar was preferred by him presumably because of his ideological affinity with the latter given their faith in the Enlightenment philosophy seeking to establish an inclusive society.

What is evident here is that, despite having compatible ideological interests, there existed ideational differences which separated Gandhi from his critics. For Ambedkar, political freedom was not a panacea since it was meant to protect the interests of the caste Hindus, which was inevitable given the well-entrenched social prejudices of mainstream nationalist leadership. In other words, it was difficult for him to be persuaded by Gandhi to fight for political freedom so long as caste division was entertained. A caveat is needed here, for the Mahatma, who vehemently opposed caste atrocities, appeared to have underplayed his opposition largely in order not to enfeeble the nationalist counteract. While Savarkar's argument for consolidation of the Indians around Hindutva was not strongly challenged by the Mahatma, Jinnah's attempt at dividing India never received approbation from him. This is illustrative of a fundamental point that is reflective of the nature of leadership that Gandhi had evinced. A true nationalist, he was under no circumstances amenable to arguments that were potentially harmful to the nationalist cause. For the Mahatma, India's political freedom was non-negotiable, which led him to oppose Ambedkar and Jinnah. This is also illustrative of Gandhi being an astute strategist who set out plans in accordance with the circumstances. There is therefore substance in the point that Gandhi was a smart politician who came up with those strategies that gave him maximum dividends. There is another caveat here because Gandhi, being true to his commitment to non-violence, had also shown that as soon as the nationalist campaign became violent, he immediately withdrew as it had struck at the foundation of the faith that he so assiduously nurtured. Fundamental here is the point that what was striking about Gandhi was his unflinching commitment to non-violence at any cost which he proved by withdrawing the 1920–1922 Non-cooperation movement following the violent attack on the police by the Congress volunteers in Chauri Chaura in 1922. The Mahatma characterized this as 'Himalayan blunder'. Nonetheless, that he completely dissociated with the campaign as soon as it ceased to be non-violent was a testimony to his steadfast commitment to non-violence. There are therefore two levels at which one needs to conceptualize Gandhi's nationalist persona: at one level, he hardly wavered as soon as non-violence was undermined and effectively challenged. So, the mainstream nationalist anti-British attack that he led largely remained non-violent. At another level, he was occupied by the counter-attacks that his colleagues launched in support of their respective ideological faiths to show that there were far more effective alternatives than what Gandhi offered. What it reveals is the fact that the critiques that Gandhi's critics developed were also responses to the main thematic that the Mahatma built by being organically linked with the campaign for political freedom.

A careful scrutiny of the available evidence suggests that critiques of Gandhi evolved out of an ideational battle in which the Mahatma and his detractors were dialectically involved. Implicit here are two points: on the one hand, Gandhi's model of nationalism was not universally accepted since those who articulated alternative ideological voices had something different to say. These alternative ideas might not have had wider acceptance, though they raised issues which the Mahatma and his colleagues were unable to scuttle presumably because of socio-economic relevance in the prevalent context. An analytical account of the differences between Gandhi and his critics also underlines, on the other hand, that without comprehending what separated them from the Mahatma, our understanding of the nationalist history shall remain incomplete. It is true that the discourses that the Gandhi revilers built in opposition to the mainstream non-violent nationalist campaign were certainly meaningful, but they did not seem to be effective enough to carve out a purposeful alternative with a wider appeal. As a result, Ambedkar's appeal was largely confined to the Dalits, though the issues that he raised were relevant; similarly, Jinnah who espoused the cause of the Muslims, was primarily a leader of the Muslims; here too, one needs to be careful since even after Pakistan was formed, a large contingent of Muslims preferred to stay in independent India, which also had exposed the obvious limitations of Jinnah's two-nation theory that drew on the assumption of Hindus and Muslims being two nations as they were religiously different. In a similar vein, Savarkar's conceptualization of Hindutva being wrongly misconstrued as political Hinduism was hardly an effective device for political mobilization cutting across caste, class and religious boundaries. It never had the appeal that Gandhi's non-violence had in the nationalist context. In a nutshell, the Mahama prevailed over those ideological experiments which attracted attention but remained confined to a segment of the population or regions in India. In other words, while Gandhi's appeal was pan-Indian, this was not so with regard to his detractors who failed to arouse the masses across regions and classes presumably because of the inherent limitations of the politico-ideological models that they evolved.

V

Politics, Ideology and Nationalism: Jinnah, Savarkar and Ambedkar versus Gandhi is about an ideational battle that unfolded in the wake of the consolidation of India's nationalist determination to wrest freedom from colonialism. Indian nationalism can be said to have created a space for multiple ideological beliefs to strike roots and flourish.

Since India was a British colony, liberal constitutionalism couched in the Enlightenment values was a dominant politico-ideological discourse which was articulated in the nationalist response during the anti-British campaign. Interestingly, a careful scan of the discourses that evolved in the nationalist period also reveals that they differed from each other not in the fundamental ideological dispositions but in terms of the means through which they were sought to be put into practice for the nationalist cause. Whether one talks about Gandhi's ideas or those of his opponents, it is clear that they all were politically baptized in the core values of the Enlightenment philosophy, namely care, concern and compassion. So, in conceptual terms, Gandhi and his detractors drew on an identical philosophical discourse. Of his opponents, V. D. Savarkar, being inspired by the Italian Risorgimento (rising again), a 19th-century politico-ideological movement that culminated in the unification of Italy in 1861, paid much attention to those aspects of indigenous sociocultural traditions with the sole purpose of galvanizing the Indian masses for the nationalist goal. Unlike Gandhi, he preferred violent resistance in line with what Mazzini and Garibaldi suggested while mobilizing the Italians for the cause. Opposed to Savarkar's inclination for violence, Gandhi never ever wavered in his choice for non-violent challenge to the colonizers. Jinnah and Ambedkar too appear to have acquiesced Gandhi's preference for constitutional means for redressal of socio-economic and political grievances. Given the fact that, in their politico-ideological beliefs, they had affinity, one may, however, get puzzled when one comes across acrimonious interactions between Gandhi and his opponents. The reasons are to be located in the goals that they pursued and the ideological tools that they had deployed towards their attainment. For Gandhi, India's partition was repugnant to his conceptualization of India as a nation; in Jinnah's perception, it was a natural choice in view of his unflinching faith in the two-nation theory; in accordance with Ambedkar, partition was perhaps the best option available since Hindus and Muslims were at loggerheads; by articulating Hindutva, a proposed template for bringing together India's disparate sociocultural communities, Savarkar did not exactly conform to the design that the Mahatma devised.

The above discussion helps us make the argument that the Gandhi detractors, despite being drawn on more or less identical philosophical discourses, resorted to a different ideological path which was tuned to their goals and objectives. So, they were similar, at one level, in terms of their ideological faith in the Enlightenment values, but they were radically separate from one another since they understood nationalism differently and undertook different steps for realizing their specific ideological goals, for Ambedkar always believed that Gandhi deceived the people because in his conceptual universe, caste was not at all despised, which Babasaheb characterized as 'natural' as the latter wanted to establish 'the Hindu Raj' at the cost of the socially peripheral Dalits. Apart from his writings in which he pursued this line of argument, as discussed in Chapter 3, the 1955 British Broadcasting Corporation (BBC) interview, where he scathingly criticized the Mahatma, is a testimony to the argument. Characterizing Gandhi as 'a mere episode and not an epoch maker', Babasaheb most candidly stated that

> [a]s I met Mr. Gandhi in the capacity of an opponent, I know him better than most of the people because he has opened his real fangs to me as I could see the inside of the man. Others failed to see this because they went there as devotees, saw nothing of him except the external appearances which he put up as a Mahatma. I saw him in his human capacity, the bare man in him.[15]

Accusing Gandhi of deceiving people, Ambedkar further mentioned in this interview that the former had two contrasting faces: on the one hand, he had shown his liberal face to impress the Western world which he pursued consistently in his writings in the English-language texts; the situation was, however, different; on the other, he underlined, in regard to those texts which he wrote in vernacular (Gujarati); there he zealously held those views which are 'supportive of those dogmas that kept India down for ages'.[16] Being a social crusader, Ambedkar's views did not seem to be startling, though they confirm

[15] https://www.youtube.com/watch?v=ZJs-BJoSzbo, B. R. Ambedkar's interview to the BBC in 1955.

[16] Ibid.

that his critique was an articulation of his ideological commitment to the Dalit cause which he never diluted even at the cost of undermining his political career.

While Ambedkar questioned Gandhi for not having paid adequate attention to the Dalit cause, Savarkar expressed his resentment since Gandhi's non-violence was neither practical nor tuned to the fulfilment of the nationalist goal. It was a well-designed device to deceive the people and was thus meant to protect the colonizers' interests. According to him,

> no programme based on the monomaniacal principle of absolute nonviolence is worth a moment's consideration. If … the extreme remedy of an armed rising on a national scale is ruled out on grounds of practical politics, this other extreme of absolute nonviolence condemning all armed resistance even to an incorrigible aggression must be ruled out not only on practical grounds alone but even on moral grounds.[17]

That Savarkar was persuaded that non-violence was not an effective anti-British strategy is evident here. In his perception, the strategy, despite being hyped as an all-embracing design, did not seem to have had the capacity to win freedom in the face of the brutal oppression by the British. He was also neither favourably disposed towards an armed resistance nor an armed revolution. By ruling out both non-violence and armed resistance/revolution, Savarkar is understood to have been tiled for liberal constitutional methods as perhaps the most effective instrument for realizing his mission. This is evident if one goes through his speeches as the Hindu Mahasabha's president between 1937 and 1941.

Given Savarkar's insistence on constitutional methods for wresting power, he created a conceptual universe similar to that of Gandhi and Ambedkar. There is, however, a difference between Ambedkar and Savarkar in regard to some personal beliefs; for instance, Ambedkar declared that though 'he was born a Hindu but would not die as one',

[17] V. D. Savarkar's address at the Hindu Mahasabha's 22nd annual session at Madura in 1940, reproduced Savarkar, *Hindu Rashtra Darshan*, 149.

while Savarkar devised Hindutva in which the religious denomination of being a Hindu remains a critical factor in his conceptualization. They came together because both of them were opposed to Gandhi because they, as it is stated sarcastically, 'didn't see a Mahatma in Gandhi'.[18] While elaborating his critique of Gandhi, Ambedkar accused Gandhi of being 'the most dishonest human being in the history of Indian polity'.[19] Savarkar also had words of disgust when he characterized Gandhi's non-violent methods as 'quit-India-but-keep-your-arms-here plea', which was not only a restrictive design but also a ploy to sustain the imperial rule in India. What it means is that both of them, being opposed to Gandhi, held views in support of their critiques. It is a matter of common knowledge that Savarkar blamed Gandhi for India's partition and also for his soft corner for Pakistan once it was created; in fact, his incarceration following Gandhi's assassination in 1948 was justified by reference to his association with the Hindu outfit, the Hindu Mahasabha. Out of this debate comes a fundamental point that held Ambedkar and Savarkar together, namely they built their politico-ideological views entirely on their opposition to those of Gandhi. In other words, Gandhi being a constant referent in their articulation of politico-ideological ideas seems to have set out the conceptual universe in which they revolved. There were constant dialogues between Gandhi and these two colleagues despite not being on the same page on many occasions. The famous Poona Pact of 1932 is illustrative here: notwithstanding his appreciation for Ambedkar for his persuasive views on social justice, the Mahatma was never persuaded to accept the imperial constitutional guarantee for a separate electorate for the Dalits because it meant further division among the Hindus. In a similar vein, Gandhi, who clearly held diametrically opposite views, admired Savarkar and his compatriots in London for their unstinting commitment to the nationalist cause in circumstances when the revolutionary nationalists were not only imprisoned but also

[18] Vaibhav Purandare, 'Two Indians Who Didn't See a Mahatma in Gandhi', *Sunday Times*, Kolkata, 29 September 2019.

[19] B. R. Ambedkar, 'What Gandhi and Congress Have Done to the Untouchables', in *Dr. Babasaheb Ambedkar's Writings and Speeches*, ed. Vasant Moon, Vol. 9 (Bombay: Education Department, Government of Maharashtra, 1982), 538.

faced death penalty. The narrative of interaction between Gandhi and his detractors, Ambedkar and Savarkar, confirms the point that it was primarily Gandhi who designed the nationalist template which was critical to them while drawing their road map for future.

The story of Jinnah's opposition to Gandhi does not seem to be radically different. As shown in Chapter 4, the Quaid-i-Azam had crafted his own unique methods to carve out Pakistan following the transfer of power even though he was a congress loyalist at the outset of his political career. The separation took place in clear terms in the First Round Table Conference in 1932 when he strongly pleaded for a separate electorate for Muslims which Mahatma did not appreciate but had to accept due to the pressing circumstances. With the announcement of the Communal Award for the Muslims, Gandhi seemed to have lost out to Jinnah who now had emerged as the unquestionable leader of the Indian Muslims. It was a strategic victory for the Quaid-i-Azam. The story later unfolded with a clear direction, namely the consolidation of the demand that Jinnah made in favour of a separate homeland for the Muslims which he justified by devising a cultural model of two-nation theory. There were two implications which need attention here: on the one hand, following the First Round Table Conference, the argument that Gandhi and the Congress were the leaders of the Muslims had not had the validity with the rise of Jinnah as an alternative power centre capable of championing their goal. The conference also set in motion, on the other, the processes supportive of the demand for a sovereign state for the Muslims. In such circumstances, it was not possible for Gandhi to reverse the cycle of history since not only Jinnah succeeded in moulding the opinion of the Indian Muslims for India's partition but also created a milieu in which he became the Quaid-i-Azam, the undisputed leader of the Indian Muslims. Again, the story is familiar. Jinnah built his ideological package for separatism in response to Gandhi's conceptualizing modes in which the division of India was never an aspired goal. It is true that the Hindu–Muslim division was acerbated largely due to specific socio-economic churning which further consolidated the division; they were permanently compartmentalized, which culminated in the 1947 partition. Although the story of India's dismemberment is now a matter of common knowledge, the fact remains that the arguments justifying the communal fissure evolved out of the interaction between Gandhi and Jinnah. In a significant way, their ideas were similar at the level of their commitment to nationalism, and, at another, they held their views steadfastly to pursue their respective points of views in support of the assiduously crafted politico-ideological mission.

To conclude, the narrative of the interaction between Gandhi and his opponents is useful to understand (a) their respective conceptualizing tools and (b) how they evolved. As regards the former, they held more or less similar inclinations for constitutional liberalism except Savarkar who, in his youth, favoured a revolutionary nationalist method. Being ideologically baptized in the Enlightenment values, both Ambedkar and Jinnah seem to have been swayed by the Westminster form of democracy that gradually flourished in India in the wake of colonialism. That they fought for specific communal segments is illustrative of a commonality in conceptualizing the plight of the socio-economic groups that they represented: for Ambedkar, the so-called Dalits needed serious attention for being recognized as citizens, with rights and benefits, just like their caste-Hindu counterparts. For Jinnah, the same logic appears to have influenced him. He also strongly felt that Indian Muslims were subject to social disdain primarily because caste prejudices were well entrenched. His solution for creating an ambience of respect for Muslims was to create an independent Muslim homeland by bifurcating India. The nature of the arguments that they offered were similar in substance, though their actual unfolding followed different trajectories. In a uniquely textured format, Savarkar put forward a scheme based on his conceptualization of India being a cultural construct in which diverse communities came together by being appreciative of similar cultural traits. The idea is novel since it went beyond the conceptualization of India being a Hindu Pakistan.

As argued above, Indian nationalism created an ambience in which multiple ideological views prospered, though their roots do not seem to be radically different. This is a process in which politico-ideological priorities were couched in a widely accepted cultural ethos. It is therefore not surprising that because of Gandhi's attire like common male Indians and his reference to Tulsidas' Ramayana or local cultural heroes while addressing the gatherings across the country, he was immediately accepted as one of their own. Similarly, Jinnah's argument for the two-nation theory was hardly effectively challenged presumably because it was culturally endorsed. The same is true for Ambedkar who became the saviour for the Dalits because he succeeded in infusing the torture that they underwent with a cultural meaning. Savarkar too raised his clamour for Hindu Sangathan presumably because of the failure of the mainstream nationalists to adequately appreciate the Hindu cultural mores and values. These examples are cited to put across the point that culture is inherently political, which means that it emerges out of the power relations pervading at a particular juncture of history. A perusal of the ideas further confirms the point that with the consolidation of multiple influences, there had emerged multiple politico-ideological responses, which is most likely to happen in a socioculturally diverse country like India. Here is a very perceptive theoretical point that needs to be highlighted to avoid misconception. The appreciation of India being a multicultural society does mean

> an acceptance of assimilationism ... that seeks to impose [the so-called] symbols of allegiance on populations [that] ... may have been inspired by [completely] different religio-ideological predispositions. ... This may pave the way towards questioning the way in which the designs meant for the multitude ... are prepared.[20]

Implicit here is the contention that multiculturalism and assimilation are neither coterminous nor complementary to each other. Multiculturalism is a mindset that evolves by being together while assimilation is a deliberate design to create oneness by essentializing certain attributes which are seemingly seen to be universal. Gandhi provided his model because he believed that the civilizational affinity

[20] Alana Lentin, 'Replacing "Race", Historizing "Culture" in Multiculturalism', *Pattern of Prejudice* 39, no. 4 (2005): 395.

among those living in the location, called India, was a cementing factor. This was one of his usually offered arguments to question Ambedkar's insistence on a separate electorate for the Dalits. By following this logic, Jinnah succeeded in carving out Pakistan, though a large segment of Muslims, especially in Uttar Pradesh, who championed the cause of the Muslim League, stayed back in India. Savarkar too faced the similar predicament when he defended his idea of India around the Hindutva axis. Nonetheless, the story, narrated so far, reveals that of all the contrasting ideologies, the philosophy of Enlightenment remains a dominant theoretical design insofar as Indian nationalism is concerned. It is therefore not odd that despite having held completely different views as regards their approaches for the fulfilment of their respective socio-economic and political goals, they were favourably disposed towards constitutional methods with certain permutations and combinations. For instance, while Gandhi felt that civil disobedience was an apt strategy, neither Jinnah nor Savarkar was persuaded to adopt this method. Ambedkar resorted to civil disobedience, as the 1927 Mahad Satyagraha demonstrates, though he strongly felt that it was not needed once India became a constitutional democracy with the adoption of the 1950 Constitution of India.

Despite being conceptually more or less compatible, Gandhi and his detractors, as the above discussion shows, differ in the sense that while the latter espoused the cause of selective segments of society, Gandhi's call was for the entire country regardless of socio-economic divisions. He appears to have set the universe around which his opponents revolve. As the evolution of Indian political reveals, the Mahatma remained a constant referent to those seeking to articulate an ideological alternative to what constituted Gandhism. The Mahatma had an edge over his colleagues and compatriots for two important reasons: first, Gandhi was undoubtedly an organic leader of the nationalist movement which acquired completely different characteristics once its constituencies went beyond the metropolis and other urban centres of political activities. Whatever the immediate response to Gandhi's arrival on the Indian political scene, it was he who galvanized the masses into action despite the obvious adverse consequences of challenging a well-entrenched colonial power. The Mahatma was perhaps the first to have realized the political inadequacies of the urban-centric national movement in a diverse society like India. With his intervention, Indian nationalism became mass-based and geographically widespread in contrast with its earlier phases when the national movement had a very social base. The territorial expansion of nationalism was directly linked with the gradual, but steady, augmentation of the Indian National Congress which was no longer a platform for mere constitutional opposition to the British rule but a forum for well-organized campaigns for freedom. By involving the socio-economically peripheral sections of India, the Mahatma let loose another significant process, empowering people to endorse and also challenge the nationalist articulation of freedom struggle by Gandhi and his colleagues in the Indian National Congress. So, the Gandhian hegemony in conceptualizing even his critiques can never be undermined. Second, despite their roots in Gandhism, these critiques also provided alternatives to what the Mahatma represented. Through a serious contestation of Gandhi's social and political modes of conceptualizing Indian nationalism, Ambedkar, for instance, drew a mental map, based on a redefinition of 'freedom' and 'justice' that remained ideologically constrained if conceptualized in caste terms. Drawing on different, if not contrasting, perspectives, these critiques are illustrative of creative nationalist responses to imperialism suggesting the theoretical inadequacies of the so-called modular forms that tend to homogenize the nationalist discourses.[21] In other words, because the modular forms gloss over the peculiar socio-economic and political milieu in which the nationalist responses are formed and articulated, they fail to grasp, let alone conceptualize, the ideological basis of the responses that the colonized put forward to espouse their distinctive causes. The Gandhi detractors provided critiques within a critique since the Indian reciprocation was a critique of the larger nationalist discourses defending the modular forms. Therefore, the claim that the nationalist discourses are nothing but 'derivative' does

[21] Benedict Anderson in his *Imagined Communities: Reflections on the Origin and Spread of Nationalism* (London: Verso, 1991) (reprint) argues for modular forms of nationalism which was severely criticized by a host of scholars for being narrowly conceptualized and politically restrictive.

not seem to be plausible by any stretch of imagination. Furthermore, even the Gandhian mode of nationalist discourse, which remained one of the major forms of nationalist discourses, had varied manifestations at different levels of the anti-British struggle in India. The major nationalist discourse was, as evident, not only differently textured due to perhaps diverse participants but also designed differently, underlining the importance of the context. So, both Gandhism and the critiques of those who critically evaluated Gandhi and his ideological views constitute an important pillar of the nationalist discourse that was neither derivative nor imitative but creative and innovative.

Bibliography

Note: Ideas do not emerge in a vacuum; they are always a product of an intense dialectical interconnections with the prevalent socio-economic and political realities. Unless the ideas are coded in a meaningful language, they are futile. As soon as they figure in dialogical interactions in the public domain, they create a voice for themselves which can both be restrictive and expansive: restrictive if it does not provoke further debate and discussion; expansive if it leads the debate and discussion to either further/new conceptualization or differently textured corroboration. Either way, it is a useful exercise reflective of a serious engagement for defence or rejection. This is usually the pattern in social sciences where the one-size-fits-all formula is simply an anathema. As a result, analysis, however, strongly evidence-based shall always remain provisional, just like biological sciences where the scientists proceed on the basis of experiments which probably shall confirm the hypothesis that they have formulated. There is probability of whether the hypothesis is correct or otherwise. The purpose of putting forward the aforementioned prefacing lines is to argue the point that the available literature remains an important source of knowledge generation because the already generated inputs shall always create a baseline for the discussion and debates that are pertinent to go ahead in this regard.

Bibliography is not merely a list of texts, it is also illustrative of academic endeavours that an author undertakes to persuasively argue a point or defend a conceptual priority. This is also a serious exercise directed to suggest that those probable areas of enquiries need further probing. In this sense, a bibliography is also a space to take off for further exploration of new conceptual domains which may not have been conceivable now. So, there are two interrelated aspects which deserve attention to further understand the purpose of a bibliography: on the one hand, by selecting a specific set of books and other textual tracts, the author clearly indicates his/her preferences for specific kinds of ideas or conceptual parameters, generally speaking. For instance, a writer favourably disposed towards liberal discourses is certain to draw on those texts which are liberal in character and predisposition. Given the fact that texts which are meaningful are inconceivable unless they are seen in a context, it can thus be persuasively argued, on the other hand, that texts and contexts are dialectically interconnected. Besides the context, one has to be sensitive to the intellectual milieu in which these texts are shaped. It is a matter of common knowledge and convincing arguments are made in its favour to defend the point that texts are generally an outcome of the argumentative traditions; a powerful conceptualization endorsing the claim that ideas, being rooted, are a context-driven intellectual design in support of a point of view. This is nothing new. The aim here is to reiterate the point that bibliography is a mirror of the intellectual debates highlighting those points which may not have received adequate attention in the available texts.

Politics, Ideology and Nationalism: Jinnah, Savarkar and Ambedkar versus Gandhi is primarily an argumentative endeavour to elaborate how the nationalist discourse evolved out of a context in which Gandhi and his critics—M. A. Jinnah, V. D. Savarkar and B. R. Ambedkar—interacted with one another on the basis of their respective politico-ideological priorities. It will not be an exaggeration to suggest that Gandhi reigned supreme in the nationalist discourse that flourished in the wake of the campaign against colonialism for freedom. Based on this assumption, the book draws heavily on *The Collected Works of Mahatma Gandhi*, published by the Ministry of Information and Broadcasting, Government of India, primarily because these volumes, besides allowing access to Gandhi's own texts, have also included the replies that the Mahatma received from his colleagues and critics. Useful not only as a collection of the Gandhi-written tracts, these volumes are directional in the sense that they provide helpful inputs to decode some of the ideas that have not been adequately elaborated by the Mahatma himself. In his response, these ideas unfolded in their full form which would not have been possible without the critics' counter to what he stated. By concentrating on those letters/exchanges, the book defends the point that by being dialogical Gandhi and his detractors contributed immensely to our understanding of their views on nation, nationalism and national identity. What is true to Gandhi is also valid in case of B. R. Ambedkar because he left enormous written tracts for the posterity which help us comprehend his own perception of social justice and freedom and constitutional democracy. Made available by the Government of India for public consumption, the 17 volume texts (*Dr Babasaheb Ambedkar Writings and Speeches*, Volumes 1–17, Ministry of Social Justice and Empowerment, Government of India) are indispensable sources of conceptualization and elaboration of the ideas that figure prominently in the book. For V. D. Savarkar, texts are in abundance. Apart from the full-length books (including *My Transportation for Life*, *The Indian War of Independence of 1857*, *Hindutva*, among others) that he wrote, his speeches (incorporated in the *Selected Works of Veer Savarkar*, Abhishek Publications, Chandigarh, 2007) as the Hindu Mahasabha president for 5 years (1937–1942) are repository of his ideas which are also critical to understand the importance of a dialogical interconnection with the Mahatma in shaping some of his ideas and *vice versa*. Similar is the case with M. A. Jinnah who also, by being involved in regular exchanges of views with the Mahatma in the public domain, created a corpus of literature to conceptualize his well thought out ideas and parameters which are also of use in defending the dialectical communion between the two. Besides these texts, the book also builds the argument on the basis of other available pertinent texts. In a nutshell, this bibliography, which is, by no means, exhaustive of all sources, is basically directional since it is sure to provoke the future inquisitive minds to get provoked for further probing into an issue that continues to remain viable primarily because ideas are inspiration to undertake something afresh!

Ambedkar, B. R. *Mr. Gandhi and the Emancipation of the Untouchables*. Bombay: Thacker and Company, 1943.

———. *Pakistan or the Partition of India*, 3rd ed. Bombay: Thacker and Company, 1946.

Anand, Dibyesh. *Hindu Nationalism in India and the Politics of Fear*. New York: Palgrave Macmillan, 2011.

Andersen, Walter K., and Shridhar D. Damle. *The Brotherhood in Saffron: The Rashtriya Swayamsevak Sangh and Hindu Revivalism*. New Delhi: Vistaar Publications, 1987.

———. *The RSS: A View to the Inside*. New Delhi: Penguin Viking, 2018.

Anderson, Benedict. *Imagined Communities: Reflections on the Origin and Spread of Nationalism*. London; New York: Verso, 1983.

Balraj, Madhok. *Why Jan Sangh*. Bombay: Popular Prakashan, 1967.

Basu, T., et al. *Khaki Shorts, Saffron Flag: A Critique of Hindu Right*. New Delhi: Orient Longman, 1993.

Baxter, Craig. *The Jana Sangh: A Biography of an Indian Political Party*. Philadelphia: University of Pennsylvania Press, 1969.

Bruce, Graham. *Hindu Nationalism and Indian Politics: The Origins and Development of the Bharatiya Jana Sangh*. Cambridge: Cambridge University Press, 1990.

Chakrabarty, Bidyut. *The Partition of Bengal and Assam, 1932–1947*. London: Routledge Curzon, 2004.

———. *Mahatma Gandhi: A Historical Biography*. New Delhi: Roli Books, 2007.

Chatterjee, Partha. *Nationalist Thought and the Colonial World: A Derivative Discourse*. New Delhi: Oxford University Press, 1986.

———. *The Nation and Its Fragments: Colonial and Postcolonial Histories*. New Delhi: Oxford University Press, 1994.

Chatterjee, Partha., and Ira Katznelson, ed. *Anxieties of Democracy: Tocquevillean Reflections on India*. New Delhi: Oxford University Press, 2012.

Chaturvedi, Vinayak. 'Vinayak & Me: Hindutva and the Politics of Naming'. *Social History* 28, no. 2 (2003): 155–173.

———. 'A Revolutionary's Biography: The Case of VD Savarkar'. *Postcolonial Studies* 16, no. 2 (2013): 124–139.

Chaube, Shibani Kinkar. *The Idea of Nation and Its Future in India*. Oxford; New York: Routledge, 2017.

Curran, J. A. *Militant Hinduism in Indian Politics: A Study of the RSS*. New York: Institute of Pacific Relations, 1951.

Dalmia, V. *Nationalism of Hindu Traditions: Bharatendu Harishchandra and Nineteenth Century*. Benaras, Delhi: Oxford University Press, 1997.

Dasgupta, Swapan. *Awakening Bharat Mata: The Political Beliefs of the Indian Right*. Gurgaon: Penguin, 2019.

De, Rohit. *A People's Constitution: The Everyday Life of Law in the Indian Republic*. Princeton, Oxford: Princeton University Press, 2018.

Deoras, B. *Social Equality and Consolidation*. Delhi: Jagarana Prakashana, 1995.

Derret, J. D. M. *Religion, Law and the State in India*. London: Faber, 1968.

Devare, Aparna. *History & The Making of a Modern Hindu Self*. New Delhi: Routledge, 2011.

Doniger, Wendy, and Martha C. Nussbaum. *Pluralism and Democracy in India: Debating the Hindu Right*. New York: Oxford University Press, 2015.

Dutta, P. K. 'Dying Hindus: Production of Hindu Communal Common Sense in Early 20th Century Bengal'. *Economic and Political Weekly* 28, no. 25 (1993): 1305–1319.

Dutta, Pradip Kumar. *Carving Block: Communal Ideology in Early Twentieth Century Bengal*. New Delhi: Oxford University Press, 1999.

Elentjimittam, A. *The Philosophy and Action of the RSS for Hindu Swaraj*. Bombay: Laxmi Publications, 1951.

Ghai, P. K. *The Shuddhi Movement in India*. New Delhi: Commonwealth Publications, 1990.

Ghosh, Partha S. *BJP and the Evolution of Hindu Nationalism: From Periphery to Centre*. Delhi: Manohar Publications, 1999.

Golwalkar, M. S. *We or Our Nationhood Defined*. Nagpur: Bharat Publications, 1939.

Gordon, R. 'The Hindu Mahasabha and the Indian National Congress. 1915–1936'. *Modern Asian studies* 9 (1975): 145–204.

Guha, Chinmoy, ed. *Bridging East & West: Rabindranath Tagore and Romain Rolland Correspondence (1919–1940)*. New Delhi: Oxford University Press, 2018.

Gupta, Dipankar. 'Communalism and Fundamentalism: Some Notes on the Nature of Ethnic Politics in India'. *Economic and Political Weekly* 26, no. 11/12 (1991): 573–582.

Hansen, Thomas Blom. 'The Ethics of Hindutva and the Spirit of Capitalism'. In *The BJP and the Compulsions of Politics in India*, edited by Thomas Blom Hansen and Christophe Jaffrelot, 291–314. Delhi: Oxford University Press, 1998.

———. *The Saffron Wave and Hindu Nationalism in Modern India*. New Delhi: Oxford University Press, 1999.

Hansen, Thomas Blom, and Christophe Jaffrelot, ed. *The BJP and the Compulsions of Politics in India*. Delhi: Oxford University Press, 1998.

Hardiman, David. *The Nonviolent Struggle for Indian Freedom, 1905–1919*. Gurgaon: Penguin/Viking, 2018.

Hasan, M. *Nationalism and Communal Politics in India, 1885–1930*. New Delhi: Manohar Publications, 1991.

Hasan, Mushirul. 'The Delhi Proposals: A Study in Communal Politics'. *Indian Economic and Social History Review* 17, no. 4 (1980): 381–396.

Hobsbawn, E. J. *Nations and Nationalism since 1780: Programme, Myth, Reality*. Cambridge: Cambridge University Press, 1992.

Jaffrelot, Christophe. 'Hindu Nationalism: Strategic Syncretism in Ideology Building'. *Economic and Political Weekly* 20, no. 12–13 (1993): 517–524.

Jaffrelot, Christophe. 'The Genesis and Development of Hindu Nationalism in the Punjab: From the Arya Samaj to the Hindu Sabha, 1875–1910'. *Indo-British Review* 21, no. 1 (1993): 3–40.

———. 'The Idea of the Hindu Race in the Writings of Hindu Nationalist Ideologues in the 1920s and 1930s: A Concept Between Two Cultures'. In *The Concept of Race in South Asia*, edited by Peter Robb, 216–233. Delhi: Oxford University Press, 1995.

———. *The Hindu Nationalist Movement and Indian Politics, 1925–1990s: Strategies of Identity-building, Implantation and Mobilization (with special reference to Central India)*. New Delhi: Viking, 1996.

———. *The Sangh Parivar: A Reader*. New Delhi: Oxford University Press, 2005.

———. *Hindu Nationalism: A Reader*. Ranikhet: Permanent Black, 2007.

Jahanbegloo, Ramin. *The Disobedient India: Towards a Gandhian Philosophy of Dissent*. Delhi: Speaking Tiger, 2018.

Jalal, Ayesha. *The Sole Spokesman: Jinnah, the Muslim League and the Demand for Pakistan*. Cambridge: Cambridge University Press, 1985.

Jayal, Niraja Gopal, ed. *Democracy in India*. New Delhi: Oxford University Press, 2015 (reprint).

Jayaprasad, K. *RSS and Hindu Nationalism: Inroads in a Leftist Stronghold*. Delhi: Manohar Publication, 2002.

Joglekar, J. D. 'Veer Savarkar: Profile of a Prophet'. In *Savarkar Commemoration Volume*, edited by Vinayak Damodar Savarkar and Sudhakar Raje, 11–41. Bombay: Savarkar Darshan Pratishthan, 1989.

Jones, K. 'Communalism in the Punjab: The Arya Samaj: The Arya Samaj Contribution'. *Journal of Asian Studies* 28, no. 1 (1968): 39–54.

Jones, K. W. *Arya Dharm: Hindu Consciousness in Nineteenth Century Punjab*. Delhi: Manohar Publications, 1976.

———. *Socio-Religious Reform Movements in British India*. Cambridge: Cambridge University Press, 1989.

Jone, K. W. ed. *Religious Controversy in British India: Dialogues in South Asian Languages*. Albay: SUNY, 1992.

Jordens, J. T. F. *Dayananda Saraswatu: His Life and Ideas*. Delhi: Oxford University Press, 1978.

———. *Swami Shraddhananda: His Life and Causes*. Delhi: Oxford University Press, 1981.

Kanungo, Pralay. *RSS's Tryst with Politics: From Hedgewar to Sudarshan*. Delhi: Manohar, 2002.

Kapila, Shruti and Faisal Devji, *Political Thought in Action: The Bhagavad Gita and Modern India*. Cambridge: Cambridge University Press, 2013.

Kaviraj, Sudipta. 'The Imaginary Institutions of India'. In *Subaltern Studies*, edited by Partha Chatterjee and Gyan Pandey, vol. VII, 1–39. Delhi: Oxford University Press, 1992.

Keer, D. *Veer Savarkar*. Bombay: Popular Prakashan, 1950.

Keer, D. *Savarkar and His Times*. Bombay: India Printing Works, 1950.

———. *Veer Savarkar*. Bombay: Popular Prakashan, 1988. (Reprint).

Lentin, Alana. 'Replacing "Race", Historicizing "Culture" in Multiculturalism'. *Patterns of Prejudice* 39, no. 4 (2005): 379–96.

Lipner, J. J. *Hindu: Their Beliefs and Practices*. London: Routledge, 1994.

Lochtefeld, J. G. 'New Wine Old Skins: The Sangh Parivar and the Transformation of Hinduism'. *Religion* 26, no. 2 (1996): 101–117.

Ludden, David, ed., *Contesting the Nation: Religion, Community and the Politics of Democracy in India*. Philadelphia: University of Pennsylvania Press, 1996.

———, ed., *Making India Hindu: Religion, Community and the Politics of Democracy in India*. Delhi: Oxford University Press, 1996.

Madhok, Balraj. *RSS and Politics*. New Delhi: Madan Printers, 1986.

Majumdar, S. K. *Jinnah and Gandhi: Their Role in India's Quest for Freedom*. Calcutta: K. L. Mukhopadhyay, 1966.

Malhotra, S. L. 'Some Aspects of Hindu Revivalism and Their Impact on Indian Politics'. *Modern Review* 3, no. 1 (1963): 18–29.

Malkani, K. R. *The RSS Story*. New Delhi: Impex India, 1980.

Mandair, Arvind. 'Hegel's Excess: Indology, Historical Difference and the Post-secular Turn of History'. *Postcolonial Studies* 9, no. 1 (2006): 15–34.

Metcalf, T. *Ideologies of the Raj*. Cambridge: Cambridge University Press, 1994.

Metz, William S. *The Political Career of Mohammad Ali Jinnah*. Karachi: Oxford University Press, 2010.

Michelutti, Lucia. *The Vernacularization of Democracy: Politics, Caste and Religion in India*. Delhi: Routledge, 2008.

Minault, Gail. 'Hinduism and Politics'. *Economic and Political Weekly* 25 (1990): 723–729.

Mishra, D. N. *RSS: Myth and Reality*. New York: Asia Book Corporation of America, 1980.

Mitra, Subrata K., and Michael Liebig. *Kautilya's Arthashastra: The Classical Roots of Modern Politics in India*. New Delhi: Rupa Publications, 2017.

Mukherjee, Hirendra Nath. *Gandhi, Ambedkar and the Extirpation of Untouchability*. New Delhi: People's Publishing House, 1982.

Mukul, Akshaya. *Gita Press and the Making of Hindu India*. Noida: HarperCollins Publishers, 2017. (Indian reprint)

Nanda, B. R. *Road to Pakistan: The Life and Times of Mohammad Ali Jinnah*. New Delhi: Routledge, 2010.

Nandy, Ashis. *The Illegitimacy of Nationalism*. Delhi: Oxford University Press, 1994.

Narayan, Vasudha. *Hinduism: Origins, Beliefs, Practices, Holy Texts, Sacred Places*. New York: Oxford University Press, 2004.

Nehru, Jawaharlal. *Autobiography*. New York: John Day Company, 1941.

Noorani, A. G. *The RSS and the BJP: A Division of Labour*. New Delhi: LeftWord, 2000.

Nussbaum, Martha C. *Political Emotions: Why Love Matters for Justice*. Cambridge, London: The Belknap Press of Harvard University Press, 2013.

Omvedt, Gail. 'Gandhi and Ambedkar'. In *Studies in Ambedkar*, edited by V. T. Patil, 270–76. Delhi: Devika Publications, 1995.

Oomen, T. K. 'Religious Nationalism and Democratic Polity: The Indian Case'. *Sociology of Religion* 55, no. 4 (1994): 455–472.

Osuri, Goldie. 'Transitional Bio/necropolitics: Hindutva and Its Avatars (Australia and India)'. *Somatechnics* 1, no. 1 (2011): 139.

Palshikar, Suhas, Sanjay Kumar, and Sanjay Lodha, ed., *Electoral Politics in India: Resurgence of the Bharatiya Janata Party*. London; New York: Routledge, 2017.

Pandey, G., ed., *Hindus and Others: The Question of Identity in India Today*. New Delhi: Viking/Penguin, 1993.

Pandey, Gyan. 'In Defence of the Fragment: Writing About Hindu-Muslim Riots in India Today'. *Economic and Political Weekly* 26, no. 11–12 (1991): 559–572.

Pandey, Anurag. 'Communalism and Separatism in India: An Analysis'. *Journal of Asian and African Studies* 42, no. 6 (2007): 533–549.

Parekh, Bhikhu. *Debating India: Essays on Indian Political Discourse*. New Delhi: Oxford University Press, 2015.

Pinto, Ambrose. 'Saffronization of Affirmative Action'. *Economic and Political Weekly* 34, no. 52 (1999): 3642–3645.

Prakash, Gyan. *Emergency Chronicles: Indira Gandhi and Democracy's Turning Point*. Gurgaon: Penguin Random House, 2018.

Prakash, Indra. *Hindu Mahasabha: Its Contribution to India's Politics*. Delhi: Akhil Bharatiya Hindu Mahasabha, 1966.

Rajagopal, Arvind. *Politics After Television: Hindu Nationalism and the Reshaping of the Public in India*. Cambridge: Cambridge University Press, 2001.

Rajagopalachari, C. 'Gandhi-Jinnah Talks: Text of Correspondence and Other Relevant Matter', *The Hindustan Times*, New Delhi, 1944.

Ram-Prasad, C. 'Hindutva Ideology: Extracting the Fundamentals'. *Contemporary South Asia* 2, no. 3 (1993): 285–309.

Rathore, Akash Singh. *Indian Political Theory: Laying Groundwork for Svaraj*. Oxford; New York: Routledge, 2017.

Roy, Ramashray. *Indian Politics and the 1998 Election: Regionalism, Hindutva and State Politics*. New Delhi: SAGE Publications, 1999.

———. *Gandhi and Ambedkar: A Study in Contrast*. Delhi: Shipra Publications, 2006.

Salam, Ziya Us. *Of Saffron Flags and Skullcaps: Hindutva, Muslim Identity and the Idea of India*. New Delhi: SAGE Publications, 2018.

Sampath, Vikram. *Savarkar: Echoes from a Forgotten Past, 1883–1924*. Gurgaon: Penguin Random House, 2019.

Sarkar, S. 'Indian Nationalism and the Politics of Hindutva'. In *Contesting the Nation: Religion, Community and the Politics of Democracy in India*, edited by D. Ludden, 111–38. Philadelphia: University of Pennsylvania Press, 1996.

Sarkar, Sumit. *Beyond Nationalist Frames: Relocating Postmodernism, Hindutva, History*. Ranikhet: Permanent Black, 2002.

Savarkar, V. D. *The Indian War of Independence of 1857*. London, 1909.

———. *Hindu Rashtra Darshan: A Collection of the Presidential Speeches Delivered from the Hindu Mahasabha Platform*. Bombay: Laxman Ganesh Khare, 1949.

———. *Hindutva: Who is a Hindu?* Bombay: Veer Savarkar Prakashan, 1989. (6th edition of the text was first published in 1923)

Sen, Amartya. *The Argumentative Indian: Writings on Indian History, Culture and Identity*. New York: Picador, 2005.

Shah, Ghanshyam. 'Caste, Hindutva and Hideousness'. *Economic and Political Weekly* 37, no. 15 (2002): 1391–1393.

Sharma, Jyotirmaya. *Hindutva: Exploring the Idea of Hindu Nationalism*. New Delhi: Penguin Random House, 2003.

———. *Terrifying Vision: MS Golwalkar, the RSS and India*. New Delhi: Penguin Random House, 2007.

Singh, Jaswant. *Jinnah: India-Partition-Independence*. New Delhi: Rupa Publications, 2009.

Singh, Neerja. *Patel, Prasad and Rajaji: Myth of the Indian Right*. New Delhi: SAGE Publications, 2015.

Spear, Percival, and Margaret. *India Remembered*. Delhi: Orient Longman, 1981.

Srivastava, Harindra. *Five Stormy Years: Savarkar in London June 1906–June 1911*. New Delhi: Allied Publishers, 1983.

Thakur, Ramesh. 'Ayodhya and the Politics of India's Secularism: A Double Standard Discourse'. *Asian Survey* 33, no. 7 (1993): 645–664.

Thapar, Romila. 'Imagined Religious Communities: Ancient History and Modern Search for a Hindu Identity'. *Modern Asian Studies* 23, no. 2 (1989): 209–231.

Vajpeyi, Ananya. *Righteous Republic: The Political Foundations of Modern India*. Cambridge: Harvard University Press, 2012.

van der Veer, P. *Religious Nationalism: Hindus and Muslims in India*. Berkeley: University of California Press, 1994.

van der Veer, Peter. 'God Must be Liberated! A Hindu Liberation Movement in Ayodhaya'. *Modern Asian Studies* 21, no. 1 (1987): 283–301.

Varshney, Ashutosh. 'Contested Meanings: India's National Identity, Hindu Nationalism and the Politics of Anxiety'. *Daedalaus* 122, no. 3 (1993): 227–261.

Yang, A. 'Sacred Symbol and Sacred Space in Rural India: Community Mobilization in the "Anti-cow Killing" Riot of 1893'. *Comparative Studies in Society and History* 22, no, 4 (1980): 576–596.

Zavos, John. *The Emergence of Hindu Nationalism in India*. New Delhi: Oxford University Press, 2000.

About the Author

Bidyut Chakrabarty is Vice-Chancellor of Visva-Bharati, West Bengal. He was a professor in the Department of Political Science, University of Delhi, until November 2018. He completed his PhD from London School of Economics and has been associated with teaching and research for more than three decades. He has taught in several prestigious educational institutions, such as the London School of Economics; Indian Institute of Management Calcutta; Monash University, Australia; National University of Singapore; and Hamburg University, Germany. He has authored several textbooks and academic books. Among his publications are *Public Administration: From Government to Governance* (2017), *Winning the Mandate: The Indian Experience* (2016, SAGE Publications), *Communism in India: Events, Processes and Ideologies* (2014), *Indian Politics and Society since Independence: Events, Processes and Ideology* (2008) and *The Governance Discourse: A Reader* (2008).

Index